# Law, Governance and Technology Series

Volume 73

The *Law, Governance and Technology Series* is intended to attract manuscripts arising from an interdisciplinary approach in law, artificial intelligence and information technologies. The idea is to bridge the gap between research in IT law and IT-applications for lawyers developing a unifying techno-legal perspective. The series will welcome proposals that have a fairly specific focus on problems or projects that will lead to innovative research charting the course for new interdisciplinary developments in law, legal theory, and law and society research as well as in computer technologies, artificial intelligence and cognitive sciences. In broad strokes, manuscripts for this series may be mainly located in the fields of the Internet law (data protection, intellectual property, Internet rights, etc.), Computational models of the legal contents and legal reasoning, Legal Information Retrieval, Electronic Data Discovery, Collaborative Tools (e.g. Online Dispute Resolution platforms), Metadata and XML Technologies (for Semantic Web Services), Technologies in Courtrooms and Judicial Offices (E-Court), Technologies for Governments and Administrations (E-Government), Legal Multimedia, and Legal Electronic Institutions (Multi-Agent Systems and Artificial Societies).

Agnieszka Jabłonowska

# Consumer Protection and Online Travel Platforms

## An EU Law Perspective

Springer

Agnieszka Jabłonowska
Institute of Private Law
Leiden University
Leiden, The Netherlands

ISSN 2352-1902 ISSN 2352-1910 (electronic)
Law, Governance and Technology Series
ISBN 978-3-031-90169-0 ISBN 978-3-031-90170-6 (eBook)
https://doi.org/10.1007/978-3-031-90170-6



This Springer imprint is published by the registered company Springer Nature Switzerland AG
The registered company address is: Gewerbestrasse 11, 6330 Cham, Switzerland

# Acknowledgements

The publication of this book would not have been possible without the generous support that I was fortunate to receive. I would especially like to thank Prof. Monika Namysłowska, Prof. Monika Jagielska, and Prof. Piotr Tereszkiewicz for their guidance and feedback. I would also like to direct my special thanks to Prof. Hans-Wolfgang Micklitz for his continued support and mentorship.

Moreover, I am grateful for the insightful consultations, which constantly enriched my thinking while I was working on this book. In alphabetical order, I want to express my gratitude to: Prof. Christoph Busch, Prof. Urs Gasser, Prof. Marie Jull Sørensen, Prof. Vanessa Mak, Prof. Giovanni Sartor, Prof. Hans Schulte-Nölke, Prof. Christian Twigg-Flesner, Prof. Aneta Wiewiórowska-Domagalska, and Prof. Fryderyk Zoll.

Last but not least, I would like to thank my parents, my sister, my partner Leo, and my dear friends, for their continuous support and trust in me.

The research leading to this publication was financed by the National Science Centre in Poland (projects no. 2015/19/N/HS5/01557 and 2018/28/T/HS5/00142).

Leiden, 2024 Agnieszka Jabłonowska

**Competing Interests** The author has no competing interests to declare that are relevant to the content of this manuscript.

# Contents

# Chapter 1
# Introduction

## 1.1 Background

This book examines how European Union law protects—and could protect—consumers concluding stand-alone contracts for single travel services in the digital economy. Single travel services include short-term accommodation rental and passenger transport services that are not sold as part of package tours. Services of this kind are increasingly popular around the world, thanks to the rise of online platforms like Booking.com or Uber. The book explores this changing market landscape and the associated EU legal framework, showing an interesting dynamic between sectoral and horizontal rules.

Travel and online commerce are both important areas of interest for EU lawmakers. They have long been the scene of considerable harmonisation efforts, aimed among others at improving consumer protection. However, the development of online travel platforms has revealed important gaps in EU sectoral rules.

Indeed, online platforms allowing consumers to conclude stand-alone contracts for single travel services are largely missed by EU travel law. To date, the most developed protections are provided to travellers engaged in package tours, encompassing at least two different types of travel services. In contracts for single travel services, issues of vital relevance to consumers—like safety and performance—are only partially addressed. The same is true for passenger rights, which only apply to standard means of transport, such as air, rail, or coach. In contrast, the carriage of passengers by car so far remains outside the scope of the EU law.

Similarly, EU e-commerce law has long missed the reality of online travel platforms. Focused on two-party relationships, it failed to take account of the more and more prominent intermediaries. This appears to be changing, as the widely



A. Jabłonowska, *Consumer Protection and Online Travel Platforms*, Law, Governance and Technology Series 73, https://doi.org/10.1007/978-3-031-90170-6_1

discussed Digital Services Act[1] demonstrates. However, a careful analysis reveals that recent platform legislation is far from a game-changer for the travel sector.

Considering the above, the book explores the reasons behind the Union's failure to take decisive action on online travel platforms. Two possible reasons are identified: firstly, the lack of EU competence and, secondly, sufficient consumer protection provided under the horizontal consumer *acquis*. The analysis of the existing competences in the internal market and common transport policy rejects the former reason as invalid and confirms that harmonised safeguards for consumers contracting via online travel platforms are supported by primary law. While the horizontal consumer *acquis* can be interpreted, in part, to close sectoral gaps, it comes with limitations. A scope therefore remains for further EU regulation of online travel platforms with an eye to improving consumer protection.

## 1.2 Structure

The book is divided into three main parts. Part I explores the transformative power of online platforms. To lay the ground for further analysis, Chap. 2 begins with a discussion of the shared characteristics of online platforms. It then zooms in on the travel sector and considers the main recent developments in the sector, associated, firstly, with the emergence of direct and mediated digital booking channels and, secondly, with the more advanced online marketplaces, including in the so-called collaborative economy. The notion of the collaborative economy is explored against the background of EU policy documents and the common definitional difficulties are addressed. The transformative impact of online platforms on the travel sector is further investigated, with a focus on the growing number of stand-alone contracts for single travel services, the rise of non-professional supply and the central position of platform operators. The chapter concludes with a review of the benefits and risks of online platforms in the travel sector.

In Chap. 3, the transformative impact of online platforms is further explored based on a selection of case studies undertaken between 2020 and 2024. Particular attention is drawn to the frameworks of private governance that platform operators may deploy to mitigate the risks associated with their business model. The focus remains on the segments of the travel sector in which online platforms are particularly present, namely short-term accommodation rental and passenger transport. As it turns out, all investigated platform operators have put in place governance frameworks of some sort, which can be seen as an important determinant of consumer trust in their business models. The chapter further evaluates the ability of the analysed frameworks to respond to the risks that online platforms bring about and identifies their limitations.

[1] Regulation (EU) 2022/2065 of the European Parliament and of the Council of 19.10.2022 on a Single Market For Digital Services and amending Directive 2000/31/EC (Digital Services Act) [2022] OJ L 277/1.

To understand the role of consumer protection in the EU legal framework, Part II of the book explores existing legislation based on Articles 91 and 114 TFEU. It highlights the economic and axiological dimensions of consumer protection in primary and secondary law, focusing respectively on the internal market (Chaps. 4 and 5) and the common transport policy (Chap. 6). Prior measures of consumer protection in digital markets and the travel sector are analysed and their main parameters (personal scope, core aspects and underlying ethics) are identified. This exercise reveals that existing sectoral rules largely miss the reality of online travel platforms, although the issues they address are also present on those platforms. The lack of EU competence does not explain this outcome. On the contrary, EU primary law lends sufficient support to more decisive measures.

The third and final part of the book considers the potential and limits of the horizontal consumer *acquis* (Chap. 7) and examines what measures could be taken to increase consumer protection in online travel platforms (Chap. 8). It is observed that the existing instruments, such as Directives 93/13/EEC on unfair terms (UCTD)[2] and 2005/29/EC on unfair commercial practices (UCPD),[3] do not apply to the underlying peer-to-peer relationships. However, they offer a degree of protection vis-à-vis professional providers, who notably include platform operators. A consumer-oriented reading of existing provisions can therefore partly fill the gaps in sectoral rules. To offer more tailored solutions, legislative reforms are nonetheless recommended, building upon the EU sectoral experiences.

[2] Council Directive 93/13/EEC of 5.4.1993 on unfair terms in consumer contracts [1993] OJ L95/29.

[3] Directive 2005/29/EC of the European Parliament and of the Council of 11.5.2005 concerning unfair business-to-consumer commercial practices in the internal market and amending Council Directive 84/450/EEC, Directives 97/7/EC, 98/27/EC and 2002/65/EC of the European Parliament and of the Council and Regulation (EC) No 2006/2004 of the European Parliament and of the Council ('Unfair Commercial Practices Directive') [2005] OJ L149/22.

# Part I
# Transformative Power of Online Platforms

# Chapter 2
# Online Platforms and Travel Transformation

## 2.1 Setting the Scene

Online platforms form a recurring theme in many present-day debates, in which they are viewed at least as a broadly distinguishable phenomenon.[1] It is widely accepted that online platforms transform—or disrupt[2]—markets, giving rise to both benefits and risks.[3] Scholars and policymakers are thus increasingly confronted with the question as to a possible "disconnection" of the existing norms from the technological state of the art and, accordingly, the need for, and means of, re-establishing a connection.[4] This overarching question can be approached from many different angles: from the broader perspectives on how to regulate innovation[5] to studies focusing on particular fields of law[6] and specific issues.[7] The present book focuses on the travel sector and adopts the consumer protection perspective.

There are several factors behind the choice of the travel sector as the primary subject of analysis. Online platforms associated with mobility and hospitality are clearly on the rise and continue to transform the ways people travel.[8] At the same

[1] For notable, cross-thematic analyses, see Hatzopoulos (2018), Devolder (2019a) and Davidson et al. (2018).

[2] Twigg-Flesner (2016), pp. 36–37.

[3] On emerging evidence on positive and negative effects of online platforms, with a strong emphasis on its inconclusive nature, see Codagnone et al. (2018), p. 6, 61.

[4] Brownsword (2018), pp. 171–172.

[5] Ranchordás (2015), p. 413.

[6] E.g. contract law, Maultzsch (2018), p. 209, Orti Vallejo (2019), p. 995, Devolder (2019b), p. 31, competition law, Lougher and Kalmanowicz (2016), p. 87 and tax law, Pantazatou (2018), p. 368.

[7] E.g. the impact of platforms facilitating the conclusion of contracts for tourism accommodation on the housing market, see Lee (2016), p. 229.

[8] OECD (2018), pp. 74–75 <https://doi.org/10.1787/tour-2018-en>.

 
A. Jabłonowska, *Consumer Protection and Online Travel Platforms*, Law, Governance and Technology Series 73, https://doi.org/10.1007/978-3-031-90170-6_2

time, risks associated with travelling, especially across borders, have long been recognized as significant. Certain indispensable components of travelling, such as the use of particular means of transport, can involve increased risks, e.g. in terms of safety. Any potential complications experienced during the journey can be additionally challenging for the traveller who is, by definition, geographically removed from his or her home. To deal with emerging problems and fulfil even basic needs, such as finding shelter, a traveller needs to get around in a new, possibly culturally and linguistically unfamiliar environment. It is for these reasons among others that services in the field of travel have long attracted the attention of lawmakers at national and supranational levels. These efforts have led to the emergence of dedicated legal rules, which are sometimes collectively described as "travel law".[9]

The travel sector has also long remained on the radar of the European Union. As an area with a strong cross-border potential, it fits well with EU integration goals. The growth of online platforms has further transformed the sector, making travelling even more manageable than before. It is nonetheless debatable whether the multiple dimensions of the transformed travel sector have been sufficiently addressed by the EU. To lay the ground for addressing this question, it is useful to first consider the concept of online platforms and their impact on the travel sector.

## 2.2 Online Platforms: A Contested Notion

Despite significant public interest in online platforms, many questions they raise remain underexplored. Indeed, on a closer look, even the understanding of the term appears to be ambiguous.[10] Its origin can be traced back to economic studies of markets characterised by the presence of two or more sides whose ultimate benefit derives from their interactions through a common platform.[11] Central to the existence of such markets are the entities that serve the relevant customer groups and give rise to a dynamic, in which the numerosity of each group creates an externality for the other (network effects).[12]

Over time, the focus of economic studies on multi-sided markets has shifted away from the role of network effects alone,[13] and the theory began to be developed

[9] Tonner et al. (2018), Karsten (2010), p. 201.

[10] The focus typically lies on "architectures", "services", "undertakings", "business models" or "markets" and it is not uncommon to use these terms interchangeably.

[11] Martens (2016). See also: Rochet and Tirole (2003), p. 990 and Luchetta (2014), p. 188.

[12] Wismer and Rasek (2017).

[13] Armstrong (2006), p. 668, Rochet and Tirole (2006), p. 645, Hagiu and Wright (2015), p. 162. See also Evans and Schmalensee (2016).

in different, sometimes diverging ways.[14] One notable account considers direct interactions between at least two groups of market actors and their affiliation with a platform to be determinative of multi-sided platforms.[15] Understood in this way, multi-sided platforms constitute a business model alternative to those of resellers and vertically integrated firms.

Economic findings on multi-sided markets have clearly had an impact on the understanding of online platforms in policy and legal scholarship. Busch et al. refer to "companies using the platform business model" distinguished by its multi-sided nature and the presence of network effects.[16] The authors recognize that the model is not new in itself. It is nonetheless argued that online platforms, due to their digital dimension, can profoundly transform market interactions.[17] Helberger et al. define online platforms as "socio-technical architectures that enable and steer interaction and communication between users through the collection, processing, and circulation of user data".[18] This takes attention away from network effects and the qualifying criteria developed by economists, and instead highlights the importance of data and the impact of platform design on users' behaviour.

Clearly, the approaches signalled above do not seek to achieve the level of precision that is imperative for economic models. Both debates, therefore, are not entirely aligned; all of them, however, take similar factors into account: heterogeneous groups of users brought together through data-driven architectures and liable to be affected by their design. Oftentimes a line is being drawn between the entity behind the architecture (providing services according to the analysed business model) and the architecture, or the business model, itself, yet it is also not uncommon to let both categories converge.

Against this background, the understanding of the online platforms adopted for this book refers primarily to business models composed of a variety of services that share some overarching features. The latter are elaborated on further below and include: direct interactions between heterogeneous groups of users, triangular settings, network effects and data-driven architectures. Since the provision of data-driven architectures forms a prominent part of platform services, the term "online platform" will hereafter be used to describe these software facilities. The entities behind them will consequently be described as either "platform providers" or "platform operators".

---

[14] Martens (2016), p. 13, Rochet and Tirole (2006), Evans and Schmalensee (2016). See also Li (2015), p. 99.

[15] Hagiu and Wright (2015), p. 163. See also Luchetta (2014), p. 192 who focuses on the two following criteria—uniqueness of transaction and reciprocal inter-side positive externalities, as a consequence of which the two sides are necessary to the operation of the platform.

[16] Busch et al. (2016), p. 3. Similarly Strowel and Vergote (2019), p. 15.

[17] Busch et al. (2016), p. 4.

[18] Helberger et al. (2018), p. 1.

## 2.3 Shared Characteristics of Online Platforms

### 2.3.1 *Direct Interactions Between Heterogeneous Groups of Users*

Online platforms provide a space where two or more groups of internet users can meet to exchange goods, services or information. In some business models, the distinction between both groups is more visible than in others. For example, it is fairly easy to identify two distinct groups of users who exchange goods or services through platforms such as eBay or Booking.com. On the one side there are suppliers of the relevant goods or services, on the other side there are customers who seek access to them. The same users can sometimes switch between the roles, depending on their needs and the specifics of the business model in which they operate. Should the two parties agree on a binding exchange, a contractual relationship is usually formed, subject to the applicable law.[19] Two heterogeneous groups of users can also be identified when both parties come together for purposes other than contractual exchange of goods and services. Notable examples include social media (e.g. Facebook) and some of the platforms in which the exchange pertains to the temporary usage of goods or the provision of services by private individuals (collaborative economy[20]), where assets can also be exchanged without the intention to create legal relations (e.g. Couchsurfing).

### 2.3.2 *Triangular Settings*

For the two groups of users to meet and exchange via online platforms, a third party must be involved, namely the platform operator (Fig. 2.1). The existence of triangular settings is thus a natural consequence of the market structure associated with online platforms.[21]

As with the interactions between users, the assessment of legal relationships between the platform operators and respective platform users must always be performed on a case-by-case basis and depends on the applicable law. In terms of contract formation, factors revealing the meeting of two wills related to the same thing as well as the intention to create legal relations will be particularly relevant.[22]

---

[19] See generally Smits (2014), pp. 41–42.

[20] European Commission, 'Communication from the Commission to the European Parliament, the Council, the European Economic and Social Committee and the Committee of the Regions. A European Agenda for the Collaborative Economy' (2016) COM(2016) 356 final.

[21] Adam and Micklitz (2017), pp. 47–48, Tereszkiewicz (2019), p. 143.

[22] Smits (2014), pp. 41–42.

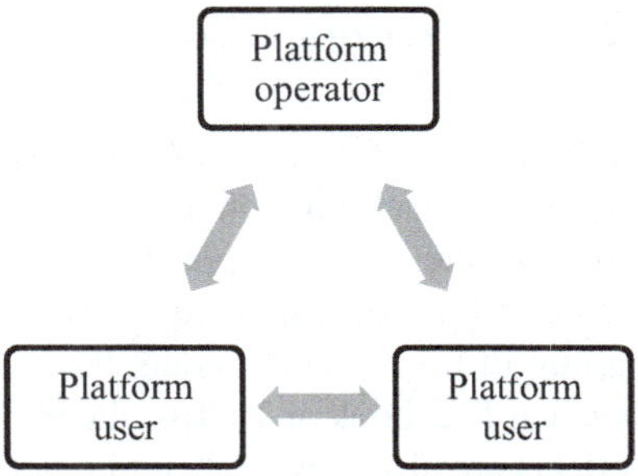


**Fig. 2.1** Triangular relationships in platform business models

In most platforms associated with the travel sector, the existence of contractual relations between the platform operator and the platform user will be fairly apparent, as evidenced by the requirement to create a user account and agree to the terms of service.[23]

The existence of an online platform as a business model does not in itself presuppose any particular alignment between the three relationships from a legal perspective or a corresponding allocation of rights and duties. Certainly, the fact that some of the relationships established through an online platform are not *contractual* in nature should not prevent a classification of a business model as an online platform.[24] More problematic are the situations in which, despite the appearance of a triangular setting, a bipolar relationship between the platform operator and the platform user is in fact established, that is where the operator is not merely an intermediary but is the actual supplier of the relevant goods, services or content.[25] In order not to limit the scope of the analysis unnecessarily, business models with a strong triangular appearance will not be excluded from the present book, but will rather be discussed as borderline cases of the platform economy.[26] The focus, nonetheless, remains on the business models in which three corresponding, and primarily contractual, relationships are established.[27] As empirical data suggests, models of this kind are most frequently deployed in the platform economy.[28]

[23] Cf. Faust (2016). Similarly Wendehorst (2016), p. 31 and Kramme (2022), p. 59. See also Maultzsch (2018), p. 211 and Meller-Hannich et al. (2019), p. 404. On the possible conclusion of the contract in the course of mere use of the platform, see Hauck and Blaut (2018), pp. 1426–1427. On the role of consideration in common law, see e.g. Mik (2016).

[24] Consider the earlier example of social media.

[25] As illustrated by the controversies surrounding the business model of Uber, for now especially under national labour law and European Union free movement law, see especially the judgment of the Supreme Court of the United Kingdom of 19.2.2021 in case *Uber BV and others v Aslam and others* [2021] UKSC 5 and the judgment of the Court of Justice of 20.12.2017 in case C-434/15 *Asociación Profesional Elite Taxi (Uber Spain)*, ECLI:EU:C:2017:981.

[26] Codagnone et al. (2018), pp. 31–34, 36. Similarly Meller-Hannich et al. (2019), pp. 404–405.

[27] Orti Vallejo (2019), p. 1000.

[28] Meller-Hannich et al. (2019), p. 404.

### *2.3.3 Network Effects*

The concept of network effects, describing the totality of the effect that one user of a good or service has on the value of that good or service to other people,[29] is central to understanding the appeal of online platforms from the user perspective and the reasons for their rapid expansion.[30] Direct network effects occur within the same group of users. To illustrate, the more people start using a social media platform, such as Facebook or TikTok, the more attractive it becomes for others to join.[31] Such effects are also at work in reputational feedback systems, covering both review and rating tools, whereby users generate value (experience) for the other users belonging to the same group.[32] By contrast, the idea behind indirect, or cross-group, network effects is that one group of users benefits from the growing presence of a different group of users.[33] For example, an increase in the number of sellers on an online marketplace, such as eBay or Airbnb, is likely to stimulate an increase in the number of buyers and *vice versa*.

There are several aspects of network effects which are worth highlighting in the context of online platforms. Firstly, markets with network effects may be additionally prone to market failures, since platform services tend to be rather "sticky".[34] Accordingly, online platforms display a tendency towards concentration, which may result in a more limited competitive pressure and limited alternatives being available to consumers.[35] Secondly, specific user groups may be more difficult to draw and maintain than others and may contribute differently to the platform's value.[36] This is especially the case when the price elasticity of supply and demand is not identical, in which case either suppliers or customers can be asked to pay for access to the platform while the other side can be subsidized.[37] On the one hand, cross-subsidization is one of the basic strategies employed by platform operators to prevent the 'chicken-and-egg' problem and maintain a functioning ecosystem.[38] On the other hand, due to incentives created by network effects and a strong position enjoyed by platform operators, the neutrality of the latter should be approached with caution.

---

[29] For a concise discussion, see Hagiu and Yoffie (2018).

[30] Strowel and Vergote (2019), p. 16.

[31] Hatzopoulos (2018), p. 10.

[32] Martens (2016), p. 10.

[33] Hagiu and Yoffie (2018), p. 1104.

[34] See, in relation to social media platforms, Wauters et al. (2014), pp. 258–261, Chiu (2011), pp. 184–193.

[35] Smorto (2018), p. 436.

[36] For an empirical illustration based on the analysis of an online dating platform, see Voigt and Hinz (2015), p. 139.

[37] Martens (2016), p. 11.

[38] Stummer et al. (2018), p. 170, Schneider (2018), pp. 30–31.

### 2.3.4 *Data-Driven Architectures*

To improve the platform's utility to its users, as well as monetize their interactions, platform operators rely on algorithms responsible for large-scale data analysis and powering a continuous flow of automated outcomes. The functioning of such architectures may be directly linked to the *raison d'être* of a given platform, namely the matching of its users. However, since data constitutes a non-rivalrous good, there are no practical barriers for the operators to extract value from it in different ways.[39] As a result, economies of scope in data collection and analysis can significantly reinforce the position of the platform provider vis-à-vis platform users as well as other market actors.[40] This informational advantage and power embedded in digital architectures, along with other regulatory tools available to operators, can be a source of risks. At the same time, the unique position of platform operators can be leveraged to achieve legitimate objectives and is something that lawmakers should also keep in mind.

The benefits and risks of online platforms, including those related to data-driven architectures, may vary depending on the type of platform and its area of activity. As this book focuses on the travel sector, it is helpful to first characterize the latter's transformation and the corresponding role of online platforms.

## 2.4 Online Platforms and Travel Sector

### 2.4.1 *Travel as Economic Sector*

The notion of travel includes any movement of persons between removed geographic locations for any purpose and duration.[41] Mobility of this kind is anything but new. It has been a part of human existence from its very beginnings, for reasons originally related to survival and subsequently trade, conquest or adventure.[42] However, the idea of travelling for leisure—which today forms a major part of the travel sector—is a more recent phenomenon, and remains closely tied to technical advances.[43]

The emergence of leisure travel as a mass phenomenon would not have been possible without historic breakthroughs in the field of transport—from the invention of

---

[39] On the non-rivalrous nature of data, see e.g. Graef (2015), p. 479.

[40] Martens (2016), p. 36.

[41] United Nations, 'International Recommendations for Tourism Statistics 2008' (2010) ST/ESA/STAT/SER.M/83/Rev.1 9.

[42] Zuelow (2016), pp. 2–4. Some issues related to travel were already addressed in Roman law, see e.g. Wyrwińska (2018), p. 609, Sobczyk (2018), p. 436, Zimmermann (1996), p. 514.

[43] Nesterowicz (2016), p. 16.

the steam engine to the birth of air travel.[44] First, railway companies offered a transport mode which allowed long-haul travel to develop on a broader scale, due to speed and affordability. The developments in the aviation industry further broadened the range of the available transport options, including for international journeys. The opportunity was taken by a new group of companies which started to offer package tours.[45] Technical development was therefore followed by business innovation, which defined leisure travel for more than a century. A similar process took place in the more recent past, with the rise of the digital age.

### 2.4.2 *Digital Booking Channels and Online Platforms*

The digital transformation of the travel sector has proceeded gradually. Firstly, the rapid increase in internet penetration rates allowed many service providers to develop their own channels for reaching customers. Airlines, for example, no longer needed to rely on the operation of computerised reservation systems by travel agencies, but instead launched their own websites and call centres.[46] Direct channels also became available for other travel-related services, such as tourism accommodation. In this case, however, the variety of service providers[47] posed a difficulty to any independent consumer search—even with the help of search engines. As a result, it was not until a new group of intermediaries began to aggregate the relevant information at one point of entry that combining a trip entirely on one's own became truly accessible. Data collection and analysis undertaken by the providers of online marketplaces, like Booking.com and Expedia, has played a key part in this process.

More recently, digital architectures of platform operators have allowed another important development to take place. In particular, the growing deployment of rating and review systems has created a new source from which mutual trust could be derived.[48] This, in turn, has allowed the activities which previously remained of marginal economic importance, such as car-sharing or private accommodation rentals, to expand on a broader scale and gain cross-border importance. Gradually, non-professional supply has become complementary and, in part, even substitutable to the services provided by established suppliers.[49] This phenomenon is widely associated with the so-called collaborative economy.

---

[44] Zuelow (2016), pp. 59, 112.

[45] Ibid, p. 62. Nesterowicz (2016), p. 16.

[46] European Commission, 'Commission Staff Working Document. Proposal for a Regulation of the European Parliament and of the Council on a Code of Conduct for Computerised Reservation Systems. Impact Assessment' (2007) SEC(2007) 1496 12.

[47] See also van Leeuwen (2017), p. 145.

[48] Busch (2016), p. 223.

[49] TNS Political & Social, 'The Use of the Collaborative Economy' (2018) Flash Eurobarometer 467 5 <http://data.europa.eu/euodp/en/data/dataset/S2184_467_ENG>.

### 2.4.3 *Collaborative Economy*

#### 2.4.3.1 Notion of Collaborative Economy

The term "collaborative economy" is one of the buzzwords aimed to capture several broader trends in modern consumption made possible by the developments of online platforms. It is often used interchangeably with other notions, such as the sharing economy,[50] collaborative consumption,[51] access-based consumption[52] and the gig economy.[53] All of these concepts broadly refer to the same phenomenon, which in either case is perceived rather vaguely.[54] References to "sharing" or "collaboration"—underlined in the original notions—emphasize the social interactions relating to a common resource. Such interactions allow new value to be extracted from already existing, underutilized assets and are well-aligned with the themes of access over ownership[55] and sustainable consumption.[56] An emphasis on peer-to-peer interactions is a further feature of these discussions: sharing is not to be turned into one's main field of activity, but rather allows individuals to capitalize on excess, idle capacity—be it time, skills or physical assets—which is generally used elsewhere.[57]

Early models which came to be associated with a collaborative, or sharing, economy indeed echoed these sentiments. Couchsurfing—a platform enabling travellers to connect with local hosts offering free accommodation—is seen as one of the forerunners of collaborative consumption in the field of short-term accommodation. Founded several years later, in 2008, Airbnb added "economy" to the equation, providing hosts with the possibility of charging guests for their stay. The business model at that time was seen as the epitome of the sharing economy, combining economic and social aspects and "unlocking the value of underused assets by matching needs and haves"[58] with the help of information technologies. What emphasised the social aspect was, among others, the system of mutual reviews, also known from Couchsurfing. The ability to share one's experience with other platform users—both as a guest and as a host—allowed for the creation of the trust needed for the economic exchange to take place, similar to the one previously derived from social ties within local communities.[59]

[50] Sundararajan (2016).

[51] Botsman and Rogers (2010).

[52] Bardhi and Eckhardt (2012), p. 881.

[53] Prassl (2018).

[54] Gobble (2017), p. 59.

[55] Meller-Hannich (2015), p. 120.

[56] Schor and Fitzmaurice (2015), p. 410.

[57] Aloni (2018), pp. 143, 146, Petropoulos (2016).

[58] Rachel Botsman, 'Defining The Sharing Economy: What Is Collaborative Consumption – And What Isn't?' [2015] *Fast Company* www.fastcompany.com/3046119/defining-the-sharing-economy-what-is-collaborative-consumption-and-what-isnt.

[59] Ranchordás (2018), pp. 132–133, Sundararajan (2016), p. 4.

The controversies began to build up around Airbnb after it emerged that an increasing number of its hosts were, in fact, full-time providers using designated capital and not excess capacity.[60] This not only created new policy dilemmas,[61] but also put the viability of the very term "collaborative economy" into question. Importantly, since suppliers using designated capital generate substantial revenues for platform operators,[62] the incentives of these actors are essentially aligned. This has led Airbnb to expressly embrace professional providers over time.[63] Given the growing openness of more established platforms, such as Booking.com, to individual hosts, pre-existing and collaborative business models appear to gradually converge.

The situation has been equally dynamic in the second major field of activity associated with the collaborative economy, namely passenger transport. A distinction in this domain is typically made between two prominent models: ride-sharing (carpooling) and ride-hailing (rides-on-demand). The former is epitomized by platforms such as BlaBlaCar, which allow drivers to list their journeys and offer to give a lift to potential passengers, usually on a cost-sharing basis. The latter, by contrast, is associated with platforms, through which passengers can order rides between specific places at a specific time, not unlike traditional taxi services.

In both ride-sharing and rides-hailing, reputational feedback systems play an important role and are usually two-sided, even though their details may vary from one provider to another.[64] Other differences, however, are even more pronounced. In the first model, the matching takes place according to supply, i.e. it is the driver who defines the available routes, on which passengers are welcome to accompany him or her—an approach which is viable especially for long-distance rides which drivers are undertaking anyway. The latter model, associated with providers like Uber or Bolt, follows an inverse logic. Here the matching remains demand-oriented, which means that service requests—usually concerning urban rides—are matched with available drivers nearby, not *vice versa*. Rather than picking up passengers on a predefined route, according to a shared objective, drivers operate on routes reflecting passenger requests. The possibility of sharing the ride by several passengers going in the same direction can be incorporated into rides-on-demand,[65] although such an alignment is generally not achieved on the drivers' part.

Motivations of drivers in rides-hailing are essentially profit-driven; the "underutilized resources" which potentially are at play here are not spots on particular

---

[60] In one study, 58.9% of 3,580,044 analysed active Airbnb listings were considered to be "professional accommodation offers", see Adamiak (2019), p. 3137.

[61] For example, concerning the impact of tourism accommodation platforms on the availability of long-term housing, see e.g. Lee (2016), p. 229 and Busch (2019), p. 39.

[62] Aloni (2018), p. 146.

[63] Airbnb, 'More Hotels are Using Airbnb' (2019) <https://press.airbnb.com/more-hotels-are-using-airbnb>.

[64] For further illustrations, see Chap. 3.

[65] See e.g. the description of UberX Share <www.uber.com/pl/en/ride/uberx-share>.

routes, but rather service providers' skills and time, not unlike in established business models. It is for this reason among others that the classification of ride-hailing platforms as a "collaborative economy" has been called into doubt.[66] The strong influence of software providers on the relationship between drivers and passengers has also raised the question as to whether ride-hailing models at all represent online platforms.[67] The judgment of the Court of Justice in *Uber Spain,*[68] discussed in Chap. 4, lends support to such doubts.

The controversies surrounding the two most developed sectors of the collaborative economy illustrate the broader difficulty with the use of the term. Part of the problem lies in the tendency to equate the collaborative economy with particular "collaborative platforms" while, in reality, a single platform may sustain differing models of exchange. Notable efforts have been made in the subject literature to organise the narrative. In one of such attempts, Codagnone and Martens distinguish between three broad categories associated with the collaborative economy: (i) recirculation of goods, (ii) increased asset utilization, and (iii) service and labour exchanges.[69] The role of platform operators is in turn located on a continuum between "pure resellers" and "pure multi-sided platforms".[70] Finally, the authors present a two-dimensional matrix, which they use to map different practices facilitated by platform providers. The most relevant dimensions are, in their view: (i) the for-profit or not-for-profit nature of suppliers' activities and, (ii) the peer-to-peer or business-to-consumer nature of the underlying relationships, with the peer-to-peer, for-profit quadrant constituting the main area of focus for policy and regulation.[71] While the framework of Codagnone and Martens is not limited to the travel sector, platforms operating in the field of tourism accommodation and passenger transport are its prominent part.

To conclude, the "collaborative economy" is a contentious notion that can hardly be used as a legal term. This, however, does not preclude its added value to the public debate. The aspects highlighted by Codagnone and Martens prove relevant for the investigation not only of the "collaborative economy" as such but also—and perhaps more importantly—of the transforming socio-economic interactions which the collaborative economy discourse brings into the spotlight. This general understanding seems also to be shared in EU policy discussions.

---

[66] Ravenelle (2017), p. 281.

[67] Garden and Leong (2018), pp. 457–458. Cf. Schneider (2017), pp. 32–38.

[68] Judgment of the Court of Justice of 20.12.2017 in case C-434/15 *Asociación Profesional Elite Taxi (Uber Spain).*

[69] Codagnone and Martens (2016).

[70] Cf. Hagiu and Wright (2015), p. 165.

[71] Codagnone and Martens (2016), pp. 12–13. See also, elaborated, in Codagnone et al. (2018), pp. 42–45.

#### 2.4.3.2 Collaborative Economy in EU Policy

Collaborative economy (back then as the sharing economy) first appeared on the European Union's agenda in the 2015 Digital Single Market Strategy.[72] Later that year, in the Single Market Strategy, the Commission announced that it would "develop a European agenda for the collaborative economy"—a term which has been consistently used ever since. The agenda was to include a guidance on how existing EU law applies to the collaborative economy along with an assessment of the possible regulatory gaps. These announcements were subsequently turned into action: first as part of the updated guidance on the implementation and application of Directive 2005/29/EC on unfair commercial practices,[73] and eventually in a self-standing communication.

The 2016 communication defines the collaborative economy as "business models where activities are facilitated by collaborative platforms that create an open marketplace for the temporary usage of goods or services often provided by private individuals".[74] The involvement of three categories of actors is emphasised: (i) service providers who share assets, resources, time and/or skills, (ii) users of these, and (iii) intermediaries that connect—via an online platform—providers with users and facilitate transactions between them. According to the communication, service providers can be both private individuals offering services on an occasional basis (peers) or service providers acting in their professional capacity and may be profit-driven or not-for-profit in motivation. Collaborative transactions, however, generally do not involve a change of ownership.

The understanding of the "collaborative economy" provided by the European Commission is not meant to define it as a legal term. The communication rather aims to discuss several dimensions of transforming online markets, focusing on the benefits and risks which they may bring. The definition rightly stresses the existence of triangular settings, in which platform operators assume a prominent role. At the same time, the document does not exclude a possibility for the platform provider to qualify as a party to the underlying legal relationship, e.g. a provider of a transport service.[75] This shows that the terms "online platform" and "collaborative platform" are not used by the Commission too rigidly and can also describe borderline cases.

---

[72] European Commission, 'Communication from the Commission to the European Parliament, the Council, the European Economic and Social Committee and the Committee of the Regions. A Digital Single Market Strategy for Europe' (2015) COM(2015) 192 final 11.

[73] European Commission, 'Commission Staff Working Document. Guidance on the Implementation/Application of Directive 2005/29/EC on Unfair Commercial Practices' (2016) SWD(2016) 163 final 119. The document was later updated, see Commission Notice, Guidance on the interpretation and application of Directive 2005/29/EC of the European Parliament and of the Council concerning unfair business-to-consumer commercial practices in the internal market [2021] OJ C526/1.

[74] European Commission, 'Communication from the Commission to the European Parliament, the Council, the European Economic and Social Committee and the Committee of the Regions. A European Agenda for the Collaborative Economy' (2016) COM(2016) 356 final.

[75] Ibid, p. 6.

In some respects, the definition of the collaborative economy in EU policy is either more, or less inclusive compared to the other definitional attempts discussed in the previous section. For example, it does not take account of the sale of goods, but rather encompasses two further categories described by Codagnone and Martens, namely asset utilization and service and labour exchanges, which from the perspective of the underlying legal relationships can broadly be considered services. Such a discrepancy is of little relevance for the present book, whose focus anyway remains on services provided in the travel sector, and not on selling goods.

It is worth noting that the Commission does not make a sharp distinction based on the personal aspects of the corresponding legal relationships. In particular, it does not consider the business-to-consumer nature of the underlying service contracts to be disqualifying. At the same time, the scale of peer-to-peer transactions and associated legal problems are clearly highlighted in the communication. A similar conclusion follows from the accompanying Staff Working Document, which notes that service providers "are, at least in the initial stages of platform development, typically consumers" (or, more precisely, peers).[76] To avoid excessive overlaps with the broader notions, the understanding of the "collaborative economy" in this book will exclude those settings in which the underlying relationships are clearly business-to-consumer ones. The focus will rather remain on peer-to-peer transactions, recognizing that the relevant classification may be ambiguous and evolving.

## 2.5 Benefits and Risks of Online Platforms

### *2.5.1 Economic and Societal Benefits*

From an economic perspective, the key benefit of platform business models lies in the efficiencies they create.[77] This is directly related to the core function of online platforms, namely the matching of a large number of users to facilitate an exchange.[78] Algorithms which underlie search rankings in Airbnb and Booking.com, as well as direct matching between drivers and passengers in Uber, can radically reduce transaction costs[79] for both sides of the exchange. Consumers and suppliers no longer need to bear many of the costs traditionally associated with finding a suitable counterparty, negotiating the contract and completing the exchange (e.g. arranging for

---

[76] European Commission, 'Commission Staff Working Document. European Agenda for the Collaborative Economy – Supporting Analysis' (2016) SWD(2016) 184 final 13.

[77] Edelman and Geradin (2016), p. 296.

[78] Martens (2016), p. 20.

[79] On the foundations of transaction costs economics, see Coase (1937), p. 386, Coase (1960), p. 1, Cheung (1969), p. 23.

payment, monitoring and evaluating counter-performance). All of this increases the potential welfare gains to society, including the platform operators.

Unlike traditional vertically integrated firms or resellers—like hotel chains or supermarkets—platform operators generate the value for the platform users without having to produce or acquire the subject-matter of the exchange. Rather, they allow a more efficient use of already existing assets, such as flats or vehicles, promising to improve the allocation of resources. For similar reasons, platform users can also be incentivized to invest more in their property or acquire new assets, thus creating an economic and societal value.[80] Customers, in turn, gain access to a greater variety of goods and services at potentially lower prices. It has been suggested, moreover, that collaborative platforms generate a particularly high value for below-median income citizens, thereby positively affecting social inclusion.[81] Finally, some of the benefits promised or delivered by online platforms cannot easily be framed in economic terms. For example, ride-sharing could potentially exert a lower environmental impact compared with traditional car transport.[82] The injection of the social aspect into economic activity can also have a community-building effect and improve social cohesion.[83]

### 2.5.2 *Economic and Societal Risks*

The overall perception of online platforms, including those that have transformed the travel sector, is, however, not unequivocally positive. Oftentimes, the extent of benefits discussed above is being called into question, particularly when viewed in a broader context.[84] For example, operators of ride-hailing platforms (Uber, Bolt) have been criticised for offering lower prices not because of the efficiencies they create, but rather by avoiding regulatory requirements associated with driver and consumer protection.[85] Arguments about the environmental benefits generated by online platforms also tend to lose force when put into perspective, e.g. when their environmental impact is compared to less polluting alternatives and when the rebound effects are taken into account.[86]

---

[80] Edelman and Geradin (2016).

[81] Fraiberger and Sundararajan (2015).

[82] Rademaekers et al. (2018), p. 81.

[83] Cf. Belk (2010), p. 725. The author distinguishes between "sharing in", which involves "regarding ownership as common", and "sharing out", which involves dividing a resource (e.g. giving to others) without necessarily engaging in a common experience. See also Belk (2014), p. 1596.

[84] For a comprehensive overview with a sceptical overall assessment, see Codagnone et al. (2018), pp. 6, 57–65.

[85] Bagińska and Majkowska-Szulc (2018), p. 35. See also Van Damme (2019), p. 89. Cf. Rogers (2015), p. 87.

[86] Rademaekers et al. (2018). Leenheer and Kuijten (2018), pp. 279–280.

In discussion about the dark sides of online platforms a distinction can be drawn between, on the one hand, platforms' internal operations, i.e. the interactions between three corresponding parties, and, on the other hand, their external consequences, such as the effect on the local housing, incumbent businesses, labour relations, environment and social cohesion.[87] Since the present book is focused on consumer protection, understood as the protection of passive market participants,[88] it is the former aspect that remains at its core.

#### 2.5.2.1 Interactions Between Users and Platforms

The principal concerns regarding interactions between platform operators and platform users relate to the potential exploitation of the asymmetry of power and information existing between both groups. Indeed, to benefit from connecting with others at a distance, information and coordination problems must be overcome.[89] Unlike previously, consumers are nowadays exposed to the problems of information overload, rather than scarcity.[90] Platform operators, therefore, increasingly assume the role of both the necessary middlemen and private regulators. This raises potential issues, including the possible distortion of their goals towards capturing profits or the prioritization of the bigger picture perspective at the expense of the detrimental outcomes experienced by individual users. For example, providers of online marketplaces may suppress negative reviews to incentivize contracting or increase the ranking of products in return for monetary benefits.[91]

While some of the risks can affect all platform users to an equal degree, others are more likely to be experienced on one side of the platform. By way of illustration, in the case of a dispute between customers and suppliers, the operator of an online marketplace may systematically favour the interest of one group over the other. Such a treatment can be a result of the different price elasticity of supply and demand as well as other factors which make one group of platform users more difficult to draw and maintain than the other.[92] To ensure a high number of active users on both sides, as required by the network effects, the platform operator may choose to subsidize one of the sides of the exchange not only in terms of price but also in terms of quality.[93] Another set of risks arises when the platform operator acts in a dual role: as both an intermediary and a direct seller or supplier of the relevant

---

[87] Similarly Finck (2018), p. 47. See also Witt et al. (2015), p. 175, Rogers (2015), p. 98, Domurath (2017), pp. 106–109, Palombo (2018), p. 307 and Lee (2016), p. 229.

[88] Reich and Micklitz (2014), p. 53.

[89] For a discussion of the problems, which increased choice and information entail for the consumers, along with the associated regulatory pitfalls, see Hanson and Kysar (1999), pp. 1438–1439, Howells (2005), pp. 356–362, Willett and Morgan-Taylor (2012), Ben-Shahar and Schneider (2014).

[90] Boudreau and Hagiu (2009), pp. 166–167, 183–184.

[91] Stemler (2017), p. 700.

[92] Voigt and Hinz (2015).

[93] Schweitzer (2019), p. 9.

goods or services. In this case, the platform operator may be tempted to abuse the knowledge generated about the market and demote competing suppliers to its own economic advantage.[94]

#### 2.5.2.2 Interactions Between Users

The success of many online platforms is due to software facilities which reduce the transaction costs for interacting parties. However, reduced *ex ante* costs of finding information or a matching party may come with additional risks that materialise at a later stage. This is because the operators of online platforms do not consider themselves responsible for the subject of the exchange, but rather focus on allowing the two corresponding parties to find each other.[95] The ability to exchange an extraordinary variety of products and services within a wide and potentially very diverse pool of platform users can create subsequent costs for the interacting parties.[96]

The nature of the relevant *ex post* risks depends on the subject of the exchange. Notably, users of online marketplaces, including travel platforms, may enter into contracts with disloyal or otherwise inappropriate counterparties, leading to injuries or monetary loss among other things.[97] To illustrate, more than half of respondents to a 2017 survey commissioned by the EU reported having experienced at least one type of problem when using peer-to-peer platforms such as: (i) product/service not being as described or of poor quality, (ii) the price not being as agreed or incurring additional costs, (iii) non-delivery of the product or cancellation, (iv) safety issues with the product or service, (v) personal data being given, resold or leaked to others, or (vi) problems with the use of the platform.[98] The identified personal detriment was generally lower in peer-to-peer (re)sale of goods compared to services offered via collaborative platforms.[99] Interestingly, only 26.4% of the peer consumers said they experienced similar problems with conventional businesses, such as webstores, hotels or taxis.[100] This percentage was, again, somewhat lower for the (re)sale of goods compared to tourism accommodation rental and passenger transport.[101] Notably, a significantly lower occurrence of issues was reported by the peer

[94] Ibid, pp. 9–10. See also European Commission, 'Antitrust: Commission accepts commitments by Amazon barring it from using marketplace seller data, and ensuring equal access to Buy Box and Prime' <https://ec.europa.eu/commission/presscorner/detail/en/ip_22_7777>.

[95] For a critical reconstruction of this discursive framework, see Gillespie (2010), p. 347.

[96] Martens (2016), p. 28.

[97] Cf. OECD, 'Protecting Consumers in Peer Platform Markets: Exploring the Issues' (OECD 2016) 2016 Ministerial Meeting on the Digital Economy Background Report 15.

[98] Hausemer et al. (2017), p. 68.

[99] Ibid, p. 72.

[100] Ibid, p. 71.

[101] Ibid.

providers. Only 14% of the total 8,498 respondents disclosed having experienced a problem, which was most of the time payment-related.[102]

Other available data shed light on specific segments of the platform economy. For example, 69 cases of sexual violence related to the use of ride-hailing applications were reported in Poland between 2016 and 2022.[103] Notably, 32 of these cases were reported in the first seven months of 2022 alone, which suggests that the problem may be escalating. This tendency is also confirmed by information provided by the Warsaw Metropolitan Police, according to which 24 reports were recorded between 2020 and 2021, while 20 cases were reported between January and the end of July 2022 alone.[104]

Official databases hardly paint a full picture and platform operators rarely share internal data on their own initiative. In one notable statement, Airbnb communicated that between 1 August 2018 and 31 July 2019, 0.05 % of trips organised through the platform had a safety-related issue reported by a host or guest.[105] Seeing that the provider declares to have facilitated 193.2 million nights and experience bookings in 2020, the absolute number of reported issues is not insignificant.[106] More detailed information about reported safety issues is unfortunately lacking at the time of writing, although the recent EU legislation may soon bring more transparency.[107] Indeed, more data has already been shared by Booking.com, which reported to have received 881 notices in the EU between 1 March 2024 and 31 August 2024. In addition, the operator moderated a multitude of items on its own account, including 645,072 items related to scams and fraud (covering both listings and reviews), 694 items related to unsafe and/or illegal products and 62 violence-related items.[108]

The above alarming findings are not unexpected. Several factors at play in the platform economy—and especially in the travel sector—are liable to increase *ex post* risk faced by the contracting parties. These include: (i) the means of contracting, (ii) contractual subject-matter and, and (iii) qualities of contracting parties. As regards the former, it is recognized that contractual relationships established at a distance carry a potentially higher level of uncertainty as the parties cannot personally inspect and exchange counter-performance or at least get to know one other.[109] Secondly, the risks of contracting appear to be additionally high in the case of

---

[102] Ibid, p. 73.

[103] Gajewska (2023) Interpelacja nr 38836 do prezesa Rady Ministrów w sprawie zmian w przepisach zwiększających poziom bezpieczeństwa pasażerów zamawiających przejazdy "na aplikację".

[104] Ibid.

[105] Airbnb, 'Trust Innovation Update: Protecting Hosts, Guests, and Communities' (2019) <https://news.airbnb.com/trust-innovation-update-protecting-hosts-guests-and-communities>.

[106] Airbnb, 'Q4 2020 Shareholder Letter' (2020) available at <https://investors.airbnb.com/home>.

[107] Article 15 of Regulation 2022/2065 (Digital Services Act). See Chap. 4 for more details.

[108] Booking.com, 'Digital Services Act. 28 October 2024 – Transparency Report prepared by Booking.com' <https://digital-strategy.ec.europa.eu/en/policies/dsa-brings-transparency>.
B.V. under the Digital Services Act.

[109] Bech Serrat (2012), p. 37, 102.

distance contracts related to the provision of certain types of services, for example, tourism accommodation rental or passenger transport. For the service recipient, the stakes are clearly higher when entering someone's car or flat, than when buying the product from an unknown seller.[110] The risks are even more pronounced when access to a service is being sought at a destination which the service recipient does not know, as is often the case in the travel sector. The qualities of contracting parties constitute an additional risk factor. In particular, the professional status of the consumer's counterparty can be seen as a proxy for a higher level of reliability, which is often supported by existing regulatory safeguards.[111] This is also true for conventional travel services, for which an extensive body of rules has been developed, as will be discussed in Chaps. 5 and 6. However, in the collaborative economy protections of this kind are often not available.

## 2.6 Conclusions

Online platforms are unquestionably a moving target. They cannot be defined in clear and static terms, and their various facets can be addressed by legal rules employing different concepts. In this book, online platforms are understood as a business model sharing a number of characteristics: the existence of triangular settings, in which the direct interactions of two distinct groups of users are taking place, network effects and data-driven architectures. This is without prejudice to the emerging legal definitions of online platforms, such as the one most recently adopted in the Digital Services Act.[112]

The transformative impact of online platforms is particularly prominent in the travel sector. Such an impact is clearly visible in the field of short-term accommodation, in which operators of online marketplaces have gradually taken the role previously assumed by package tour organisers and travel agents. Today prospective travellers can choose between a myriad of single travel services in different Member States, and directly make a booking through digital architectures provided by the operators. What is more, online platforms have also allowed new, non-professional, suppliers to join the market, leading to a broader phenomenon described as the collaborative economy. The impact of online marketplaces had originally remained limited in the field of passenger transport. More recently, however, innovative services have also emerged in this domain. The platform-driven transformation has made it possible for consumers to easily book accommodation, also in private homes, or agree on shared rides. In addition, platforms for rides-on-demand can be accessed in different jurisdictions from a single mobile application and are

[110] Sundararajan (2017).

[111] Hausemer et al. (2017), p. 14.

[112] Article 3(i) of Regulation 2022/2065 (Digital Services Act). See also Chap. 4.

increasingly used by consumers instead of more traditional means of transport, both at home and abroad.

The development of the platform economy comes with both benefits and risks. As far as interactions between the users are concerned, online platforms reduce transaction costs, i.e. the costs of finding relevant information or a matching party for an exchange, which is liable to lower prices and increase consumer choice. At the same time, the ability to exchange with a wide and potentially very diverse pool of suppliers can expose consumers to additional risks, which materialise at a later stage. Risks of this kind relate, among others, to injuries or adverse effects on health and the non-performance of the contract. Considering their particular severity in the travel sector, the question can be asked if platform operators are taking any measures to reduce the risks linked to their operation.

## References

Adam L, Micklitz H-W (2017) Verbraucher und Online-Plattformen. In: Micklitz H-W, Reisch LA, Joost G, Zander-Hayat H (eds) Verbraucherrecht 2.0 – Verbraucher in der digitalen Welt. Nomos, pp 45–102

Adamiak C (2019) Current state and development of Airbnb accommodation offer in 167 countries. Curr Issues Tourism 25(19):3131–3149

Aloni E (2018) Pluralism and regulatory responses. In: Davidson NM, Finck M, Infranca JJ (eds) The Cambridge handbook of the law of the sharing economy. Cambridge University Press, pp 143–155

Armstrong M (2006) Competition in two-sided markets. Rand J Econ. 37(3):668–691

Bagińska E, Majkowska-Szulc S (2018) Granice prawne "uberyzacji" – glosa do wyroku Trybunału Sprawiedliwości z 20.12.2017 r., C-434/15, Asociación Profesional Elite Taxi przeciwko Uber Systems Spain SL. Europejski Przegląd Sądowy 5:30–36

Bardhi F, Eckhardt GM (2012) Access-based consumption: the case of car sharing. J Consum Res 39(4):881–898

Bech Serrat JM (2012) Selling tourism services at a distance: an analysis of the EU consumer *acquis*. Springer

Belk R (2010) Sharing. J Consum Res 36(5):715–724

Belk R (2014) You are what you can access: sharing and collaborative consumption online. J Bus Res 67(8):1595–1600

Ben-Shahar O, Schneider CE (2014) More than you wanted to know the failure of mandated disclosure. Princeton University Press

Botsman R, Rogers R (2010) What's mine is yours: the rise of collaborative consumption. Harper Collins

Boudreau KJ, Hagiu A (2009) Platform rules: multi-sided platforms as regulators. In: Gawer A (ed) Platforms, markets and innovation. Edward Elgar, pp 163–191

Brownsword R (2018) The E-Commerce Directive, consumer transactions, and the digital single market – questions of regulatory fitness, regulatory disconnection and rule redirection. In: Grundmann S (ed) European contract law in the digital age. Intersentia, pp 165–204

Busch C (2016) Crowdsourcing consumer confidence. How to regulate online rating and review systems in the collaborative economy. In: De Franceschi A (ed) European contract law and the digital single market: the implications of the digital revolution. Intersentia, pp 223–243

Busch C (2019) Regulating Airbnb in Germany – status quo and future trends. Eur Consum Mark Law 8(1):39–41

Busch C, Schulte-Nölke H, Wiewiórowska-Domagalska A, Zoll F (2016) The rise of the platform economy: a new challenge for EU consumer law? Eur Consum Mark Law 5(1):3–10
Cheung SNS (1969) Transaction costs, risk aversion, and the choice of contractual arrangements. J Law Econ 12(1):23–42
Chiu AT (2011) Irrationally bound: terms of use licenses and the breakdown of consumer rationality in the market for social network sites. South Calif Interdiscip Law J 21(1):165–197
Coase RH (1937) The nature of the firm. Economica 4(16):386–405
Coase RH (1960) The problem of social cost. J Law Econ 3:1–44
Codagnone C, Martens B (2016) Scoping the sharing economy: origins, definitions, impact and regulatory issues. Institute for Prospective Technological Studies – Digital Economy Working Paper 2016/01. European Commission
Codagnone C, Karatzogianni A, Matthews J (2018) Platform economics: rhetoric and reality in the "sharing economy". Emerald Publishing Limited
Davidson NM, Finck M, Infranca JJ (eds) (2018) The Cambridge handbook of the law of the sharing economy. Cambridge University Press
Devolder B (ed) (2019a) The platform economy: unravelling the legal status of online intermediaries. Intersentia
Devolder B (2019b) Contractual liability of the platform. In: Devolder B (ed) The platform economy: unravelling the legal status of online intermediaries. Intersentia, pp 31–88
Domurath I (2017) Verbraucherrecht in der Plattformökonomie. In: Micklitz H-W, Reisch LA, Joost G, Zander-Hayat H (eds) Verbraucherrecht 2.0 – Verbraucher in der digitalen Welt, Nomos, pp 103–134
Edelman BG, Geradin D (2016) Efficiencies and regulatory shortcuts: how should we regulate companies like Airbnb and Uber? Stanf Technol Law Rev 19:293–328
Evans DS, Schmalensee R (2016) Matchmakers: the new economics of multisided platforms. Harvard Business Review Press
Faust F (2016) Gutachten A zum 71. Deutschen Juristentag. Digitale Wirtschaft – Analoges Recht: Braucht das BGB ein Update? C.H. Beck
Finck M (2018) Digital co-regulation: designing a supranational legal framework for the platform economy. Eur Law Rev 43(1):47–68
Fraiberger SP, Sundararajan A (2015) Peer-to-peer rental markets in the sharing economy. NYU Stern School of Business Research Paper 4
Garden C, Leong N (2018) The platform identity crisis: responsibility, discrimination, and a functionalist approach to intermediaries. In: Davidson NM, Finck M, Infranca JJ (eds) The Cambridge handbook of the law of the sharing economy. Cambridge University Press, pp 449–458
Gillespie T (2010) The politics of "platforms". New Media Soc. 12(3):347–364
Gobble MM (2017) Defining the sharing economy. Res Technol Manage 60(2):59–63
Graef I (2015) Market definition and market power in data: the case of online platforms. World Competition 38(4):473–505
Hagiu A, Wright J (2015) Multi-sided platforms. Int J Ind Organ 43:162–174
Hagiu A, Yoffie DB (2018) Network effects. In: Augier M, Teece DJ (eds) The Palgrave encyclopedia of strategic management. Palgrave Macmillan
Hanson JD, Kysar DA (1999) Taking behavioralism seriously: some evidence of market manipulation. Harv Law Rev 112(7):1420–1572
Hatzopoulos V (2018) The collaborative economy and EU law. Hart Publishing
Hauck R, Blaut H (2018) Die (quasi-)vertragliche Haftung von Plattformbetreibern. NJW 20:1425–1430
Hausemer P, Rzepecka J, Dragulin M, Vitiello S, Rabuel L, Nunu M, Rodriguez Diaz A, Psaila E, Fiorentini S, Gysen S, Meeusen T, Quaschning S, Dunne A, Grinevich V, Huber F, Baines L (2017) Exploratory study of consumer issues in online peer-to-peer platform markets – final report. European Union

Helberger N, Pierson J, Poell T (2018) Governing online platforms: from contested to cooperative responsibility. Inform Soc 34(1):1–14

Howells G (2005) The potential and limits of consumer empowerment by information. J Law Soc 32(3):349–370

Karsten J (2010) Travel law. In: Twigg-Flesner C (ed) The Cambridge companion to European Union private law. Cambridge University Press, pp 201–215

Kramme M (2022) Qualitätsanforderungen der Digitale-Inhalte-Richtlinie an Online-Suchmaschinen. In: Schmidt-Kessel M, Möllnitz C (eds) . Grundfragen des Digitalvertragsrechts, Mohr Siebeck, pp 57–75

Lee D (2016) How Airbnb short-term rentals exacerbate Los Angeles's affordable housing crisis: analysis and policy recommendations. Harv Law Policy Rev 10(1):229–253

Leenheer J, Kuijten M (2018) Are sharing platforms sustainable (business models)? A consumer survey on the drivers of using sharing platforms in the travel industry. In: Moratis L, Melissen F, Idowu SO (eds) Sustainable business models. Springer, pp 261–283

Li J (2015) Is online media a two-sided market? Comput Law Secur Rev 31(1):99–111

Lougher G, Kalmanowicz S (2016) EU competition law in the sharing economy. J Eur Compet Law Pract 7(2):87–102

Luchetta G (2014) Is the Google platform a two-sided market? J Compet Law Econ 10(1):185–207

Martens B (2016) Economic policy perspective on online platforms. Institute for Prospective Technological Studies – Digital Economy Working Paper 2016/05. European Commission

Maultzsch F (2018) Contractual liability of online platform operators: European proposals and established principles. Eur Rev Contr Law 14(3):209–240

Meller-Hannich C (2015) Share economy and consumer protection. In: Schulze R, Staudenmayer D (eds) Digital revolution: challenges for contract law in practice. Nomos/Hart, pp 119–134

Meller-Hannich C, Krausbeck E, Wittke R (2019) Der Verbraucher in der Sharing Economy. VuR 11:403–412

Mik E (2016) Problems of intention and consideration in online transactions. In: Furmston M, Tolhurst G (eds) Contract formation: law and practice, 2nd edn. Oxford University Press

Nesterowicz M (2016) Prawo turystyczne, 5th edn. Wolters Kluwer

OECD (2018) OECD tourism trends and policies 2018. OECD Publishing, pp 74–75

Orti Vallejo A (2019) Contractual relationships in collaborative economy platforms. Eur Rev Priv Law 27(5):995–1022

Palombo D (2018) A tale of two cities: the regulatory battle to incorporate short-term residential rentals into modern law. Am Univ Bus Law Rev 4(2):287–321

Pantazatou K (2018) Taxation of the sharing economy in the European Union. In: Davidson NM, Finck M, Infranca JJ (eds) (2018) The Cambridge handbook of the law of the sharing economy. Cambridge University Press, pp 368–380

Petropoulos G (2016) An economic review on the collaborative economy. In-depth analysis for the IMCO Committee. European Parliament

Prassl J (2018) Humans as a service: the promise and perils of work in the gig economy. Oxford University Press

Rademaekers K, Svatikova K, Vermeulen J, Smit T, Baroni L (2018) Environmental potential of the collaborative economy. European Union

Ranchordás S (2015) Does sharing mean caring? Regulating innovation in the sharing economy. Minn J Law Sci Technol 16(1):413–475

Ranchordás S (2018) Online reputation and the regulation of information asymmetries in the platform economy. Crit Anal Law 5(1):127–147

Ravenelle AJ (2017) Sharing economy workers: selling, not sharing. Camb J Reg Econ Soc 10(2):281–295

Reich N, Micklitz H-W (2014) Economic law, consumer interests, and EU integration. In: Reich N, Micklitz H-W, Rott P, Tonner K (eds) . European consumer law, Intersentia, pp 1–66

Rochet J-C, Tirole J (2003) Platform competition in two-sided markets. J Eur Econ Assoc 1(4):990–1029

Rochet J-C, Tirole J (2006) Two-sided markets: a progress report. Rand J Econ 37(3):645–667
Rogers B (2015) The social costs of Uber. Univ Chi Law Rev 82(1):85–102
Schneider H (2017) Uber: innovation in society. Palgrave Macmillan
Schneider S (2018) Digitale Plattform-Geschäftsmodelle: Zunehmende Relevanz riner umfassenden Ecosystem-Perspektive. In: Rott P, Tonner K (eds) . Online-Vermittlungsplattformen in der Rechtspraxis, Nomos, pp 27–38
Schor JB, Fitzmaurice CJ (2015) Collaborating and connecting: the emergence of the sharing economy. In: Reisch LA, Thøgersen J (eds) Handbook of research on sustainable consumption. Edward Elgar, pp 410–425
Schweitzer H (2019) Digitale Plattformen als private Gesetzgeber: Ein Perspektivwechsel für die europäische "Plattform-Regulierung". ZEuP 27(1):1–12
Smits JM (2014) Contract law: a comparative introduction. Edward Elgar
Smorto G (2018) The protection of the weaker parties in the platform economy. In: Davidson NM, Finck M, Infranca JJ (eds) The Cambridge handbook of the law of the sharing economy. Cambridge University Press, pp 431–446
Sobczyk M (2018) Siła wyższa jako okoliczność zwalniająca od odpowiedzialności osobę utrzymującą zarobkowo hotel za rzecz wniesioną przez gościa. Uwagi historyka prawa. In: Cybula P (ed) Prawne aspekty podróży i turystyki – historia i współczesność. Prace poświęcone pamięci profesora Janusza Sondla. Jagiellonian University Press, pp 435–448
Stemler A (2017) Feedback loop failure: implications for the self-regulation of the sharing economy. Minn J Law Sci Technol 18:673–712
Strowel A, Vergote W (2019) Digital platforms: to regulate or not to regulate? Message to regulators: get the economics right first, then focus on the right regulation. In: Devolder B (ed) The platform economy: unravelling the legal status of online intermediaries. Intersentia, pp 3–30
Stummer C, Kundisch D, Decker R (2018) Platform launch strategies. Bus Inf Syst Eng 60:167–173
Sundararajan A (2016) The sharing economy: the end of employment and the rise of crowd-based capitalism. MIT Press
Sundararajan A (2017) The collaborative economy: socioeconomic, regulatory and policy issues. In-depth analysis for the IMCO Committee. European Parliament
Tereszkiewicz P (2019) Digital platforms: regulation and liability in EU law. In: DiMatteo LA, Cannarsa M, Poncibò C (eds) The Cambridge handbook of smart contracts, blockchain technology and digital platforms. Cambridge University Press, pp 143–159
Tonner K, Bergmann S, Blankenburg D (eds) (2018) Reiserecht. Nomos
Twigg-Flesner C (2016) Disruptive technology – disrupted law? How the digital revolution affects (contract) law. In: De Franceschi A (ed) European contract law and the digital single market: the implications of the digital revolution. Intersentia, pp 21–48
Van Damme N (2019) Law evasion in the platform economy: the Uber case. In: Devolder B (ed) The platform economy: unravelling the legal status of online intermediaries. Intersentia, pp 89–124
van Leeuwen B (2017) European standardisation of services and its impact on private law: paradoxes of convergence. Hart Publishing
Voigt S, Hinz O (2015) Network effects in two-sided markets: why a 50/50 user split is not necessarily revenue optimal. Bus Res 8:139–170
Wauters E, Lievens E, Valcke P (2014) Towards a better protection of social media users: a legal perspective on the terms of use of social networking sites. Int J Law Inform Technol 22(3):254–294
Wendehorst C (2016) Platform intermediary services and duties under the E-Commerce Directive and the Consumer Rights Directive. EuCML 5(1):30–33
Willett C, Morgan-Taylor M (2012) Recognising the limits of transparency in EU Consumer law. In: Devenney J, Kenny M (eds) European consumer protection: theory and practice. Cambridge University Press, pp 143–163
Wismer S, Rasek A (2017) Market definition in multi-sided markets. OECD

Witt A, Suzor N, Wikström P (2015) Regulating ride-sharing in the peer economy. Commun Res Pract 1(2):174–190

Wyrwińska K (2018) *Fide, sed cui, vide*... niektóre aspekty odpowiedzialności *ex recepto* armatorów, oberżystów i gospodarzy stajen w kontekście ryzyka podróży lądowych i morskich w antycznym Rzymie. In: Cybula P (ed) Prawne aspekty podróży i turystyki – historia i współczesność. Prace poświęcone pamięci profesora Janusza Sondla. Jagiellonian University Press, pp 609–624

Zimmermann R (1996) The law of obligations: Roman foundations of the civilian tradition. Oxford University Press

Zuelow EGE (2016) A history of modern tourism. Palgrave Macmillan

# Chapter 3
# Private Governance in Online Travel Platforms

## 3.1 Private Governance and Regulatory Environment in the Platform Economy

### *3.1.1 Notion of Regulatory Environment*

The previous discussion highlighted the role of data-driven architectures among the key characteristics of online platforms. Thanks to those architectures, and related contract-based strategies, platform operators can channel users' behaviour in ways that they consider optimal for their business models. In the most elaborate online platforms, the deployed regulatory instruments and modalities are so extensive, that they can together be perceived as private governance systems.[1]

The potential of technology for steering human conduct finds support in the extensive literature, dating back to mid-1990s and the observations of Lawrence Lessig about the coexistence of several regulatory modalities: law, market, social norms and architecture.[2] In-depth research has also been carried out on the role and means of private ordering in commercial and consumer relations, describing a variety of governance mechanisms which reduce the likelihood of opportunistic behaviour among contracting parties, as well as their interactions with international and domestic institutions.[3] The regulatory theory has likewise gradually acknowledged that capacities and resources relevant to the exercise of power

---

[1] Petersen et al. (2018), p. 39. Similarly Schweitzer (2019), pp. 4–6.

[2] Lessig (1999a), pp. 501, 506–509. Lessig (1999b). For an overview of later works exploring the effects of regulatory signals other than formal legal rules on individual behaviour, see Leiser and Murray (2016).

[3] See e.g. Calliess (2008), p. 226, Cafaggi (2015), p. 875, Purnhagen (2015), p. 309, Grundmann et al. (2015), Grundmann and Hacker (2018), pp. 14–26.



A. Jabłonowska, *Consumer Protection and Online Travel Platforms*, Law, Governance and Technology Series 73, https://doi.org/10.1007/978-3-031-90170-6_3

may be dispersed among a wide range of state, non-state and supranational actors,[4] with some authors observing, or arguing for, a shift towards "new governance"[5] or "smart regulation".[6]

From the present perspective, a particularly helpful analytical lens can be found in the notion of "regulatory environment" as understood by Roger Brownsword.[7] At the most general level, the concept refers to the totality of different signals—regulatory instruments and modalities—designed to channel the conduct of regulatees.[8] Central to this concept is the understanding, in line with the prior work of Lessig, that legal norms are not the only type of signals channelling human behaviour. Other elements, such as social norms, can also convey the message to regulatees what they ought or ought not to do, and thus have a normative dimension. Norms of this kind can be followed out of moral or prudential reasons, or the agents can choose not to comply and face potential consequences.[9] Crucially, besides normative signals, there are also other elements, especially associated with architecture, which can affect human behaviour for reasons of possibility and practicability, rather than moral or prudential ones.

The above findings are directly relevant to the platform economy. Platform operators are increasingly managing risks in underlying relations by excluding actions or actors through their technological design. In addition, data-driven architectures can be used to "nudge"[10] individuals towards particular actions, thus triggering a set of moral or prudential signals.[11] However, Brownsword warns about potential negative impacts of technological management, especially in terms of autonomy and liberty, the moral community and the rule of law.[12] Strong emphasis is therefore placed on the need to ensure that the adoption of regulatory technologies finds support in an appropriate social license.[13] In general, the regulatory environment is seen as adequate when, on top of maintaining the basic preconditions for a viable social existence, the fundamental values of a community are respected and legitimate interests are reasonably balanced.[14]

---

[4] Scott (2004), p. 145, Hodges (2016), pp. 252–254.

[5] Lobel (2004), p. 342. In the EU context, see Scott and Trubek (2002), p. 1.

[6] Gunningham and Sinclair (2017), p. 133.

[7] Brownsword (2019), p. 39.

[8] Brownsword and Goodwin (2012), pp. 27–28.

[9] Brownsword (2019), pp. 65–66.

[10] Thaler and Sunstein (2008).

[11] Finck (2018b), pp. 266–267.

[12] Ibid, p. 12–19.

[13] Ibid, p. 91.

[14] Ibid, p. 102.

### 3.1.2 *Societal Values and Normative Patterns in the Normative Field*

Brownsword underlines the connection between the regulatory environment and fundamental values of a community as well as the balance of competing interests. The author does not prejudge what constitutes the relevant set of values in every case and notes that this may be for the relevant community to decide.[15] The evolving relationship between the values of a community and its governance mechanisms is also prominent in the theory of law as normative patterns in a normative field, developed by Anna Christensen. The theory is not concerned with the aspects of technological management or, in general, the elements of non-normative nature. However, it provides a valuable lens through which regulatory instruments in particular communities and their relationship with societal developments can be looked at.

The theory of law as normative patterns in a normative field draws attention to the polycentricity of the legal order, reflected in the role of normative signals beyond and beneath the formal legal rules.[16] The focus remains on the different basic normative patterns, which can be distinguished in the multitude of legal norms and which, according to the author, are part of the cultural values upon which society is built.[17] These patterns do not form hierarchical structures but are rather put in play in a normative field for the given area of life and law, and potentially remain in tension.[18] Indeed, moral habits of particular groups of society may differ and different kinds of relations may call for different moral norms.[19] Importantly, the understanding of moral norms within this framework is not limited to the ones associated with the "big moral issues", but begins with the habits "penetrating all parts of daily life", such as keeping one's promises.[20] As Christensen observes, the positions in the normative field—that is, the way in which particular patterns affect the normative content of the legal rules—are not fixed and stable, but can rather change over time. Explanation for this variability is sought in a functional relationship between law and society, whereby changes in societal conditions set ground for movements in the normative field.[21] Such movements and tensions can also be identified in the legal norms of relevance to consumers, as Hans-W. Micklitz demonstrates in his extensive research.[22]

In light of the above, there is arguably a level of alignment between the prominence of particular normative patterns expressed in legal norms and the values deemed societally important in relevant communities and points in time. One could

[15] Ibid, pp. 95–101, in relation to the right to be forgotten.

[16] Christensen (1995), p. 238.

[17] Christensen (1999), p. 89.

[18] Ibid, pp. 90–91.

[19] Christensen (1995), p. 238.

[20] Ibid, pp. 236–237.

[21] Numhauser-Henning (2013), p. 27.

[22] Micklitz (2018), pp. 225–238.

therefore hypothesise that the expansion of the EU consumer law over past decades, which is discussed in more detail in the following chapter, reflects the importance attached in the EU society to the particular values embedded in this field of law. Considering the major role of private governance in the platform economy, a question can be asked about the values that emerge from it. Arguably, the spotlight in which platform operators are placed due to their strong market position may render them receptive to societal perceptions discussed above, communicated either directly by the users and affected third parties or indirectly by the law- and policymakers.[23] Platform operators may thus take voluntary steps to ensure that the values of respective communities are safeguarded, or at least seek to create such an impression.

### 3.1.3 *Private Governance in Online Travel Platforms*

In the remainder of this chapter, specific private governance frameworks employed in online travel platforms are discussed.[24] The focus remains on the providers who not only have the highest EU market share but also demonstrate notable differences in their business models. The selection includes, for tourism accommodation rental—Airbnb and Booking.com, for passenger transport—BlaBlaCar and Uber. Some of these platforms have largely been associated with the collaborative economy (Airbnb, BlaBlaCar), others have relied on more established service providers and have shown certain openness towards non-professional supply (Booking.com). Still others have long remained the subject of controversial debates, in which their classification as "platforms" has been called into doubt (Uber). As was explained in Chap. 2, these conceptual difficulties are recognized, but do not preclude the added value of analysing all selected models in more detail. The observed development rather shows that platform-based governance structures, which reduce risks of contracting, can play an important role in a variety of online settings and as such, be of potential relevance to the EU law- and policymakers.

The analysis covers the features of relevant data-driven architectures, such as reputational feedback systems, which may steer the behaviour of the platform users and help eliminate harsh outcomes.[25] It further includes the available mechanisms for identity verification, performance monitoring or payment processing, which can have similar effects. Furthermore, platform providers can directly define the standards of user behaviour in their terms of service and automatically enforce those standards by means of technological management, e.g. by suspending or blocking

---

[23] Compare with Christensen's discussion of the Bismarck system in social security law: Christensen (1999), p. 95. On the economic considerations concerning platform-based mechanisms of quality and behaviour control, see Engert (2018), pp. 352–354.

[24] Petersen et al. (2018), p. 39.

[25] Helberger et al. (2018), p. 4, Cantero Gamito (2017), pp. 60–63, Busch (2020), pp. 119–120.

user accounts.[26] Finally, the risk of contracting can be reduced through mechanisms which are not *per se* implemented in the platform design, such as undertaking more traditional background checks, providing assistance in case of problems or engaging in dispute resolution.

The following discussion is organised according to the stages of underlying relationships, where the relevant problems might arise, from the perspective of a new user and his or her first offline interaction mediated via the platform. As was signalled in Chap. 2, the existence of a contract between the platform provider and the user is usually unquestioned in the travel sector. The situation may not be equally clear for some of the underlying relationships, especially where no money changes hands.[27] In the continental legal systems, on which this book is focused, particular importance is ascribed to the meeting of two wills related to the same thing, along with the intention to create legal relations. In business models with a strong social component and perceived informality, such an intention may at times be lacking. However, even in those cases, the establishment of contractual relationships cannot be ruled out.[28] Moreover, legal relationships between the parties can also be established irrespectively of, or in addition to, a contract, particularly when one party has suffered from damage as a result of the culpable conduct of the other party. In the following, I will operate with a more neutral notion of an interaction which is meant to include but is not limited to obligatory relationships of a contractual and non-contractual nature.

The analysis is largely informed by the documents, such as the terms of service, made available by platform operators. Such documents were consulted at two points in time—in 2020 and 2024—so as to take account of possible changes in governance frameworks.

## 3.2 Private Governance in Short-Term Accommodation Rental Platforms

### *3.2.1 Airbnb*

#### 3.2.1.1 Background Information

Airbnb (originally Airbed & Breakfast) was founded in 2008 in San Francisco, United States with an underlying concept similar to the one known from Couchsurfing—to connect guests with hosts willing to offer overnight accommodation to strangers.[29] Unlike its predecessor, however, Airbnb does not prohibit hosts

[26] Finck (2018a), p. 55.

[27] Consider the case of Couchsurfing. See Meller-Hannich (2014), pp. 2338–2339.

[28] Ibid, p. 2339.

[29] Hausemer et al. (2017a), p. 20.

from charging guests for a stay but rather seeks to provide them with a monetization opportunity.[30] This likely contributed to its remarkable success, as epitomized by the number of its listings, exceeding 8 million globally as of 2024.[31] The company's revenues stem from the commission which it collects from both parties to the transaction.

Airbnb originally only allowed hosts to list spare rooms, but has gradually developed to include entire apartments, houses and vacation rentals (traditional bed and breakfasts, boutique hotels).[32] Over the years, the company further expanded by allowing experiences (e.g. guided tours or cooking classes) to be organised via the platform.[33] The following discussion focuses on the core Airbnb segment, namely tourism accommodation. The operator has made significant changes to its terms of service in the studied period, partly in response to EU legislation and enforcement.[34]

#### 3.2.1.2 Before Interaction

To be able to use core Airbnb services, such as publishing or booking a listing, users are required to register and accept the operator's terms of service.[35] The relevant terms, as well as the functioning of the platform, significantly affect users' position at all stages of their interactions. The platform provider nonetheless underlines that it merely provides an online marketplace and is not a party to, or other participant in, any contractual relationship between users.[36] The details of applicable terms of service differ depending on the user's country of residence. The following analysis of carried out from the perspective of European users.

Airbnb defines eligibility requirements and procedures for establishing a user account. For individuals, the minimum age is set at 18 years. A user account can be created using an email address or through a social login. Users are contractually obliged to provide accurate, current and complete information during the registration process and keep the relevant information up-to-date.[37]

Airbnb's approach to users' identity verification has evolved over time. Confirming one's identity was initially a voluntary measure that users could undertake free of charge. In 2023, the company announced that identity verification would become mandatory for all guests and primary hosts, although this commitment is

---

[30] Ikkala and Lampinen (2015), p. 1033.

[31] Airbnb, 'Q3 2024 Shareholder Letter' (2024) available at https://investors.airbnb.com/home.

[32] Airbnb, 'More Hotels are Using Airbnb' (2019) https://news.airbnb.com/more-hotels-are-using-airbnb.

[33] Airbnb, 'Airbnb Experiences Update' (2019) https://news.airbnb.com/airbnb-experiences-update.

[34] See also Chaps. 4 and 7.

[35] Airbnb, 'Terms of Service for European Users' (2024) www.airbnb.com/help/article/2908#EUTOS.

[36] Ibid, sec. 17.

[37] Ibid, sec. 18.

not so far reflected in its terms of service.[38] The latter merely state that the platform operator may, as far as legally permitted, but has no obligation to "(i) ask [users] to provide identification or other information, (ii) undertake checks designed to help verify [users'] identity or background, (iii) screen [users] against third-party databases or other sources and request reports from service providers, and (iv) obtain reports from public records of criminal convictions or sex offender registrations or their local equivalents".[39] This remains somewhat at odds with the newly added section for business hosts, who are explicitly required to provide Airbnb, among others, with a copy of their identification document and a number in the relevant trade register.[40] As is further discussed in Chap. 4, the legal background for this dedicated section can be found in Article 30 of the Digital Services Act. The somewhat inconsistent terms of service reflect the operator's strategy to respond to changes in the law only as far as necessary, further adding to the non-transparency of the platform policies.[41]

In addition to the above, hosts are contractually required to provide complete and accurate information about their services, and disclose any rules and requirements that apply.[42] Part of this information is disclosed by way of checking boxes predefined by the platform operator. Hosts are prompted, among others, to indicate whether or not their accommodation is equipped with a fire extinguisher, first aid kit as well as carbon monoxide detectors. The terms of service further prohibit a range of behaviours, including the offering of services that violate the laws or agreements applicable to the host.[43]

The platform operator assumes no general obligation to monitor the content provided by and stored on behalf of users.[44] Neither does it consider itself obliged to act upon user reports, beyond the degree required by law.[45] It nevertheless reserves broad rights to take action aimed *inter alia* at improving the platform, ensuring users' compliance with the terms of service, and responding to any content that it deems objectionable.[46] Airbnb further undertakes to notify the users whose content it has removed or disabled and provide the reasons for its measure, unless such

---

[38] Airbnb, 'An update on identity verification on Airbnb' (2023) https://news.airbnb.com/an-update-on-identity-verification-on-airbnb.

[39] Airbnb, 'Terms of Service for European Users' (2024), sec. 18.

[40] Ibid, sec. 26.

[41] Note that information about additional measures taken by the provider has so far been scarce and, if at all, shared via press releases. For example, in a statement from 2017, the operator mentioned that it was running background checks on every host and guest in the United States. See Airbnb, 'Perfect Strangers: How Airbnb is building trust between hosts and guests' (2017) https://news.airbnb.com/perfect-strangers-how-airbnb-is-building-trust-between-hosts-and-guests/.

[42] Airbnb, 'Terms of Service for European Users' (2024) sec. 5.4.

[43] Ibid, sec. 11.1.

[44] Ibid, sec. 12.1.

[45] Ibid, sec. 11.2.

[46] Ibid, sec. 17.

notification would prevent or impede the detection or prevention of fraud or other illegal activities, among other things.[47]

To find a suitable listing, a guest makes use of search tools provided by the operator. The parameters of the offer are determined by the host within the architecture defined by the operator. This includes the setting of the price and the choice of a cancellation policy, which applies in addition to the terms about "major disruptive events" (previously termed "extenuating circumstances").[48] Applicable fees, including Airbnb commission, are generally collected upon the host's confirmation[49] and the users are prohibited from requesting, accepting or making any payments outside the platform.[50] The relevant pay-outs, however, are only initiated 24 hours after the guest's scheduled check-in time.[51]

If a booking is cancelled by the host, the guest receives a full refund of the fees paid via the platform. For cancellations occurring within 30 days of the check-in, Airbnb also undertakes to help the user "find a similar place, depending on availability at comparable pricing" as an alternative to the total refund.[52] However, Airbnb notes that it is not obligated to pay for, or contribute to, the cost of new accommodations, although it may choose to do so.[53] Guests, in principle, are not compensated otherwise.[54]

Airbnb has over time improved the clarity of its terms about host cancellations. The terms retrieved in 2024 define specific amounts that can be charged from hosts who cancel reservations. The fees depend on the time of cancellation and represent a relevant percentage of the reservation amount. In addition, Airbnb may keep the calendar of the host unavailable or blocked for the dates of the cancelled booking. The consequences are not drawn if the cancellation was made for a valid reason, such as circumstances beyond the host's control.[55]

Finally, in a quite recent section, Airbnb discloses that it uses "various processes and tools to identify, review, and moderate [user content]".[56] The provider further submits that such processes and tools "may include human review, automated review, or a combination of both".[57] The above formulations appear to implement Article 14 of the Digital Services Act, which is discussed in more detail in Chap. 4.

---

[47] Ibid.

[48] Airbnb, 'Major Disruptive Events Policy' (2024) https://www.airbnb.com/help/article/1320.

[49] Airbnb, 'Payments Terms of Service for European Users' (2024), sec. 2.5 www.airbnb.com/help/article/2909#euptos.

[50] Airbnb, 'Terms of Service for European Users' (2024), sec. 11.1.

[51] Airbnb, 'Payments Terms of Service for European Users' (2024), sec. 3.3.

[52] Airbnb, 'Rebooking and Refund Policy' (2024) www.airbnb.com/help/article/2868. See also the discussion in the following sections. The same applies if the guest is unable to access the property.

[53] Airbnb, 'Rebooking and Refund Policy' (2024).

[54] Anecdotal evidence shows that the operator may offer additional vouchers for future reservations.

[55] Airbnb, 'Host Cancellation Policy' (2023) www.airbnb.com/help/article/990.

[56] Airbnb, 'Terms of Service for European Users' (2024), sec. 12.

[57] Ibid.

While these descriptions are still far from transparent, more details on the actions taken can be expected in the future.[58]

#### 3.2.1.3 During Interaction

Airbnb terms of service make it clear that the users are entering into a contract directly with one another and are alone responsible for their behaviour. The platform operator further purports that it does not become a party to any contractual relationship between the users, nor is it an agent for any user, except in the context of payments. Despite this self-declared role, Airbnb does not shy away from steering user's offline behaviour to a certain extent. As was already mentioned, there is an extensive list of activities in which the users are prohibited from engaging towards one another according to their contract with Airbnb.[59]

Airbnb recognizes that interactions established through the platform may pose a risk of harm to a person or property. The terms of service advise the users to contact competent authorities as well as the operator if situations of this kind occur.[60] Notably, as of 2020, a dedicated hotline has been made available to the users, enabling contact with Airbnb safety team 24/7.[61]

If a host claims and presents evidence of damage occasioned by the guest's stay, Airbnb provides an avenue for dispute resolution.[62] Should the guest fail to pay for the damage caused, the platform operator can reimburse the costs under its host protection programme.[63] The operator also undertakes to address several "reservation issues" experienced by the guests.[64] These include, in particular: (i) host cancellations, (ii) inability to access the accommodation, and (iii) inaccuracy of the online listing. In contrast to the earlier terms, Airbnb's current commitments seem to be actionable, and not just aspirational. In addition, Airbnb provides insurance to hosts for their liability for bodily injury or property damage to guests.[65] The lack of such

---

[58] Recent press releases suggest that machine learning systems are put in place to identify potential violators of the terms on parties. See Airbnb, 'An update on our work to crack down on parties and disruptive behavior' (2023) https://news.airbnb.com/an-update-on-our-work-to-crack-down-on-parties-and-disruptive-behavior. More details should follow in compliance with Article 15 of Regulation 2022/2065 (Digital Services Act).

[59] Airbnb, 'Terms of Service for European Users' (2024), sec. 11.1. Airbnb, 'Host and guest safety' www.airbnb.com/help/article/3063. Airbnb, 'Illegal and prohibited activities' www.airbnb.com/help/article/3064.

[60] Airbnb, 'Terms of Service for European Users' (2024), sec. 11.2.

[61] Airbnb, 'Expanding the Urgent Support Line' (2021) https://news.airbnb.com/expanding-the-urgent-support-line.

[62] Airbnb, 'Terms of Service for European Users' (2024), sec. 16.

[63] Airbnb, 'AirCover for Hosts' www.airbnb.com/aircover-for-hosts.

[64] Airbnb, 'Rebooking and Refund Policy' (2024).

[65] Airbnb, 'Host Liability Insurance Program Summary' (2024) www.airbnb.com/help/article/3145.

coverage had previously been reported as an issue by the guests concerned.[66] However, the insurance includes notable limitations, e.g. for the bodily injury or property damage that the insured should have expected to happen.

#### 3.2.1.4 After Interaction

A prominent protection instrument available to users after their offline interaction is the system of ratings and reviews. Within 14 days after completing a booking, guests and hosts can leave a public review and submit a star rating about each other. According to Airbnb terms of service, reviews must be accurate and may not contain any offensive or defamatory language. The operator admits, however, that the user feedback is not verified for accuracy and may be incorrect or misleading.[67]

The feedback system deployed by Airbnb follows a double-blind approach.[68] First of all, Airbnb allows guests to rate their overall experience as well as its particular elements, such as cleanliness, location and communication. Guests are further asked to provide private and public feedback in the form of a short message, to which the recipient can respond. Similar feedback is also provided by the hosts, which underlines the social dimension of platform-mediated interactions, even though Airbnb has long remained open to providers with designated capital.[69] Airbnb has over time improved the presentation of reviews, e.g. by offering more sorting options.[70]

Besides leaving ratings and reviews, guests who completed their stay are prompted to provide Airbnb with information about its various aspects, such as the availability of kitchen amenities, check-in process, type of accommodation, etc. The system also includes a facility to report any dangerous or inappropriate activity, including sexual harassment or violent behaviour, yet it is difficult to assess how the corresponding data is being used.

As mentioned, Airbnb has established procedures to be followed in case of different problems experienced during offline interactions. Under the host damage protection terms, Airbnb agrees to make a monetary payment to the host to repair or replace the property damaged or destroyed, subject to the conditions set out in the policy.[71] The scope of the protection has been adjusted over time and currently covers e.g. physical damage to different types of property as well as reasonable, customary and unexpected cleaning costs. The limit has gradually increased from one to three million USD or its equivalent in the local currency.[72]

---

[66] Interview with an Airbnb user concerning a reservation in Lisbon, Portugal (2 January 2019, Lodz, Poland). See also Mak (2018), pp. 94–95.

[67] Airbnb, 'Terms of Service for European Users' (2024), sec. 8.

[68] For an illustration, see Hausemer et al. (2017a), pp. 36–38.

[69] Aloni (2018), p. 146.

[70] See also Airbnb, 'Airbnb 2023 Winter Release: Introducing Guest Favorites, a collection of the two million most-loved homes on Airbnb' (2023) https://news.airbnb.com/airbnb-2023-winter-release.

[71] Airbnb, 'Host Damage Protection Terms' (2024) www.airbnb.com/help/article/2869.

[72] Ibid.

Airbnb further operates a separate policy for guest refunds in the case of reservation issues described in the previous section. Guests wishing to benefit from this policy must fulfil several conditions, for example, contact the host or Airbnb within 72 hours after discovery.[73] The acceptance of a guest's claim concerning a reservation issue by Airbnb is not without consequences for the host who may have his or her payout reduced. Guests can also indirectly benefit from the host liability insurance, even though the company does not provide any details on that process from the guest's perspective.[74]

## *3.2.2 Booking.com*

### 3.2.2.1 Background Information

Booking.com represents another business model in the short-term accommodation rental sector. Launched in 1996 in Amersfoort, the Netherlands, the company has over time established itself as one of the leading European platform operators. Unlike Airbnb, which focuses on non-professional hosts, Booking.com primarily provides an online distribution channel for regular hotels and hotel-like accommodations. While the platform has more recently expanded to include private accommodations, the original concept remains at its core.

Contract terms governing the relationships between the platform operator and its users are not identical for guests and hosts. Rather, publicly available terms of service are directed primarily at guests. The relationship between the platform operator and the host is, in turn, governed by separate agreements between both parties. The following analysis is mostly carried out from the guests' perspective.

Notably, at the time of writing, Booking.com is the only online travel platform designated by the European Commission as a "very large online platform" within the meaning of the Digital Services Act.[75]

### 3.2.2.2 Before Interaction

As in all analysed business models, to make a booking through the platform users need to establish an account.[76] Guests can browse through a multitude of available listings with the help of search tools. The default ranking is created via the

---

[73] Airbnb, 'Rebooking and Refund Policy' (2024). Guests.

[74] Airbnb, 'Host Liability Insurance Program Summary' (2024).

[75] Article 33 of Regulation 2022/2065 (Digital Services Act). See Chap. 4 for more details.

[76] Booking.com, 'Customer terms of service' (2023), sec. 5 www.booking.com/content/terms.en-gb.html.

operator's algorithm and may differ from one search to another. Guests also can adjust the presentation of the ranking according to different criteria (price, review scores, etc).[77]

Information about particular listings, including the description of accommodation, the indicated standard, and availability, is provided by the hosts. While the platform operator insists that it cannot guarantee that everything is accurate, it does undertake to take reasonable care and act with professional diligence.[78] The company disclaims liability for any errors, interruptions, or missing information unless the above duty was violated or the provider acted with negligence.[79] Such a formulation constitutes an improvement compared to the previously applicable terms, which contained a broader limitation.

Users can book accommodations directly through the platform and the price paid by the users reflects the price set by the hosts, who alone are charged a commission by Booking.com. All bookings are instantly confirmed online and, in principle, give rise to a contractual relationship between the users. The platform operator stresses that it is not a party to these contracts and hosts alone are responsible for underlying services.[80]

Before making the reservation, guests are expected to familiarize themselves with applicable cancellation, payment and no-show policies as well as any other terms and conditions of the host (such as the house rules). It is up to the hosts whether or not the guests should be allowed to choose between refundable and non-refundable reservations and under what conditions. The same applies to the accepted payment methods and the requirement to provide a security deposit.

In the business model of Booking.com, the payment system does not fulfil similar regulatory functions as it does in Airbnb. In principle, hosts can choose between three payment options: payment at the accommodation, advance payment not organised by Booking.com (in which case the operator simply forwards the payment details of the guest to the host), and advance payment organised by Booking.com (in which case the provider is also providing payment services).[81] The applicable policy may influence the prospects of obtaining a refund in case something goes wrong. At the same time, the distinction between the last two options may not be obvious to the users.

An important policy adjustment applies to new hosts, who are only allowed to charge guests at the property. Even in that case, however, the operator allows hosts

---

[77] Booking.com, 'How we work' (2023), sec 1F https://secure.booking.com/content/how_we_work.en-gb.html.

[78] Booking.com, 'Customer terms of service' (2023), sec. A4.1. Service providers, for instance, can be removed from the platform if they have breached their contract with the operator, see Booking.com, 'How we work' (2023), sec. 1K.

[79] Booking.com, 'Customer terms of service' (2023), sec. A4.1.

[80] Ibid, sec. A4.4.

[81] Booking.com, 'How we work' (2023), sec. 1H.

to view and charge guests' credit cards in cases of no-shows or cancelled non-refundable reservations. The details of this policy are not disclosed to users.[82]

#### 3.2.2.3 During Interaction

While hosts can protect themselves from the consequences of guest cancellations and no-shows by selecting preferable policies, the protection of guests in analogous situations is more standardized. A host, who realises that he or she can no longer accommodate the guest, is responsible for covering the cost of relocating the guest to a nearby accommodation of a similar standard.[83] If the host refuses to cooperate, the guest can cancel the booking at no cost. As noted earlier, however, the time and prospects of obtaining the refund may differ depending on the applicable payment policy. The traveller can also ask the platform operator for support in finding alternative lodging. Under the recent terms of service, the company undertakes to refund the price difference, if the new accommodation is "a bit more expensive".[84] Unlike in Airbnb, no similar policy appears to be in place if it turns out that the original accommodation does not meet the expected standard (instead of being overbooked). Moreover, according to media reports, the assistance offered by Booking.com may not be adequate in practice.[85]

Over time, Booking.com has expanded its protection of hosts against the damage caused by guests. Hosts can, firstly, request guests to provide a damage deposit or, secondly, choose to participate in the damage programme. In the former case, the platform operator is not involved in any related financial settlement, which means that guests have limited options for challenging respective claims. Like with the payment system, the platform operator appears to prioritize the interests of service providers and leaves them a margin of discretion.

In a positive development, as of March 2022, Booking.com began to offer a liability insurance programme to partners with residential or home-like properties.[86] Similarly to Airbnb, the programme can indirectly protect guests, by ensuring that their claims for bodily injury and property damage are covered, but likely suffers from similar limitations.

[82] Booking.com, 'New partner restrictions: credit cards and prepayments' https://partner.booking.com/en-gb/help/first-steps/first-reservations/new-partner-restrictions-credit-cards-and-prepayments.

[83] Booking.com, 'How we work' (2023), sec. 1L.

[84] Ibid.

[85] Sobolak (2019) Rezerwujesz nocleg przez Booking.com? Nawet płacąc z góry, nie masz pewności zakwaterowania. Gazeta Wyborcza, 8 August 2019.

[86] Booking.com, 'Partner Liability Insurance' https://partner.booking.com/en-gb/help/legal-security/security/partner-liability-insurance.

#### 3.2.2.4 After Interaction

The principal mechanism of user protection after interaction is the feedback system. The system is not mutual as in the case of Airbnb. Only guests are invited to comment on and score particular aspects of their stay. Hosts, in turn, have the possibility of responding to a review. Reviews can only be submitted within a limited period after a stay and each review is available for a limited period after posting.[87] The default ranking order is by date of submission and a few additional criteria, such as language. Users who wish to consult reviews prior to their booking can sort them according to several parameters. Booking.com moderates user reviews and describes this process in a dedicated policy.[88] Besides the rating system, both guests and hosts can report misconduct to the operator through reporting features. As a very large online platform within the meaning of the DSA, Booking.com is under particular scrutiny concerning its content moderation practices.[89]

### *3.2.3 Assessment*

To assess the described private governance frameworks from a consumer protection perspective it is useful to distinguish between consumer self-reliance and need ethics, as proposed by Chris Willett.[90] The former allows businesses to escape responsibility for poor quality outcomes and to legitimise the imposition of outcomes that are harsh on consumers, due to a focus on the business "inputs" or "processes".[91] The latter, in turn, prioritises the protection of consumers from poor quality and harsh "outcomes" due to their position of weaknesses (vulnerability).[92] The framework thus offers a useful benchmark for distinguishing the level of protection provided to consumers through different instruments.

Overall, the analysis of practices of Airbnb and Booking.com shows an impressive range of contract-based and other voluntary mechanisms protecting platform users from the risks associated with tourism accommodation rental. Mechanisms of this kind seem to be capable, at least in part, of mitigating the most frequent

---

[87] The respective periods are 3 months and 36 months, respectively, at the time of writing, and have been extended over time. See Booking.com, 'How we work' (2023), sec. 1F.

[88] Booking.com, 'Content standards and guidelines' www.booking.com/content-moderation-policy/overview-page.en-gb.html.

[89] Articles 15 and 42 of Regulation 2022/2065 (Digital Services Act). See Chap. 4 for more details.

[90] Willett (2018), p. 179.

[91] Ibid, p. 180.

[92] Ibid. Note that the author uses the notions of "weakness" and "vulnerability" interchangeably. Such an understanding is not entirely aligned with the emerging notion of vulnerability in EU law, referring to qualified consumer weaknesses, such as physical, intellectual and, to some extent, economic disabilities. See Reich (2016), p. 141. For reasons of clarity, the more general concept of weakness will be referred to in this book.

problems faced by the guests—the service not being as described or of poor quality (inadequate performance), and ones which can lead to particularly harsh outcomes—the service not being provided at all (non-performance) or experiencing a safety issue (injury and adverse effects on health). Noteworthy is the emergence of certain common baseline practices in both analysed models, such as standardised registration processes requiring a minimum set of information to be provided, reputational feedback systems covering at a minimum the opinions of guests as well as automated reporting tools.

All of the baseline protection mechanisms listed above assist the users in making a decision on the level of risk they wish to accept or, at best, allow them to express their dissatisfaction with an experience, thus following a self-reliance ethic.[93] An approach focusing on achieving expected outcomes, characteristic of a need ethic, appears to be less robust and differs across platforms.

A fundamental outcome awaited by the traveller is to receive counter-performance for his or her payment. This has a twofold dimension: a monetary and a non-monetary one. Indeed, a traveller who arrives at an accommodation which remains unavailable not only loses money but can also be stranded in an unfamiliar environment. To prevent this from happening, Airbnb implements safeguards in its payment system. The solution of Booking.com, whereby hosts can choose a payment system, is less favourable to travellers. These limitations are somewhat mitigated by restrictions for the new providers who may only accept payment in cash.

When it comes to rebooking assistance, safeguards provided by Airbnb seem quite extensive, as they cover host cancellations, inability to check in and inaccurate listings. By contrast, Booking.com undertakes to assist stranded guests only in the case of overbooking. While the relevant terms of both platforms have notably improved in the last few years, they continue to contain vague terms that leave uncertainty about user rights. Moreover, doubts can be raised about the level of assistance that users actually receive when facing a problem.

Being left to one's own devices is certainly a risk to which travellers are exposed. Other harsh outcomes can occur after the guests enter the property. For example, the traveller can suffer from bodily injury or property damage as a result of poor-quality equipment or the host's behaviour. In this regard, the switch from a voluntary to a mandatory identity verification process in Airbnb can be seen as a step in the right direction. The same is true for its urgent support line which remains available 24/7. However, other measures taken by platform operators to prevent and respond to harsh outcomes remain largely unknown, as does the scale of reported issues.

Overall, platform operators appear to recognize consumer protection as an important community value and adopt measures that are aligned with it, at least to some extent. Indeed, the adverse impact of unexpected outcomes can be particularly significant for travellers who can not only be affected monetarily, but also experience loss of time, distress, and personal inconvenience—all of this in a potentially

---

[93] Willett (2018), pp. 185–187.

unknown place.[94] Suppliers, and particularly business suppliers, are generally less likely to be affected in these ways. An exception applies to the peer providers who choose to share their personal space with strangers. Even in this case, however, harsh outcomes mainly take the form of property damage and can be limited by taking adequate precautions. What is more, as the previous analysis has shown, platform providers can afford extra protection to the hosts, considering their importance from the network effects perspective.[95]

## 3.3 Private Governance in Passenger Transport Platforms

### *3.3.1 BlaBlaCar*

#### 3.3.1.1 Background Information

As previously observed, the platform-driven transformation of passenger transport can be linked to the rise of two predominant business models: ride-sharing (carpooling) and ride-hailing (rides-on-demand). Launched in 2004 in France, BlaBlaCar is the epitome of the former.[96] The platform connects passengers planning relatively long-distance journeys with drivers heading the same way. In 2023, the company reported to have reached 100 million users in more than 20 countries.[97] However, this impressive number does not say much about current user activity. As of 2024, the number of average monthly active users in the EU was estimated at approx. 3.28 million.[98]

Unlike in traditional hitchhiking, the coordination between drivers and passengers takes place before the journey and is largely facilitated by the data-driven architectures provided by the platform operator. Rides are not offered for free, although drivers are not allowed to make a profit: the idea is for both parties to share the costs of travelling, such as petrol and road charges. Like in many other areas of the platform economy, the monetization model and even the core services of the operator have evolved over time. The original commission-free model has gradually been replaced with a transaction or subscription fee, yet the extent of this transition has differed across jurisdictions.[99] The following analysis is based primarily on the Polish market.

[94] Sundararajan (2017), p. 19.

[95] Consider Airbnb's protection programme for hosts and the possibility of requesting a security deposit or a no-show payment in Booking.com.

[96] The platform was originally named Covoiturage. See also Hausemer et al. (2017b), p. 12.

[97] BlaBlaCar, 'We are 100 million on BlaBlaCar!' https://blog.blablacar.com/blog/blablalife/events/we-are-100-million-on-blablacar.

[98] BlaBlaCar, 'Regulamin' (2024), sec. 17.1 https://blog.blablacar.pl/about-us/terms-and-conditions.

[99] Hausemer et al. (2017b), pp. 15–19.

#### 3.3.1.2 Before Interaction

To make full use of the service, which includes posting a listing or booking a journey, both drivers and passengers are required to open user accounts. The minimum age threshold for registering an account is set at 18 years. Users are further encouraged to complete their profiles by uploading a profile picture and a short personal description. Providing accurate and true information and keeping it up to date is a contractual obligation.[100] Nonetheless, the information provided is generally not verified by the platform operator. Over time, an identity verification feature has been made available to service recipients, but its use is in principle voluntary.

After establishing the account, the user can freely choose if, at a given time, he or she will use the platform as a passenger or as a driver. This feature of BlaBlaCar shows certain similarities to Airbnb, which also allows users to switch between roles. Drivers can post listings on the platform indicating the relevant date and time, the places of departure and arrival, the requested remuneration (referred to in the terms of service as "cost contribution") as well as further information about the car and journey.[101] Drivers agree to limit their remuneration to the costs they actually incur to make the trip. BlaBlaCar suggests an amount for the given trip, yet drivers are generally allowed to increase or reduce it within the limits set by the provider.[102]

According to the terms of service, drivers are only allowed to post a listing if several conditions are fulfilled. These include: holding a valid driving licence, using one's own vehicle or a vehicle, the use of which for the purposes of carpooling was expressly permitted by the owner, remaining the main driver during the journey, holding valid third party insurance, having no contraindication or medical incapacity for driving, offering no more seats than the number available in the vehicle or seats without a seatbelt, and using a vehicle in good working order and compliant with applicable legal provisions and customs.[103] Once again, however, the fulfilment of these requirements remains the user's contractual duty, which is generally not verified by the platform operator. The latter, nonetheless, reserves the right, at its sole discretion and without notice, not to post or to remove any listing that does not comply with the terms of service or that it considers as damaging to its image.[104] Although the terms of service describe the content moderation policies rather superficially, more details about the actions taken can be expected in the future.[105]

On their part, passengers make use of a search form to identify the rides that are best suited to their needs. Following an indication of the points of departure and arrival and the relevant time, a ranking of available rides is presented. The passenger can consult more detailed information about particular rides, including the driver's

---

[100] BlaBlaCar, 'Regulamin' (2024), sec. 3.2.

[101] For an illustration, see Hausemer et al. (2017b), p. 10.

[102] BlaBlaCar, 'Regulamin' (2014), sec. 5.1. See also Hausemer et al. (2017b), p. 15.

[103] BlaBlaCar, 'Regulamin' (2014), sec. 4.1.

[104] Ibid.

[105] Ibid, sec. 4.3.2. On the role of the Digital Services Act, see Chap. 4.

first name, age, the level of experience (reflected in the number of published trips and the date of joining the platform) as well as reviews from other users. Contact with particular drivers can further be established via a messaging system provided by the platform operator. Before agreeing on a journey it is necessary to verify one's mobile phone number using an SMS code. The numbers are not publicly viewable but only shared between the parties who agree on a shared ride.

The booking process begins with the passenger's request. At the time of the booking, a service fee is charged by the platform operator.[106] Depending on the country, the cost contribution can be either collected through the platform or paid directly to the driver.[107] After payment and driver's validation, the passenger receives a booking confirmation. The payment method has consequences for potential refunds. In markets where the drivers are paid in person, no-shows and cancellations merely trigger the question of whether the service fee should be refunded.[108] In markets where all payments are made online, the rules on refunds are more comprehensive.[109]

#### 3.3.1.3 During Interaction

The platform operator is generally not engaged at the stage of physical interaction between the users. Although user behaviour is addressed in BlaBlaCar terms and conditions,[110] there is nothing to suggest that users could seek the operator's support to ensure that performance complies with respective provisions.

The company does not provide a helpline, but only an online contact form, the usefulness of which seems limited to the post-interaction stage. The terms of service further stress that the platform provider is not party to any agreement entered into between the users and has no control over and assumes no liability for their behaviour.[111] In 2018, the company announced that it would roll out an insurance programme across the European market, covering a breakdown cover and an onward journey.[112] In the analysed car-pooling model, insurance of this kind is vital. Rides undertaken by BlaBlaCar can cover significant distances, which means that users affected by an accident can find themselves stranded away from both the place of

[106] BlaBlaCar, 'Regulamin' (2014), sec. 5.2.

[107] In Poland, the payment takes place in cash while in the UK a fee is collected via an online system, cf. BlaBlaCar, 'Regulamin' (2024), sec. 5.4 and BlaBlaCar, 'Terms & Conditions' (2024), sec. https://blog.blablacar.co.uk/about-us/terms-and-conditions.

[108] BlaBlaCar, 'Regulamin' (2024), sec. 7.1.

[109] See e.g. BlaBlaCar, 'Terms & Conditions' (2024), sec. 7.1.

[110] BlaBlaCar, 'Regulamin' (2024), sec. 8.

[111] Ibid, sec. 12.

[112] AXA, 'BlaBlaCar and AXA launch first-of-its-kind ridesharing insurance product' (2015) www.axa.com/en/press/press-releases/blablacar-insurance-ridesharing. For an overview as of 2017, Hausemer et al. (2017b), pp. 33–35.

departure and the relevant destination. Unfortunately, no detailed information about the insurance in question is available at the time of writing.

#### 3.3.1.4 After Interaction

Like all other investigated platforms, BlaBlaCar provides a reputational feedback system. After completing a shared ride, or following the non-performance of a ride, both passengers and drivers are encouraged to leave feedback about their counterpart, consisting of a star rating on a scale from 1 to 5 and a descriptive review.[113] The feedback system deployed by BlaBlaCar follows a double-blind approach. Respective comments thus become visible either immediately after both parties have left a review, or 14 days after the review written by the first party, should the other one refrain from doing so.[114] It is possible to write a response to a review, which is published on the platform alongside the review. The platform operator reserves the right not to publish or to delete any review, any question, any comment or any response if it deems its content breaches its terms of service. It further reserves the right to suspend a user account or terminate the contract with the user who received at least three reviews and one or the average review was less than or equal to 3, depending on the severity of the feedback.[115]

The definition of criteria for suspending or blocking user accounts in case of a poor rating is certainly noteworthy and distinguishes BlaBlaCar from other platforms in the travel sector. The use of the platform can also be limited in other cases, such as when BlaBlaCar has "genuine reason to believe that [such an action] is necessary to protect its security and its integrity, that of the Members or third parties, or for the purpose of investigations or prevention of fraud".[116] The user is to be notified of these measures "when this is necessary" and the platform operator reserves the right to decide whether or not to lift the measures put in place, taking into account "all circumstances of each case and severity of the violation".[117] Negative consequences of such restrictions primarily involve the loss of prior reputational capital, as no procedures appear to be in place to prevent re-entry to the platform. The user affected may appeal the operator's decision among others through the internal complaint-handling system.[118]

---

[113] Hausemer et al. (2017b), pp. 28–30.

[114] BlaBlaCar, 'Regulamin' (2024), sec. 4.3.1.

[115] Ibid, sec. 4.3.3. The formulation of this term has become stricter over time.

[116] Ibid, sec. 9.

[117] Ibid.

[118] Ibid, sec. 15.1.

## 3.3.2 *Uber*

### 3.3.2.1 Background Information

The platform operator—in a broad sense of the word—who has arguably triggered the most heated debate is Uber, headquartered in San Francisco, United States. Unlike in BlaBlaCar, passengers using Uber do not choose among the available long-distance rides, but rather order (principally urban) rides between specific places at a specific time. The company's business model originally focused on connecting professional drivers with persons wishing to make urban journeys through a smartphone application.[119] This distribution model constituted a novelty in the early 2010s and its appeal was growing with the soaring uptake of smartphones.[120] Over time, the diversity of services offered under the Uber brand has expanded to include, among others, a rides-on-demand service involving non-professional drivers with private vehicles,[121] a car-pooling service in which on-demand rides could be shared with other passengers,[122] and even a food delivery service.[123]

The expansion of Uber has met with controversy around the world, leading to gradual adjustments in the company's approach to various issues. In particular, the regulatory pressure has prompted Uber to tighten the conditions of accessing the platform in different jurisdictions, bringing it closer to its initial concept.[124] The following analysis is carried out primarily from the perspective of Poland and the ride-hailing service UberX, at a time when the worldwide debate about the company's role appears to be maturing.[125] The functioning of UberX in Poland—as well as other applications following a similar approach, e.g. Bolt—reflects a certain tension between the operator's attempts to maintain low barriers to entry for drivers, while

---

[119] Today a variety of services can be observed in this segment. For an illustration see Uber Black www.uber.com/pl/en/ride/uberblack and Uber Green www.uber.com/pl/en/ride/ubergreen.

[120] OECD, 'Measuring the Digital Economy: A New Perspective' (2014), p. 30–31 www.oecd-ilibrary.org/science-and-technology/measuring-the-digital-economy_9789264221796-en.

[121] Vaughan and Daverio (2016), pp. 14–15, Hatzopoulos and Roma (2017), pp. 81–93.

[122] The service was originally called UberPool and was later rebranded as UberX Share. See www.uber.com/pl/en/ride/uberx-share.

[123] UberEats www.ubereats.com/pl-en.

[124] See e.g. in Germany: Uber, 'Von Berlin Kreuzberg Zum Münchner Marienplatz: Uber in Deutschland' (2018) www.uber.com/de/blog/uber-in-deutschland. On the diversity of ride-hailing models, see also Hacker (2018), p. 91.

[125] For an illustration of early controversies in different European jurisdictions see the series of country reports in the Journal of European Consumer and Market Law introduced by Podszun (2015), p. 59.

responding, at least in part, to public concerns. This tension appears to be one of the factors behind the regional diversity in Uber conditions.[126]

#### 3.3.2.2 Before Interaction

The number of steps to be taken by the user before ordering the first ride or providing the first passenger transport service is not identical for both parties to the exchange. The passenger merely needs to download the mobile application, accept the terms of service and register an account by providing his or her name, phone number, email address, and a payment instrument. According to the terms of service, the minimum age of the passenger is set, in general, at 18 years and users are not allowed to use their application to book rides for others, yet no additional mechanisms appear to be in place to ensure compliance with these requirements.[127]

Drivers also begin the relevant process by downloading the application and registering an account. As a next step, however, they are asked to take follow-up actions, the extent of which appears to differ across jurisdictions.[128] In Poland, this includes attendance at an in-person meeting and the provision of numerous documents, such as a government-issued ID, a driving license (obtained at least 1 year prior), a vehicle registration certificate with a valid technical inspection, a civil liability insurance, profile picture and a certificate of no conviction.[129] Additional documents are required if the driver intends to use his or her vehicle, including a valid taxi license, which constitutes a novelty compared to the previous terms.[130] If the driver instead decides to join a "partner fleet", an excerpt from the partner's license is to be provided. Following this process, the driver can begin to accept passenger requests. As of 2017, the platform operator was reported to charge drivers a transaction fee of approx. 20% of the ride price.[131]

The booking process is initiated by the passenger who provides information about the route and decides to place a request based on the price estimate displayed. After the request is accepted by one of the drivers, the passenger is informed of that fact, along with the driver's name and his or her star rating. The scope of additional information provided to the users appears to differ from country to country. Passengers who change their mind, or do not feel comfortable with the driver they

[126] For an overview of Uber's business model in different European markets as of 2017, see Hausemer et al. (2017c).

[127] Uber, 'General Terms of Use – Poland' (2024), sec. 5.3 and 6.3 www.uber.com/legal/en/document/?name=general-terms-of-use&country=poland&lang=en.

[128] Hausemer et al. (2017c), p. 23.

[129] Uber, 'How to drive with Uber in Poland' www.uber.com/pl/en/drive/requirements.

[130] Ibid. Cf. Toroń and Wiese (2017), p. 17.

[131] Hausemer et al. (2017c), p. 25.

were matched with, can cancel the confirmed booking. However, failing to do so within 2 min of sending the request entails a cancellation fee.[132]

#### 3.3.2.3 During Interaction

Even though users acknowledge that Uber does not provide a transport service,[133] the company's involvement during the offline interaction between the driver and the passenger is quite extensive. Besides the usual rules of behaviour, drivers and passengers are provided with more concrete protection tools. Firstly, before entering the vehicle passengers can verify the profile picture and the license plate of the car with the ones provided in the application. Secondly, while on the way, the vehicle's route continues to be tracked through GPS. Following gradual updates in the safety features, passengers can currently share their route with a trusted person and contact the emergency services directly from the application.[134] Furthermore, the RideCheck system, which has been gradually implemented in different geographic markets, proactively surfaces these tools when an irregularity, such as a possible crash or an unexpected long stop, is detected.[135] The platform provider further assures its readiness to promptly assist the users in case of an emergency, yet the types of available communication channels were reported to vary from country to country.[136] Similarly to BlaBlaCar, Uber also informs about the insurance coverage it offers to drivers, yet the scope of such protection and its applicability across geographic markets is not clear.[137] In particular, a question arises if such a policy could fill the gaps in the liability insurance of vehicle keepers.

#### 3.3.2.4 After Interaction

After completing the ride, the driver indicates this fact on the mobile application and the amount is charged from the passenger's payment instrument. Both users are subsequently prompted to leave their counterpart a star rating. The ratings provided by individual users are not disclosed; only an average rating is visible both to the rated user and his or her subsequent counterparts. Users can also report any issues they have experienced with the ride to the platform operator, which may lead Uber, for example, to re-adjust the collected fee. Based on the rating, as well as other relevant feedback, the platform operator may undertake numerous steps, up until the termination of the user agreement. The minimum average rating, which can be

[132] Uber, 'General Terms of Use – Poland' (2024), sec. 8.4.

[133] Ibid, sec. 3.1.

[134] Uber, 'Driving safety forwards' www.uber.com/pl/en/ride/safety.

[135] Ibid.

[136] Hausemer et al. (2017c), p. 35.

[137] Ibid, p. 41.

reached by the driver without risking deactivation varies for each city, arguably due to cultural differences.[138] Finally, a special provision is made for cases of unlawful damage (e.g. leaving stains) caused by the passenger.[139]

### 3.3.3 *Assessment*

The analysis of BlaBlaCar and Uber reveals a picture similar to the one observed in the tourism accommodation sector. First of all, a variety of contract-based and other voluntary mechanisms protecting platform users can be identified in the passenger transport segment. Mechanisms of this kind can mitigate at least some of the problems faced by passengers. Equally noteworthy is the emergence of common baseline practices in both analysed models, including standardised registration processes requiring a minimum set of information to be provided, reputational feedback systems, automated reporting tools and help centres, accessible at a minimum via online forms. A tendency can also be observed to adopt ID verification mechanisms, which are mandatory in Uber and for now voluntary in BlaBlaCar.

Like in the tourism accommodation segment, most of the common baseline protection mechanisms follow a self-reliance ethic.[140] Rather than focusing on outcomes, they assist users in making a decision on the level of risk they wish to accept or, at best, allow them to express dissatisfaction with their experience. The degree of this assistance depends on the particularities of a given mechanism—for example, verified information about the driver's identity may not be available at all in BlaBlaCar, while in Uber such information is available at least to the operator. Further differences concern the ratings and reviews, which in BlaBlaCar include more comprehensive information than they do in Uber.

As for the measures reflecting the need ethic, the analysis of private governance frameworks reveals a mixed picture. Like in tourism accommodation, a position of weakness can especially be identified on the part of service recipients. This is due to both specific risks associated with travelling to a removed location and the operation of motor vehicles. An elementary outcome is to ensure that a passenger's payment is not made without counter-performance, and platform operators can contribute to its achievement. Mechanisms geared towards this goal have indeed been identified in both analysed models.[141]

The second, and particularly important outcome relates to the prevention and compensation of injuries and adverse effects on health. This has to do, on the one hand, with the condition of the vehicle and characteristics of the driver, and, on the

---

[138] Ibid, p. 34. See also Holder (2019) For ride-hailing drivers, data is power. Bloomberg, 22 August 2019.

[139] Uber, 'General Terms of Use – Poland' (2024), sec. 7.1.3.

[140] Willett (2018), pp. 185–187.

[141] Note, however, the differences in the model of BlaBlaCar depending on whether payments is made by cash or via an online system.

other hand, with on-the-spot assistance and available paths for claiming compensation in case harm is incurred. Like in tourism accommodation, the definition of behavioural standards and the possibility for the operator to act upon violations are characteristic of both analysed models. In other respects, the steps taken by particular operators appear to diverge. For example, BlaBlaCar fully relies on drivers' declarations, while Uber imposes minimal requirements concerning the age of the vehicle and requires the submission of documentation. Uber also appears to operate a more robust help centre compared to BlaBlaCar and addresses the issue of damage caused by passengers. Both Uber and BlaBlaCar maintain that users are covered by accident insurance, yet the terms of those policies are not disclosed to passengers.

Overall, both in tourism accommodation and in transport platforms the values of protecting the weaker parties enjoy a growing recognition. However, due to the broad margin of discretion reserved by platform operators, the afforded protection may not always be based on solid legal grounds.[142]

## 3.4 Conclusions

The development of consumer markets, and especially the development of travel as a mass phenomenon, has not remained without legal response, mindful of the position of consumers. While details of this process will be discussed hereafter, we can observe already now that changes in the legal framework reflect the corresponding shifts in social practice.[143] As a society, we recognize that travelling involves considerable risks and expect those risks to be mitigated.

The importance attached to the protection of the weaker party is also reflected in the analysed private governance frameworks of selected online travel platforms. Frameworks of this kind might even be perceived as instrumental to those platforms' success, as they help to win and maintain consumer trust. The discussion focused on four platform operators in two main market segments and was carried out as their business models appeared to be maturing. Arguably, the spotlight in which these providers are placed is rendering them increasingly receptive to societal perceptions, communicated either directly by users and affected third parties or indirectly by the law- and policymakers. The development of platform operators' practices therefore reflects—at least to some extent—the values considered to be societally important and desirable.

The analysis revealed an important role of travellers' protection in all examined business models. However, the scope of the protection measures appears to differ across platforms. Moreover, due to a margin of discretion often reserved by platform operators and the opacity of many underlying processes, the protection afforded in specific cases may be more apparent than real. Accordingly, private

[142] Petersen et al. (2018), p. 59.

[143] Cf. Christensen (1999), p. 89.

governance frameworks may be successful in earning users' trust without necessarily being worthy of it.[144] In the following chapters, the protection of consumers in online travel platforms is analysed from the perspective of the EU *acquis*.

## References

Aloni E (2018) Pluralism and regulatory responses. In: Davidson NM, Finck M, Infranca JJ (eds) The Cambridge handbook of the law of the sharing economy. Cambridge University Press, pp 143–155

Brownsword R (2019) Law, technology and society: reimagining the regulatory environment. Routledge

Brownsword R, Goodwin M (2012) Law and the technologies of the twenty-first century: text and materials. Cambridge University Press

Busch C (2020) Self-regulation and regulatory intermediation in the platform economy. In: Cantero Gamito M, Micklitz H-W (eds) The role of the EU in transnational legal ordering. Edward Elgar, pp 115–134

Cafaggi F (2015) The many features of transnational private rule-making: unexplored relationships between custom, jura mercatorum and global private regulation. Univ Pa J Int Law 36(4):875–938

Calliess G-P (2008) Transnational consumer law: co-regulation of B2C e-commerce. In: Dilling O, Herberg M, Winter G (eds) Responsible business: self-governance and law in transnational economic transactions. Hart Publishing, pp 225–258

Cantero Gamito M (2017) Regulation.com: self-regulation and contract governance in the platform economy: a research agenda. Eur J Legal Stud 9:53–67

Christensen A (1995) Polycentricity and normative patterns. In: Petersen H, Zahle H (eds) Legal polycentricity: consequences of pluralism in law. Dartmouth, pp 235–242

Christensen A (1999) Normative patterns and the normative field: a post-liberal view on law. In: Wilhelmsson T, Hurri S (eds) From dissonance to sense: welfare state expectations, privatisation, and private law. Ashgate/Dartmouth, pp 83–98

Engert A (2018) Digitale Plattformen. AcP 218(2):304–376

Finck M (2018a) Digital co-regulation: designing a supranational legal framework for the platform economy. Eur Law Rev 43(1):47–68

Finck M (2018b) The sharing economy and the EU. In: Davidson NM, Finck M, Infranca JJ (eds) The Cambridge handbook of the law of the sharing economy. Cambridge University Press, pp 261–273

Grundmann S, Hacker P (2018) The digital dimension as a challenge to European contract law – the architecture. In: Grundmann S (ed) European contract law in the digital age. Intersentia, pp 3–46

Grundmann S, Möslein F, Riesenhuber K (eds) (2015) Contract governance: dimensions in law and interdisciplinary research. Oxford University Press

Gunningham N, Sinclair D (2017) Smart regulation. In: Drahos P (ed) Regulatory theory: foundations and applications. ANU Press, pp 133–148

Hacker P (2018) UberPop, UberBlack, and the regulation of digital platforms after the Asociación Profesional Elite Taxi judgment of the CJEU. Eur Rev Const Law 14(1):80–96

Hatzopoulos V, Roma S (2017) Caring for sharing? The collaborative economy under EU law. Common Mark Law Rev 54(1):81–127

Hausemer P, Rzepecka J, Dragulin M, Vitiello S, Rabuel L, Nunu M, Rodriguez Diaz A, Psaila E, Fiorentini S, Gysen S, Meeusen T, Quaschning S, Dunne A, Grinevich V, Huber F, Baines

[144] Helberger et al. (2022), p. 189.

L (2017a) Exploratory study of consumer issues in online peer-to-peer platform markets: task 4 – case study: AirBnB. European Commission

Hausemer P, Rzepecka J, Dragulin M, Vitiello S, Rabuel L, Nunu M, Rodriguez Diaz A, Psaila E, Fiorentini S, Gysen S, Meeusen T, Quaschning S, Dunne A, Grinevich V, Huber F, Baines L (2017b) Exploratory study of consumer issues in online peer-to-peer platform markets: task 4 – case study: BlaBlaCar. European Commission

Hausemer P, Rzepecka J, Dragulin M, Vitiello S, Rabuel L, Nunu M, Rodriguez Diaz A, Psaila E, Fiorentini S, Gysen S, Meeusen T, Quaschning S, Dunne A, Grinevich V, Huber F, Baines L (2017c) Exploratory study of consumer issues in online peer-to-peer platform markets: task 4 – Uber – case study report. European Commission

Helberger N, Pierson J, Poell T (2018) Governing online platforms: from contested to cooperative responsibility. Inform Soc 34(1):1–14

Helberger N, Sax M, Strycharz J, Micklitz H-W (2022) Choice architectures in the digital economy: towards a new understanding of digital vulnerability. J Consum Policy 45(2):175–200

Hodges C (2016) The consumer as regulator. In: Leczykiewicz D, Weatherill S (eds) The images of the consumer in EU law: legislation, free movement and competition law. Hart Publishing, pp 245–256

Ikkala T, Lampinen A (2015) Monetizing network hospitality: hospitality and sociability in the context of Airbnb. In: CSCW'15 Proceedings of the 18th ACM conference on computer supported cooperative work & social computing. ACM, pp 1033–1044

Leiser M, Murray A (2016) The role of non-state actors and institutions in the governance of new and emerging digital technologies. In: Brownsword R, Scotford E, Yeung K (eds) The Oxford handbook of law, regulation, and technology. Oxford University Press, pp 670–702

Lessig L (1999a) The law of the horse: what cyberlaw might teach. Harv Law Rev 113(2):501–549

Lessig L (1999b) Code and other laws of cyberspace. Basic Books

Lobel O (2004) The renew deal: the fall of regulation and the rise of governance in contemporary legal thought. Minn Law Rev 89:342–470

Mak V (2018) Regulating online platforms – the case of Airbnb. In: Grundmann S (ed) European contract law in the digital age. Intersentia, pp 87–102

Meller-Hannich C (2014) Zu einigen rechtlichen Aspekten der "Share-Economy". WM 68(50):2337–2344

Micklitz H-W (2018) The politics of justice in European private law: social justice, access justice, societal justice. Cambridge University Press

Numhauser-Henning A (2013) Understanding law as normative patterns in a normative field. In: Numhauser-Henning A, Rönnmar M (eds) . Hart Publishing, Normative patterns and legal developments in the social dimension of the EU, pp 27–52

Petersen CS, Ulfbeck VG, Hansen O (2018) Platforms as private governance systems—the example of Airbnb. Nord J Commer Law 1:37–60

Podszun R (2015) UBER—a pan-European regulatory challenge. Eur Const Mark Law 4(1-2):59–60

Purnhagen KP (2015) Mapping private regulation—classification, market access and market closure policy and law's response. J World Trade 49(2):309–323

Reich N (2016) Vulnerable consumers in EU law. In: Leczykiewicz D, Weatherill S (eds) The images of the consumer in EU law: legislation, free movement and competition law. Hart Publishing, pp 139–158

Schweitzer H (2019) Digitale Plattformen als private Gesetzgeber: Ein Perspektivwechsel für die europäische "Plattform-Regulierung". ZEuP 27(1):1–12

Scott C (2004) Regulation in the age of governance: the rise of the post-regulatory state. In: Jordana J, Levi-Faur D (eds) The politics of regulation: institutions and regulatory reforms for the age of governance. Edward Elgar, pp 145–174

Scott J, Trubek DM (2002) Mind the gap: law and new approaches to governance in the European Union. Eur Law Rev 8(1):1–18

Sundararajan A (2017) The collaborative economy: socioeconomic, regulatory and policy issues. In-depth analysis for the IMCO Committee. European Parliament
Thaler RH, Sunstein CR (2008) Nudge: improving decisions about health, wealth, and happiness. Yale University Press
Toroń M, Wiese K (2017) Aplikacja UBER lub jak ująć sharing economy w istniejące ramy prawne? iKAR 5(6):8–27
Vaughan R, Daverio R (2016) Assessing the size and presence of the collaborative economy in Europe. European Commission
Willett C (2018) Re-theorising consumer law. Cambridge Law J 77(1):179–210

# Part II
# Online Travel Platforms and EU Consumer Protection

# Chapter 4
# Internal Market Policy and Consumer Protection in Digital Markets

## 4.1 Preliminary Remarks

The scope and content of EU rules are closely related to the Union's competences and policy priorities. According to Article 5 of the Treaty on European Union (TEU),[1] the limits of EU competences are governed by the principle of conferral, while the use of such competences is governed by the principles of subsidiarity and proportionality. Under the principle of conferral, the EU shall act only within the limits of the competences conferred upon it by the Member States in the Treaties to attain the objectives set out therein. Under the principle of subsidiarity, in areas which do not fall within its exclusive competence, the EU shall act only if and in so far as the objectives of the proposed action cannot be sufficiently achieved by the Member States, but can rather, by reason of the scale or effects of the proposed action, be better achieved at EU level. The principle of proportionality requires that the content and form of EU action do not exceed what is necessary to achieve the objectives of the Treaties.

The principle of conferral in EU law can be described as a soft principle, in that it allows the holder of the competence to interpret its scope using teleological reasoning.[2] The margin for interpretation is particularly broad when a competence norm is directed towards a general EU goal, such as the establishment and functioning of the internal market.[3] Pursuant to Article 4(2)(a) of the Treaty on the

[1] Treaty on European Union (consolidated version) [2012] OJ C326/13.

[2] Schütze (2015), p. 77.

[3] Weatherill (2016b), pp. 59–60. Pursuant to Article 26(2) TFEU, the internal market shall comprise an area without internal frontiers in which the free movement of goods, persons, services and capital is ensured in accordance with the provisions of the Treaties.

 
A. Jabłonowska, *Consumer Protection and Online Travel Platforms*, Law, Governance and Technology Series 73, https://doi.org/10.1007/978-3-031-90170-6_4

Functioning of the European Union (TFEU),[4] the relevant competence is shared between the EU and the Member States. For the EU, it encompasses both judicial control of national restrictions to inter-state trade (negative integration) and positive measures aimed at establishing or ensuring the functioning of the internal market (positive integration).[5]

Both digital markets and the travel sector have long been affected by the process of negative and positive integration under the internal market policy. The present chapter, as well as the subsequent one, examines this development from the perspective of consumer protection. In particular, it considers when, why, and how the EU has been protecting consumers in digital markets and who exactly is covered by the consumer notion. The analysis reveals divergent justifications for relying on Article 114 TFEU as the basis for EU legislative action: some more supplier-, other more consumer-oriented. As the law-making practice shows, the potential of this competence norm has not been fully exploited by the existing legislation, which all too often remains fragmentary.

## 4.2 Development of Internal Market Policy and Consumer Protection

### *4.2.1 Article 114 TFEU as the Legal Basis for Consumer Protection Measures*

The emergence of a harmonised framework on consumer protection can be linked to the Council resolution of 1975 on a preliminary programme for a consumer protection and information policy and the second programme of 1981.[6] Even though "consumer policy" is a commonly used notion,[7] its development cannot be viewed in isolation from the internal market policy. Indeed, consumer protection measures have traditionally relied on internal market authorisation, which was originally

[4]Treaty on the Functioning of the European Union (TFEU (consolidated version) [2012] OJ C326/47.

[5]On the interplay between negative and positive harmonisation (integration) in the context of EU consumer law, see e.g. Stuyck (2013), pp. 388–390, Unberath and Johnston (2007), p. 1237.

[6]Council resolution of 14.4.1975 on a preliminary programme of the European Economic Community for a consumer protection and information policy [1975] OJ C92/1, Council Resolution of 19.5.1981 on a second programme of the European Economic Community for a consumer protection and information policy [1981] OJ C133/1.

[7]European Commission, 'Three Year Action Plan of Consumer Policy in the EEC 1990-1992' (1990) COM(90) 98 final, European Commission, 'Communication from the Commission. Priorities for Consumer Policy 1996-1998' (1995) COM(95) 519 final, European Commission, 'Communication from the Commission to the European Parliament, the Council, the Economic and Social Committee and the Committee of the Regions—Consumer Policy Strategy 2002-2006' (2002) COM(2002) 208 final.

contained in Article 100 of the Treaty establishing the European Economic Community[8] (currently Article 115 TFEU). The latter was later complemented with Article 114 TFEU, a norm which can now be described as the "heartland of harmonisation".[9] The central role of Article 114 TFEU in EU market regulation has remained unshaken, even as further competence norms were added to the Treaty.[10]

Article 114 TFEU contains an authorisation of the European Parliament and the Council to adopt measures for the approximation of the provisions laid down by law, regulation or administrative action in the Member States which have as their object the establishment and functioning of the internal market. The adoption of relevant measures follows an ordinary legislative procedure, initiated by a proposal from the European Commission and concluded by majority voting. The provision allows for full harmonisation, which prevents Member States from maintaining or adopting diverging laws, also where they seek to protect consumers at a higher level.[11] At the same time, Article 114(3) TFEU explicitly requires that proposals concerning health, safety, environmental protection and consumer protection take as a base a high level of protection.[12] The European Parliament and the Council should also seek to achieve this objective within their respective powers.

Recourse to Article 114 TFEU by the EU legislature is not frequently reviewed by the Court of Justice. Except for the widely discussed *Tobacco Advertising* case,[13] the Court remained reluctant to strike down Union measures.[14] Reliance on Article 114 TFEU has been accepted not only when legislative differences give rise to obstacles to the exercise of fundamental freedoms or distortion of competition (e.g. make it difficult for the suppliers to adopt a common strategy for the cross-border market), but also when heterogeneous development of national laws would likely lead to further disparities.[15] Over time, harmonisation began to also be perceived from the perspective of consumers. This opened up a possibility of viewing common safeguards for consumers as capable of improving the internal market, independent from the position of sellers and service providers.

---

[8] Treaty establishing the European Economic Community signed on 25.3.1957 in Rome.

[9] Weatherill (2016b), p. 57.

[10] This, most notably, includes Article 169(2)(b) TFEU which relates to measures supporting, supplementing and monitoring national policies on consumer protection.

[11] As opposed to Article 169(3) TFEU, which is likely the reason why its practical importance has remained limited. See Weatherill (2016a), p. 288.

[12] Article 114(3) TFEU.

[13] Judgment of the Court of Justice of 5.10.2000 in case C-376/98 *Germany v Parliament and Council* (*Tobacco Advertising*), ECLI:EU:C:2000:544.

[14] Weatherill (2012), p. 1308–1310. See e.g. judgment of the Court of Justice of 8.6.2010 in case C-58/08 *Vodafone and Others*, ECLI:EU:C:2010:321, para. 32.

[15] Judgment of the Court of Justice of 5.10.2000 in case C-376/98 *Germany v Parliament and Council* (*Tobacco Advertising*), para. 86. See also Weatherill (2002), p. 508.

The self-standing role of consumers in the internal market is linked to the idea of "consumer confidence".[16] According to this logic, a common set of rules can make consumers confident to shop across borders, thus activating the internal market.[17] This narrative is not uncontroversial and meets with criticism from two different angles. Critics of the EU regulatory expansion warn that the concept could justify far-reaching powers to regulate the internal market, without a sufficiently strong basis in primary law.[18] Consumer advocates, in turn, criticise the rhetoric for treating consumers as a pretext for internal market-building, while the social aspects of consumer protection get pushed to the background.[19]

Both types of criticisms are not unfounded and, indeed, consumer confidence is not convincing as an over-arching basis for harmonisation. Nevertheless, I would argue, a scope remains for its valid usage. In particular, the former line of critique does not apply with equal force to areas, like travel and e-commerce, in which cross-border contracts are truly viable and supported by market data. The latter concern, in turn, can be mitigated if the requirement of ensuring a "high level of protection" is duly realised.[20] Indeed, the EU legislature should not seek merely to build consumer confidence but to ensure that it remains well-founded.[21] Moreover, the acknowledgement of consumer confidence as a ground for recourse to Article 114 TFEU does not necessitate full harmonisation. On the contrary, a minimum set of key common safeguards may be enough from that perspective, leaving further protection to the Member States.[22]

While harmonisation justified by the need to foster "consumer confidence" in the internal market appears to already be a step away from the traditional focus on removing barriers to trade and distortions of competition, an even broader reading of Article 114 TFEU can be imagined. According to Martijn Hesselink, the establishment of a high level of protection of consumer interests as well as health and safety could be viewed as a non-exhaustive exemplification of the "proper functioning" of the internal market. As observed by the author, a properly functioning internal market can be understood as a market that is equipped with institutions which provide at least a minimal level of protection against unjust market conduct, including violations of private rights and obligations—not merely against narrowly defined

[16] For the origins, see Sutherland (1992) The Internal Market after 1992: meeting the challenge. Report presented to the Commission by the High Level Group on the Functioning of the Internal Market, SEC(92) 2044 final. See e.g. recital 6 of Directive 2011/83/EU on consumer rights: "Certain disparities create significant internal market barriers affecting traders and consumers. Those disparities increase compliance costs to traders wishing to engage in the cross-border sale of goods or provision of services. Disproportionate fragmentation also undermines consumer confidence in the internal market".

[17] For an overview, see Wilhelmsson (2004), p. 320.

[18] Roth (2003), p. 944. Similarly Unberath and Johnston (2007), pp. 1254–1255.

[19] See Wilhelmsson (2004) and Bartl (2020), p. 245. This point is also highlighted by Stuyck (2013), p. 390.

[20] Article 114(3) in conjunction with Article 169(1) TFEU.

[21] On a similar distinction between trust and trustworthiness, see Helberger et al. (2022), p. 189.

[22] Wilhelmsson (2004), p. 322.

consumers, but also against professionals and peers.[23] The argument reflects a certain uneasiness with the personal scope of the EU safeguards, which is addressed in more detail below.

## 4.2.2 *Personal Scope of Consumer Protection Measures*

### 4.2.2.1 Development of Status-Based Consumer Protection

While the notion of the "consumer" features numerously in EU Treaties—both in previously discussed provisions as well as other titles—it has not been defined under primary law.[24] In the most general sense, accepted among others in rules on competition, it is linked to the position of "passive market participants", persons entering into legal relationships to satisfy their needs without producing the product or service themselves.[25] As far as secondary law is concerned, the Treaty leaves it to the EU legislature to define the consumer concept.[26] The analysis of positive harmonisation measures concerned with "consumer protection", undertaken over past decades, reveals a tendency towards a narrower, status-based approach.[27] Such an approach is connected, firstly, to the purposes for which the consumer is acting, and, secondly, to the status of his or her counterparty. The described tendency has largely been maintained until today, although some deviations from it can be identified.[28]

Indeed, a significant part of the first generation of consumer directives,[29] adopted in 1980s and 1990s, applied to so-called business-to-consumer (B2C) relationships, understood as relationships between two formally defined categories of legal subjects. To illustrate, Council Directive 85/577/EEC on contracts negotiated away from business premises[30] (currently replaced with Directive 2011/83/EU on consumer rights, CRD),[31] limited its personal scope to contracts between a "consumer", defined as a natural person acting for purposes which can be regarded as outside his trade or profession, and a "trader", referring to a natural or legal person acting in his commercial or professional capacity, and anyone acting in the name or on behalf of

[23] Hesselink (2016), pp. 450–451.

[24] Gnela (2008), p. 50.

[25] Reich and Micklitz (2014), p. 6, Cseres (2016), pp. 11–12.

[26] Reich (2008), pp. 18–19.

[27] Cafaggi (2013), p. 327.

[28] See, especially in services markets: Nijenhuis (2013), pp. 55–60, Karsten (2007), p. 135, Johnston (2016), pp. 94–99, Południak-Gierz (2016), p. 61.

[29] Tonner (2014), p. 701.

[30] Council Directive 85/577/EEC of 20.12.1985 to protect the consumer in respect of contracts negotiated away from business premises [1985] OJ L372/31, also referred to as directive on doorstep selling.

[31] Directive 2011/83/EU of the European Parliament and of the Council of 25.10.2011 on consumer rights, amending Council Directive 93/13/EEC and Directive 1999/44/EC of the European Parliament and of the Council and repealing Council Directive 85/577/EEC and Directive 97/7/EC of the European Parliament and of the Council [2011] OJ L304/64.

a trader. The same has been true for many other instruments of the emerging consumer protection *acquis*, such as Directive 97/7/EC on distance contracts,[32] but interestingly not Directive 90/314/EEC on package travel.[33] The specificity of package travel law will be addressed later in the book.

Justification for the status-based approach is usually linked with the weaker position of non-professional participants of the internal market vis-à-vis their more experienced counterparties. It is precisely this asymmetry—particularly as regards the bargaining power, the level of knowledge and legal experience—that provides a basis for consumer protection measures.[34] In *Kamenova*, the Court noted that the notions of "trader" and "consumer" are interconnected[35] and, taken together, reveal the weaker position of consumers in commercial transactions.[36] However, it did not go on to explore whether the relevant asymmetry could be identified in the analysed context—that of an occasional sale of goods via an online platform.[37] Overall, the Court can be credited for highlighting the rationale of interpreted norms, focused on the protection of the weaker party. As regards the personal scope of the relevant secondary legislation, the case law remains tied to its rather unambiguous wording and explicit limitations to B2C transactions.

#### 4.2.2.2 Status-Based Approach and Competing Ethics of Consumer Protection

The protection of weaker parties, highlighted by the Court of Justice, brings to mind regulatory justification that Willett associates with the need ethic. To recall, while the self-reliance ethic is focused on the business "inputs" or "processes", the need ethic can lend support to stronger consumer protection, aimed directly at outcomes.[38] According to the author, the premise of legal norms following the latter approach is that "consumers are especially vulnerable to detriment, and require greater protection".[39] Crucially, Willett points to the multifaceted nature of consumer weak-

---

[32] Directive 97/7/EC of the European Parliament and of the Council of 20.5.1997 on the protection of consumers in respect of distance contracts [1997] OJ L144/19.

[33] Council Directive 90/314/EEC of 13.6.1990 on package travel, package holidays and package tours [1990] OJ L158/59.

[34] Schüller (2012), pp. 125–126. See e.g. judgment of the Court of Justice of 9.11.2010 in case C-137/08 *VB Pénzügyi Lízing*, ECLI:EU:C:2010:659, para. 46. ("[T]he system of protection introduced by the Directive [93/13/EEC on unfair terms in consumer contracts] is based on the idea that the consumer is in a weak position vis-à-vis the seller or supplier, as regards both his bargaining power and his level of knowledge".)

[35] Judgment of the Court of Justice of 4.10.2018 in case C-105/17 *Kamenova*, ECLI:EU:C:2018:808, para. 33.

[36] Ibid, para. 34.

[37] The Court instead limited itself to studying the purposes for which the supplier was acting, see ibid., para. 36.

[38] Willett (2018), p. 180.

[39] Ibid, p. 187.

nesses.[40] In particular, he argues, a distinction can be made between "the weaker position of consumers as loss bearers" and "the perception that consumers struggle to exercise self-reliance to protect themselves from [...] detrimental outcomes".[41]

As observed in the literature, the status-based approach often fails to account for asymmetries associated with the second dimension mentioned above, in particular as regards the bargaining power and the level of knowledge, in relations other than B2C.[42] Relationships between large enterprises and small and medium-sized ones (SMEs) are the key illustration of this problem. In my view, however, an equally important misalignment between the status-based approach and the EU commitment to the protection of "weaker parties" can be observed with regard to the first dimension, namely the weaker position of consumers as loss bearers.

Although some impacts, which are particularly detrimental to passive market actors, may be captured by the business-to-consumer proxy, this is not necessarily the case for other matters.[43] The status-based approach may partly capture the idea that traders are generally better placed to absorb the losses suffered or the lower-than-expected gains, which for consumers is usually not the case. Other consumer weaknesses, however, may not be linked to the status of their counterparty. This is true for the impact of the breach of contract on the consumers' private sphere, including effects such as the loss of time, distress, inconvenience in personal lives, and frustration of obtaining no redress. In at least certain types of contracts—most notably for the provision of services—consumers are more likely to be affected in these ways than not only traders but suppliers more generally.[44]

### 4.2.3 *Interim Conclusions*

To sum up, consumer roles in the internal market can be perceived from several perspectives. The most traditional approach views diverging national safeguards as an impediment to cross-border trade. A more consumer-centred account is linked to the idea of consumer confidence. Crucially, when the EU legislature relies on this idea, it should not only seek to create consumer confidence. Rather, it should also ensure that the relevant confidence is indeed well-founded, i.e. that a high level of consumer protection is achieved. Otherwise, the requirements of Articles 114(3) and 169(1) TFEU would not be fulfilled.

Consumer protection is being achieved, in essence, through measures targeting consumer weaknesses. From a primary law perspective, there is no reason to narrow down the scope of the protection addressees, by default, to consumers in B2C

---

[40] Ibid.

[41] Ibid.

[42] See Stuyck (2014), p. 359, Roppo (2009), p. 304.

[43] Similarly: Cafaggi (2013), p. 327.

[44] Sanches Lima (2018), pp. 155–173. See also Enchelmaier (2005), pp. 237–238.

relationships.[45] While the B2C scenario can serve as a proxy for identifying the position of weakness, it does not paint a full picture. Thus, when exercising competences under Article 114(1) in conjunction with Articles 114(3) and 169(2)(a) TFEU, a broader category of passive market participants can be the starting point.

The analysis of consumer weaknesses can also guide the content of adopted rules. For example, consumers who struggle to exercise self-reliance due to a lack of knowledge may require access to information. By contrast, consumers who are exposed to injury may be in need of measures targeting this problem. This diversity of potential issues finds support in Article 169(1) TFEU, which points to the protection of health, safety and economic interests of consumers, as well as the consumers' right to information, education and to organise themselves to safeguard their interests.

For each aspect of the consumer's weaker position, a plethora of measures can be envisaged. For example, consumer information can be improved by requiring disclosure from suppliers or via independent product testing (or a combination of both). Similarly, consumer injury can be addressed through *ex ante* monitoring or *ex post* compensation. The conceivable measures can be located on the continuum between the ethics of self-reliance and need, with the latter generally offering a higher level of protection.[46]

The cross-border context of contracting may lend support to more protective rules, since consumer weaknesses can be exacerbated in those situations. For example, Twigg-Flesner notes that consumer confidence in cross-border contracting is more likely to be achieved through direct regulation of products and services than through *ex post* rights.[47] Arguing along similar lines, Wilhelmsson supports the adoption of rules promoting "easy access to a counterparty".[48] Conceptually, these seem to be the most coherent views on the role of consumers as weaker parties in the internal market. They embrace the competence-supportive dimension of the "consumer confidence" rhetoric—which in areas like e-commerce and travel seems to be well-founded—and combine it with a high level of consumer protection. The law-making practice, however, is not equally clear-cut and continues to be shaped by different policy goals.[49] The result is a mixture of norms adopting a varied level of protection for different addressees, often without aiming to be comprehensive.[50] This landscape is analysed in more detail below, focusing on the norms relating to e-commerce and their application to the platform economy.

---

[45] Reich (2008), p. 19. Similarly, in the context of Polish constitutional law, see Jagielska and Jagielski (2012), p. 342.

[46] Willett (2018), p. 185. Similarly in Willett and Morgan-Taylor (2012), pp. 147–151.

[47] Twigg-Flesner (2016), p. 200.

[48] Wilhelmsson (2004), pp. 329–332.

[49] The Court recognized, among others, that "although consumer protection is one of the objectives of the [Union], it is clearly not the sole objective". See judgment of the Court of Justice of 13.5.1997 in case C-233/94 *Germany v Parliament and Council*, ECLI:EU:C:1997:231, para. 48. See also Micklitz (2018), p. 240.

[50] Micklitz observes that "the current consumer law has lost a clear direction", see Micklitz (2018), p. 233.

## 4.3 Two Directions of EU Legislation

Online platforms are the key topic in many present-day discussions about digital markets. However, the EU interest in that sphere dates much further back. Due to their undeniable potential for increased cross-border activity and economic growth, digital markets appeared to be a perfect match for the internal market project. Explicit recognition of the "information society" came with the 1993 White Paper considering the challenges and ways forward into the twenty-first century.[51] A growing interest in this topic was also reflected in documents concerned with consumer protection. Already the second consumer programme took note of the potential impact, which the use of "new data processing and telecommunications technology" may have on consumption patterns and relationships between market participants,[52] while the measures designed to "enable consumers to benefit from the opportunities presented by the information society" were envisaged as one of the consumer policy priorities in 1996–1998.[53] What emerges from these discussions is an effort to, on the one hand, support the growth of the digital economy and, on the other hand, ensure that the interests of its participants are safeguarded. Both dimensions are connected to some extent, as illustrated by the following examples.

### *4.3.1 Removing Barriers to Growth*

#### 4.3.1.1 E-Commerce Directive and Liberalisation of Information Society Services

Country-of-Origin Principle

One of the central measures aimed to promote the growth of online trade is Directive 2000/31/EC on electronic commerce (E-Commerce Directive, ECD).[54] The act was adopted on a mixed legal basis consisting of what is now Article 114 TFEU as well as Articles 53(1) and 62 TFEU on the freedom of establishment and free movement

[51] European Commission, 'White Paper, Growth, Competitiveness, Employment. The Challenges and Ways Forward into the twenty-first Century' (1993) COM(93) 700 final. See also European Commission, 'Communication from the Commission to the Council, the European Parliament, the Economic and Social Committee and the Committee of the Regions. Europe's Way to the Information Society. An Action Plan' (1994) COM(94) 347 final.

[52] Council resolution of 19.5.1981 on a second programme of the European Economic Community for a consumer protection and information policy [1981] OJ C133/1.

[53] European Commission, 'Communication from the Commission. Priorities for Consumer Policy 1996-1998' (1995) COM(95) 519 final.

[54] Directive 2000/31/EC of the European Parliament and of the Council of 8.6.2000 on certain legal aspects of information society services, in particular electronic commerce, in the Internal Market ('Directive on electronic commerce') [2000] OJ L178/1. Cf. Pearce and Platten (2000), p. 366.

of services. Recourse to these provisions hints at the importance of the de-regulatory prong of the internal market policy and the goal of supporting its growth by removing barriers to trade.

The E-Commerce Directive has facilitated the growth of the digital economy in several ways. Firstly, it defined a broad liberalisation framework for information society services, following the country-of-origin principle.[55] Secondly, it established a liability safe harbour for intermediary service providers,[56] which will be addressed further below in the context of the Digital Services Act.

Under the country-of-origin principle, the providers of information society services are required to comply with national provisions applicable in the Member State in which they are established and other Member States may not, for reasons falling within the coordinated field, restrict the freedom to provide services from that Member State.[57] The principle is subject to several exceptions. Most notably, in line with Article 3(4) ECD, Member States may take measures to derogate from Article 3(2) in respect of a given information society service if the measures are: (i) necessary for one of the listed reasons, among others consumer protection, (ii) taken against a given information society service which prejudices such objectives or presents a serious and grave risk of prejudice to those objectives, as well as (iii) proportionate to those objectives. Member States are, however, in principle, required to first raise their concerns with the Member State of establishment and, failing action from that Member State, notify it as well as the Commission of its intention to take relevant measures.[58]

The country-of-origin principle is not the only mechanism aimed at promoting the growth of information society services. The E-Commerce Directive also limits the scope of the requirements which the Member States can provide for under national law. Under Article 4(1), Member States shall ensure that the taking up and pursuit of the activity of an information society service provider is not made subject to prior authorisation or any other requirement having equivalent effect, unless the authorisation scheme is not specifically and exclusively targeted at information society services. In addition, a separate framework—developed already before the adoption of Directive 2000/31/EC—ensures that the European Commission is notified about any draft national rules on information society services.[59] The application

---

[55] ibid. 369–370. On the interpretation of the country-of-origin principle see judgment of the Court of Justice of 25.10.2011 in joined cases C-509/09 and C-161/10 *eDate Advertising and Others*, ECLI:EU:C:2011:685, paras. 53–68.

[56] Articles 12–15 of Directive 2000/31/EC on electronic commerce, later replaced with Articles 4–8 of Regulation 2022/2065 (Digital Services Act).

[57] Articles 3(1) and 3(2) of Directive 2000/31/EC on electronic commerce.

[58] Exceptions apply in case of urgency, see Article 3(5) of Directive 2000/31/EC on electronic commerce.

[59] Directive 98/34/EC as amended by Directive 98/48/EC, currently repealed and replaced by Directive 2015/1535 of the European Parliament and of the Council of 9.9.2015 laying down a procedure for the provision of information in the field of technical regulations and of rules on Information Society services [2015] OJ L241/1. See also the judgment of the Court of Justice of 12.9.2019 in case C-299/17 *VG Media*, ECLI:EU:C:2019:716.

of the EU liberalisation framework depends on the interpretation of key notions, which are discussed in more detail below.

### Distinction Between Online and Offline Spheres: From *Ker-Optika* to *Uber Spain*

As was noted before, the broad liberalisation framework set out in the E-Commerce Directive only applies within the so-called coordinated field. Under Article 2(h)(ii) of Directive 2000/31/EC, the coordinated field does not cover requirements applicable to goods as such, delivery of goods, and services not provided by electronic means.[60]

The scope of the coordinated field was clarified by the Court of Justice more than a decade ago, in C-108/09 *Ker-Optika*. The case dealt with national prohibitions relating to the online sale of contact lenses. The Court considered these provisions to fall within the scope of the coordinated field, arguing, among others, that the definition of information society services extends to the selling of goods online, as apparent from recital 18.[61] National requirements relating to an online offer and conclusion of contracts by electronic means thus needed to comply with the E-Commerce Directive. The same conclusion, however, did not apply to the requirements pertaining to contact lenses as such and to their delivery, to which Directive 2000/31/EC was deemed inapplicable.[62] Against this background, one could expect that digital aspects of services provided by platform operators would generally be covered by the E-Commerce Directive.[63] In its more recent case law, however, the Court of Justice has opted for a shift of focus.

The new interpretation of the online/offline divide in the context of the platform economy came with the judgment in C-434/15 *Asociación Profesional Elite Taxi* (*Uber Spain*) and was reiterated in C-320/16 *Uber France*.[64] Both cases dealt with the qualification of the ride-hailing platform as an information society service, with all the consequences discussed above. The Court opted for an interpretation which was least favourable to the platform provider and left the widest margin of discretion to national authorities. In doing so, it developed the analysis of what Advocate-General Szpunar referred to as "composite services".[65]

The Court began its interpretation by admitting that the intermediation service consisting of connecting non-professional drivers with passengers using a smartphone application is, in principle, a separate service from the underlying transport

60 Article 2(h) of Directive 2000/31/EC on electronic commerce.

61 Judgment of the Court of Justice of 2.12.2010 in case C-108/09 *Ker-Optika*, ECLI:EU:C:2010:725, paras. 23–28.

62 Ibid, paras. 29–31.

63 Schaub (2018), pp. 109–111. Similarly Wendehorst (2016), p. 31 and Orti Vallejo (2019), p. 1006.

64 Judgment of the Court of Justice of 10.4.2018 in case C-320/16 *Uber France*, ECLI:EU:C:2018:221.

65 Opinion of Advocate General Szpunar delivered on 11.5.2017 in case C-434/15 *Asociación Profesional Elite Taxi (Uber Spain)*, ECLI:EU:C:2017:364, para. 28.

service and, as such, it is liable to be qualified as an "information society service".[66] However, according to the Court, the specific service provided by Uber was more than an intermediation service. Rather it formed an integral part of an overall service whose main component was a transport service.[67] In reaching this conclusion, the Court relied on the following two criteria. The first consideration referred to the provider's position as a market maker.[68] According to the Court, without the contested application, neither the relevant drivers would be led to provide transport services, nor persons who wish to make an urban journey would use the services provided by those drivers.[69] The second factor concerned the "decisive influence" exercised by the operator over the conditions of transport services' provision. This included, in particular, its influence on prices, the processing of payments as well as the engagement in quality control, which, in some circumstances, could lead to drivers' exclusion.[70] Consequently, services provided by the company could not be classified as information society services but were rather defined as services in the field of transport.

The qualification of Uber activities as services in the field of transport did not only exclude them from the scope of the E-Commerce Directive. Due to sector-specific exclusions, services of this kind also remained outside the scope of Directive 2006/123/EC on services in the internal market (Services Directive)[71] and even Article 56 TFEU on the free movement of services. They were, by contrast, covered by Article 58(1) TFEU as well as Article 91(1) TFEU authorising the European legislature to lay down provisions on the common transport policy. Because, however, no such common rules had been established for this type of service, Member States enjoyed a wide margin of discretion in their regulation. Even though the *Uber* judgments have been welcomed by some commentators,[72] others criticise the reasoning of the Court as inconsistent and, eventually, counter-productive.[73] The impact of the judgments on consumer protection will be elaborated on later in the book.

#### Further Clarification in *Airbnb Ireland*

The *Uber* jurisprudence has brought a certain level of uncertainty as to the qualification of different platform services, raising the question about the unintended side effects of the new distinction. Against this background, case C-390/18 *Airbnb*

[66] Judgment of the Court of Justice of 20.12.2017 in case C-434/15 *Asociación Profesional Elite Taxi (Uber Spain)*, ECLI:EU:C:2017:981, paras. 34–35.

[67] Ibid, paras. 38, 40.

[68] Busch (2018), p. 173.

[69] Judgment of the Court of Justice of 20.12.2017 in case C-434/15 *Asociación Profesional Elite Taxi (Uber Spain)*, para. 39.

[70] Ibid.

[71] Directive 2006/123/EC of the European Parliament and of the Council of 12.12.2006 on services in the internal market [2006] OJ L376/36.

[72] Hacker (2018), p. 94.

[73] See Schaub (2018), pp. 113–114, Adamski (2018), pp. 742–748 and Delimatsis (2018), p. 246.

*Ireland*[74] provided the Court with an opportunity to clarify how its prior case law applies to other prominent business models. Questions referred in *Airbnb Ireland* were similar to those in *Uber Spain*. Essentially, the controversy was whether national provisions requiring a license to mediate and manage real property could be applied to a service provider, established in another Member State, that connects hosts with guests via an online platform. To reply to this question it needed to be established, as a first step, whether services provided by Airbnb qualified as information society services within the meaning of Directive 2000/31/EC. Interestingly, the Court came to a different conclusion than in the previous *Uber* cases.[75]

Technically, the analysis of the E-Commerce Directive in *Airbnb Ireland* does not contradict the reasoning in *Uber* but rather elaborates on those arguments and applies them to a new factual setting. To establish whether an intermediation service, which *prima facie* qualifies as an information society service, forms an integral part of an overall service whose main component is a service of a different kind (passenger transport, accommodation rental), the "market maker" and "decisive influence" criteria have to be assessed. On a closer look, however, one can wonder whether the Court did not, in fact, "reverse engineer" the facts to make them fit the theory.[76] Either way, the interpretation in *Airbnb Ireland* is likely to alleviate the concerns of those who considered the *Uber* judgments to be too far-reaching.

The Court took a rather conventional approach to describing the business model of Airbnb and considered its essential features to consist in the creation of a list of offers for the benefit of hosts and guests.[77] Unlike in *Uber Spain*, the Court did not hold services of this kind to be indispensable to the provision of accommodation services. The Court further found that Airbnb did not exercise decisive influence over the conditions under which accommodation services were provided, in particular, it did not determine (directly or indirectly) the rental price charged.[78] Also, the provision of ancillary services—such as those related to posting listings and reviews, processing payments, and covering damage—did not affect the separate nature of the intermediation service.[79] Consequently, services provided by Airbnb, assessed in the commented judgment, qualified as "information society services" and could benefit from the liberalisation framework laid down in the E-Commerce Directive.

As noted, the E-Commerce Directive limits the scope of Member States' regulatory discretion and allows service providers to rely, in principle, on legislation in the country of origin. Another notable way in which EU law promotes online growth is via liability exemptions, to which we now turn.

---

[74] Judgment of the Court of Justice of 19.12.2019 in case C-390/18 *Airbnb Ireland*, ECLI:EU:C:2019:1112.

[75] Ibid, para. 69. See also opinion of Advocate General Szpunar delivered on 30.4.2019 in case C-390/18 *Airbnb Ireland*, ECLI:EU:C:2019:336, paras. 86–91.

[76] Van Acker (2020), p. 79. Cf. Hacker (2018), pp. 93–94.

[77] Judgment of the Court of Justice of 19.12.2019 in case C-390/18 *Airbnb Ireland*, para. 53.

[78] Ibid, para. 56.

[79] Ibid, paras. 58–64.

#### 4.3.1.2 Liability Exemptions: From E-Commerce Directive to Digital Services Act

Two decades following the adoption of the E-Commerce Directive, the EU legislature recognized that existing rules may need to be updated. After several years of preparations, in 2022, the Digital Services Act was eventually adopted. For the most part, the new regulation complements its predecessor, without rendering it inapplicable. One important exception concerns the liability exemptions, which have been moved to the DSA and partly amended.

According to Article 1(1), the DSA aims to "contribute to the proper functioning of the internal market for intermediary services by setting out harmonised rules for a safe, predictable and trusted online environment that facilitates innovation and in which fundamental rights enshrined in the Charter, including the principle of consumer protection, are effectively protected". It does so by establishing: (i) a framework for the conditional exemption from liability of providers of intermediary services, (ii) rules on specific due diligence obligations tailored to certain specific categories of providers of intermediary services, and (iii) rules on the implementation and enforcement.[80] The following discussion will focus on provisions supporting platforms' growth. By contrast, the provisions dealing directly with consumer protection will be elaborated on later in the chapter.

The focus of the DSA remains on "intermediary services" which are defined in Article 3(g) DSA as one of the following information society services: (i) a 'mere conduit' service, (ii) a 'caching' service, or (iii) a 'hosting' service. The latter is particularly relevant from the present perspective and relates to a service consisting of the storage of information provided by, and at the request of, a service recipient. A notable sub-group of hosting services are "online platforms", which the DSA defines as hosting services that, at the request of a service recipient, store and disseminate information to the public, unless that activity is a minor and purely ancillary feature of another service or a minor functionality of the principal service and, for objective and technical reasons, cannot be used without that other service, and the integration of the feature or functionality into the other service is not a means to circumvent the applicability of the DSA.[81] While the attempt to situate online platforms within existing EU notions is generally to be welcomed, the connection established between that definition and the notion of an "information society service" may lead to an undesirable exclusion of some platform providers.[82]

Article 6 DSA maintains the liability exception for providers of hosting services, which was originally established in Article 14 of the E-Commerce Directive. Providers of such services shall not be liable for the information stored at the request of a recipient of the service, on condition that they: (i) do not have actual knowledge of illegal activity or illegal content and, as regards claims for damages, are not

---

[80] Article 1(2) of Regulation 2022/2065 (Digital Services Act).

[81] Ibid, Article 3(i).

[82] Consider the *Uber* case law, discussed earlier in this chapter.

aware of facts or circumstances from which the illegal activity or illegal content is apparent, or (ii) upon obtaining such knowledge or awareness, act expeditiously to remove or to disable access to the illegal content. The relevant limitation does not apply where the service recipient is acting under the authority or the control of the service provider.

The above formulations reproduce the wording of the previously applicable Article 14 ECD. What constitutes a novelty is Article 6(3) DSA, pursuant to which the liability exemption in Article 6(1) also does not apply with respect to the liability under consumer protection law of online platforms that allow consumers to conclude distance contracts with traders, if further conditions are fulfilled. This is the case where an online platform presents a specific item of information or otherwise enables the specific transaction at issue in a way that would lead an average consumer to believe that the information, or the product or service that is the object of the transaction, is provided either by the online platform itself or by a recipient of the service who is acting under its authority or control.

*Prima facie*, Article 6(3) DSA looks like a significant improvement from a consumer protection standpoint. On a closer look, however, the assessment is more ambivalent. Firstly, the act offers no further guidance about the relevant criteria. Secondly, what the DSA ultimately achieves is merely the removal of the liability exemption, leaving it to "consumer protection law" to determine conditions for liability. It is not even entirely clear what the latter is supposed to encompass and what exactly is the added value of the new provision.

Indeed, the safe harbour in Article 6(1) DSA relates to liability "for the information stored at the request of a recipient of the service". The exception in Article 6(3) DSA must thus also pertain to this liability. What the new provision does not cover is the liability of the hosting service provider for his or her activities, e.g. a failure to comply with any applicable due diligence obligations or failure to provide consumers with mandatory information. Such obligations may notably arise under consumer law, e.g. the Consumer Rights Directive and the Unfair Commercial Practices Directive. This, however, is not the context to which Article 6(3) DSA relates.

Against this background, Article 6(3) DSA seems to pertain primarily to the secondary liability of hosting service providers for consumer law violations committed by the providers of information stored. This could be the case, for instance, where a trader active on an online platform is offering goods or digital services that do not comply with the conformity requirements. What constitutes "consumer protection law" may not always be easy to establish. In particular, a question arises whether EU and national rules protecting broadly defined consumers, without adopting a status-based approach, are also covered.

In addition to amended liability exemptions, the DSA clarifies that providers of intermediary services shall not be deemed ineligible for such exemptions solely because they, in good faith and in a diligent manner, carry out voluntary own-initiative investigations into, or take other measures aimed at detecting, identifying and removing, or disabling access to, illegal content, or take the necessary measures to comply with the requirements of Union law and national law in compliance with

Union law.[83] This is a welcome development ensuring that platform operators will not be penalised for taking measures to protect consumers. At the same time, Article 8 DSA continues to prevent the Member States from establishing any general obligations to monitor the information which providers of intermediary services transmit or store, or actively to seek facts or circumstances indicating illegal activity. While such general obligations could indeed negatively affect the users of some platforms, this is not necessarily the case for all platform services. In particular, specific risks observed in the travel sector could justify the imposition of further-reaching monitoring duties.

#### 4.3.1.3 Interim Conclusions

In summary, both the E-Commerce Directive and the DSA, as well as related requirements on notification, provide a powerful framework supporting the growth of the platform economy. Platform providers seek to rely on EU law when faced with national requirements constraining their activities. The Court attempts to mitigate the associated tensions through a multi-layered reading of "information society services". In light of the diversity and complexity of online platforms, the notion will likely occupy the courts in the years to come.[84]

The emerging case law confirms that a significant part of services provided in the platform economy qualify as information society services and, as such, are covered by the relevant liberalisation framework. This, however, does not necessarily mean that their providers are shielded from any kind of liability. Even if platform operators qualify as hosting service providers, the exemption in Article 6(1) DSA is not absolute. Firstly, it does not extend to the providers' own violations, but only to the information stored at the request of service recipients. Secondly, the liability exemption is subject to several limitations, including a new one established in Article 6(3) DSA. Although the DSA maintains a prohibition of general monitoring duties, it does encourage voluntary own-initiative investigations targeting illegal content or aiming to ensure legal compliance.

Most importantly for the present book, the above supplier-friendly legislation does not exhaust the EU's involvement in digital markets. On the contrary, it is recognized that market integration may exacerbate the risks for certain market actors, notably consumers. In response to these risks, negative integration in the EU tends to go hand in hand with an expansion of harmonised safeguards. This process is discussed in the following, with a focus on consumer protection in digital markets.

[83] Article 7 of Regulation 2022/2065 (Digital Services Act).

[84] See e.g. the subsequent judgment of the Court of Justice of 3.12.2020 in case C-62/19 *Star Taxi App*, ECLI:EU:C:2020:980.

## 4.3.2 *Protecting Consumers*

### 4.3.2.1 Status-Based Instruments of Consumer Protection

Forerunner: Directive 97/7/EC on Distance Contracts

The first instrument directly concerned with the challenges of contracting at a distance was Directive 97/7/EC. The act set out several information duties for traders in B2C transactions and provided consumers with a right to withdraw from a contract within at least seven working days.[85] While the relevant information duties appear to follow the self-reliance ethic, the consumer's right to withdraw seems more akin to the need ethic.[86] The decision to equip consumers with this robust safeguard can be explained by their weak position; especially, the difficulties in picturing the goods or services offered due to the lack of face-to-face contact.[87] At the same time, the right to withdraw could also foster confidence in distance contracting.[88]

Besides imposing information duties on traders and providing consumers with a right to withdraw, Directive 97/7/EC included additional rules concerning contractual performance. Most notably, under Article 7(2), a supplier who failed to perform the contract on the grounds that the goods or services ordered were unavailable, was required to inform the consumer of this situation and refund any sums already paid as soon as possible and in any case within 30 days. The provision sought to respond to the consumer's weaker position as a party making payment before, and eventually without, having received counter-performance. Besides requiring the payment made by the consumer to be refunded within a specified period, the provision helped to ensure that the consumer was informed of the supplier's inability to perform and could make alternative arrangements. Article 7(3) of Directive 97/7/EC allowed Member States to opt in favour of alternative performance as a first-stage remedy, provided that the consumer was informed of it in advance. Additional protection was also afforded to consumers in case of fraudulent use of their payment cards.[89]

The overall level of protection afforded by Directive 97/7/EC can only be established when the act's scope and the level of harmonisation are considered. As regards the former, one cannot fail to note that several important contracts concluded at a distance—including contracts for the provision of accommodation and transport services on a specific date or within a specific period—were excluded from the Directive's provisions on information and withdrawal. These negative

---

[85] Article 6 of Directive 97/7/EC on distance contracts.

[86] Willett (2018), p. 209.

[87] Bech Serrat (2012), p. 36. For a discussion of similar factors as sources of market failures, see Iamiceli (2019), p. 402.

[88] Article 8 of Directive 97/7/EC on distance contracts. See also Loos (2009), pp. 246–247.

[89] Currently covered under Articles 73 and 74 of Directive 2015/2366 on payment services in the internal market.

consequences have been counterbalanced to some extent by the principle of minimum harmonisation, which allowed the Member States to introduce or maintain more stringent provisions compatible with the Treaty, to ensure a higher level of consumer protection.[90] Crucially as well, Article 7(2) on supplier's non-performance remained fully applicable to these types of contracts.

The use of a minimum harmonisation approach is characteristic of the European consumer policy at an early stage.[91] Conceptually, the principle of minimum harmonisation seems to be particularly well-aligned with the "consumer confidence" rationale[92] as well as with the theoretical concept of "fair internal market".[93] While not incompatible *per se* with the more traditional rationales of removing obstacles to trade or distortions to competition, it may admittedly weaken the case for positive integration on those grounds.[94] Due to this tension, the European legislature has over time moved away from establishing a minimum level of protection towards a full harmonisation approach. The choice of full harmonisation highlights the importance of the more traditional internal market thinking, focused on facilitating business operations. Crucially, the commonality of the applicable consumer protection standard is the key benefit that full harmonisation offers to suppliers. In line with Article 114(3) TFEU, the standard itself should still afford a high level of consumer protection, perhaps even more so than in the case of minimum harmonisation. Overall, the fact remains that the shift towards full harmonisation has made the legislative negotiations significantly more complex and continues to attract criticism from consumer advocates.[95] The consequent difficulties may sometimes result in gaps in the personal and substantive scope of the legal norms, with potentially negative consequences for both active and passive participants of the internal market.

#### Successor: Directive 2011/83/EU on Consumer Rights

The replacement of Directive 97/7/EC on distance contracts with Directive 2011/83/EU on consumer rights marks the next major step of the EU legal evolution. The reform reflects the move towards full harmonisation, first announced in the Consumer Policy Strategy 2002–2006.[96] While Directive 2011/83/EU is predominantly focused on distance and off-premises contracts, its original conception was

---

[90] Article 14 of Directive 97/7/EC on distance contracts.

[91] Jagielska (2016), pp. 164–165.

[92] Wilhelmsson (2004), p. 322.

[93] Hesselink (2016), p. 451.

[94] Cf. judgment of the Court of Justice of 5.10.2000 in case C-376/98 *Germany v Parliament and Council* (*Tobacco Advertising*), para. 101–104 and judgment of the Court of Justice of 16.12.2008 in case C-205/07 *Gysbrechts and Santurel Inter*, ECLI:EU:C:2008:730, paras. 57–63. See also Reich and Micklitz (2008), p. 349.

[95] Jagielska (2016), pp. 167–171.

[96] European Commission, 'Communication from the Commission to the European Parliament, the Council, the Economic and Social Committee and the Committee of the Regions—Consumer

more comprehensive. According to the Commission's proposal,[97] the act was intended to incorporate four pre-existing directives, including those on unfair terms and consumer sales. The failure of this plan reveals the tensions associated with full harmonisation.

The scope of Directive 2011/83/EU broadly corresponds with that of Directives 85/577/EEC and 97/7/EC, with several exceptions. To illustrate, the CRD elaborates on information duties and extends them to some other contracts. Moreover, Article 7 of Directive 97/7/EC on contractual performance was replaced with Article 18 CRD, which only applies to sales contracts. The Consumer Rights Directive also maintains the exclusion of several important services, most notably in the travel sector. Specifically, the act does not apply, in principle, to passenger transport services[98] and the right to withdraw does not apply to contracts for the provision of accommodation other than for residential purposes.[99] An asymmetry therefore exists in the protection standard enjoyed by consumers in sale and service contracts.

The Consumer Rights Directive did not originally engage with new market developments, such as triangular relationships established via online platforms and the growth of peer-to-peer transactions.[100] However, the Court of Justice has been increasingly called upon to interpret key concepts with regard to platforms. Moreover, a recent legislative reform of the EU consumer *acquis* explicitly brought platform operators within the act's scope.

An important question raised before European courts was whether a platform operator can qualify as a "trader" not only concerning its own services but also goods and services offered by platform users.[101] The problem revolved around the reading of Article 2(2) CRD, which defines traders as natural and legal persons who are acting for purposes relating to their trade, business, craft or profession, including *through any other person* acting in their name or on their behalf. In a non-binding guidance, the European Commission argued that "other persons", mentioned in that provision, could also include platform operators.[102] In case C-536/20 *Tiketa*, the Court confirmed that intermediaries who act in the name of or on behalf of other

Policy Strategy 2002-2006' (2002) COM(2002) 208 final. For a more comprehensive account of this process, see Tonner (2014), p. 702. See also Reich (2012), p. 3 and Krämer (2021), p. 13.

[97] European Commission, 'Proposal for a Directive of the European Parliament and of the Council on Consumer Rights' (2008) COM(2008) 614 final.

[98] Article 3(3)(k) of Directive 2011/83/EU on consumer rights.

[99] Ibid, Article 16(l).

[100] Iamiceli (2019), p. 417.

[101] de Vries and Jabłonowska (2019), p. 107. See also judgment of the Court of Justice of 25.10.2005 in case C-229/04 *Crailsheimer Volksbank*, ECLI:EU:C:2005:640, paras. 41–45. For a critical assessment, see Wendehorst (2016), pp. 32–33.

[102] European Commission DG Justice, 'DG Justice Guidance Document Concerning Directive 2011/83/EU of the European Parliament and of the Council of 25 October 2011 on Consumer Rights, Amending Council Directive 93/13/EEC and Directive 1999/44/EC of the European Parliament and of the Council and Repealing Council Directive 85/577/EEC and Directive 97/7/EC of the European Parliament and of the Council' (2014) 31 <https://commission.europa.eu/system/files/2019-07/crd_guidance_en_0_updated_0.pdf>.

professional parties qualify as "traders".[103] The judgment further stated that both traders are in this case required to ensure compliance with CRD requirements.[104] At the same time, the Court distinguished its finding from an earlier *Wathelet* ruling, noting that the consumer's knowledge about the intermediary status is irrelevant under the CRD.[105]

The *Tiketa* judgment could be read to increase the responsibility of platform operators in the context of the CRD. However, the very fact that platform providers qualify as intermediaries does not yet mean that they are in fact acting "on behalf" of platform users.[106] Moreover, the impact of an extended trader definition would in any case be limited to scenarios in which the direct seller or service provider is him or herself a trader, thus leaving the peer-to-peer relationships out of scope. The latter issue was addressed more recently through a legislative change, undertaken through the Modernisation Directive.[107]

Following the 2019 reform, Article 6a was added to the CRD, requiring online marketplace providers to inform consumers who make use of their service about several matters before they are bound by a distance contract or any corresponding offer. More specifically, the consumer should be informed: (i) about the main parameters determining the ranking of offers and their relative importance as opposed to other parameters, (ii) whether the third party offering the goods, services or digital content is a trader or not, (iii) that the consumer rights stemming from Union consumer protection law do not apply to the contracts that do not qualify as B2C contracts, and (iv) where applicable, how the obligations related to the contract are shared between the third party offering the goods, services or digital content and the provider of the online marketplace. Notably, Article 6a(2) CRD establishes an exception from the principle of full harmonisation, allowing Member States to impose additional information requirements for providers of online marketplaces.

The newly introduced Article 6a CRD remains of direct relevance to online travel platforms. Indeed, the providers of such platforms will typically qualify as providers of online marketplaces, i.e. services using software, operated by or on behalf of a trader, which allow consumers to conclude distance contracts with other traders or consumers.[108] The information duty about the status of one's counterparty responds to the growth of peer-to-peer transactions, which is a prominent development in the travel sector. However, the level of protection offered by this provision is rather

[103] Judgment of the Court of Justice of 24.2.2022 in case C-536/20 *Tiketa*, ECLI:EU:C:2022:112, para. 31.

[104] Ibid, para. 35.

[105] Ibid, para. 33–34.

[106] Sørensen (2022), pp. 1029–1030.

[107] Directive (EU) 2019/2161 of the European Parliament and of the Council of 27.11.2019 amending Council Directive 93/13/EEC and Directives 98/6/EC, 2005/29/EC and 2011/83/EU of the European Parliament and of the Council as regards the better enforcement and modernisation of Union consumer protection rules [2019] OJ L328/7.

[108] Article 2(17) of Directive 2011/83/EU, as amended.

limited.[109] Firstly, Article 6a CRD maintains the status-based approach of the EU consumer *acquis*, without analysing if there are any relevant consumer weaknesses beyond the B2C scenario. Secondly, when making the disclosure, online marketplace providers may rely on declarations of relevant third parties.[110] It may well be that the latter in fact act as traders but inaccurately present themselves as peers. In such cases, information that consumer rights do not apply may deter consumers from exercising legal rights that they do enjoy.[111]

Overall, consumer protection in the CRD is primarily achieved through information duties and withdrawal rights. With regard to performance, Directive 2011/83/EU represents a backward step as it no longer contains a provision similar to Article 7(2) Directive 97/7/EC as far as services are concerned. The 2019 reform took note of the platform economy and added information duties for online marketplace providers. Rules of this kind, however, offer a comparably low level of consumer protection, more akin to the self-reliance ethic.

While the right to withdraw does provide stronger protection, its personal and substantive scope reveals important limitations. The rationale for excluding certain types of travel services from the scope of withdrawal rules is not immediately apparent. After all, such choice-enhancing instruments can foster consumer confidence in distance contracting, regardless of the subject matter. On a closer look, the exclusion seems to be justified not by the function of the right, but rather by its burden on the travel industry.[112] This broad-brush exception from the right to withdraw has been criticised by Bech Serrat, who argues that the impact of withdrawal rights on the tourism industry should be re-assessed.[113] The author points to alternative means of protecting relevant interests, such as through cancellation clauses. In my view, such re-examination should also take into account non-B2C transactions concluded in the platform economy.

The analysis in Chap. 3 revealed the existence of different types of cancellation clauses in all analysed platforms. Considering such clauses not as additional, contractually granted consumer benefits, but rather a lower form of protection than the exceptionally inapplicable right to withdraw, changes the perspective on their assessment. When revisiting this problem, it is worth taking note of existing instruments of travellers' protection in both national and EU law, such as the right to transfer the package travel contract to another traveller or to terminate the contract

[109] Prastitou Merdi (2020), pp. 360–361, 365.

[110] Article 6a(1)(b) *in fine* of Directive 2011/83/EU, as amended.

[111] For another possible confusion, associated with the application of national law, see Sørensen (2022), pp. 1025–1026.

[112] Similarly, with relation to the notion of "transport services" in Directive 97/7/EC on distance contracts in the context of car hire, see judgment of the Court of Justice of 10.3.2005 in case C-336/03 *easyCar*, ECLI:EU:C:2005:150, para. 28. For a different conclusion, see the opinion of Advocate General Stix-Hackl delivered on 11.11.2004 in case C-336/03 *easyCar*, ECLI:EU:C:2004:716. With regard to leisure activities, see judgment of the Court of Justice of 31.3.2022 in case C-96/21 *CTS Eventim*, ECLI:EU:C:2022:238.

[113] Bech Serrat (2012), p. 42.

in return for an appropriate and justifiable termination fee in Directive 2015/2302[114] or similar national rules for certain contracts for the carriage of passengers,[115] which are further discussed in Chap. 5.

### Potential and Limits of Directive 2019/770 on Digital Services

Until recently, there was no standard for reviewing the performance of digital services under EU law. This changed following the adoption of Directive 2019/770 on certain aspects concerning contracts for the supply of digital content and digital services (DSD).[116] The act shares conceptual similarities with the rules on sales, which were updated as part of a related initiative.[117]

Article 2(2) DSD defines digital services as: (i) services that allow the consumer to create, process, store or access data in digital form, or (ii) services that allow the sharing of or any other interaction with data in digital form uploaded or created by the consumer or other users of that service. The notion thus applies to services provided by many platform operators, including in the travel sector. Such operators typically act as traders, while travellers who make use of their services will typically qualify as consumers.[118]

The Directive lays down rules on the conformity of digital services with the contract as well as remedies in the event of a lack of such conformity or a failure to supply. The relevant conformity requirements are both subjective and objective. The former include the features of digital services that have been promised in the contract, the latter, in turn, derive directly from the EU law. A notable objective criterion is found in Article 8(1)(b) DSD which provides that digital services shall "be of the quantity and possess the qualities and performance features (…) normal for digital content or digital services of the same type and which the consumer may reasonably expect, given the nature of the digital content or digital service and taking into account any public statement made by or on behalf of the trader, or other

---

[114] Articles 9 and 12(1) of Directive (EU) 2015/2302 of the European Parliament and of the Council of 25.11.2015 on package travel and linked travel arrangements, amending Regulation (EC) No 2006/2004 and Directive 2011/83/EU of the European Parliament and of the Council and repealing Council Directive 90/314/EEC [2015] OJ L326/1.

[115] Article 17(1) of the Polish Act of 15.11.1984 – Carriage law (*Prawo przewozowe*), consolidated text Dz.U. 2024 poz. 1262, regulating passenger carriage by road, rail and inland waterways, as well as Article 175(1) of the Polish Act of 18.9.2001 – Maritime code (*Kodeks morski*), consolidated text Dz.U. 2023 r. poz. 1309. See also Dąbrowski (2017), p. 62.

[116] Directive (EU) 2019/770 of the European Parliament and of the Council of 20.5.2019 on certain aspects concerning contracts for the supply of digital content and digital services [2019] OJ L136/1.

[117] Directive (EU) 2019/771 of the European Parliament and of the Council of 20.5.2019 on certain aspects concerning contracts for the sale of goods, amending Regulation (EU) 2017/2394 and Directive 2009/22/EC, and repealing Directive 1999/44/EC [2019] OJ L136/28.

[118] See Articles 2(5) and 2(6) of Directive 2019/770 on digital services.

persons in previous links of the chain of transactions" (with several exceptions). Two distinct criteria must therefore be fulfilled: normality and reasonableness.[119]

Both criteria are known from the pre-existing rules on consumer sales, yet their application to digital services is not straightforward.[120] As noted, digital markets tend to be rather concentrated. A risk therefore exists that "normal" features of digital services may be determined by a small group of companies. Such risk is mitigated by two important factors, coming from both outside and within the DSD. Firstly, the scope of legitimate design choices may be determined by other legal norms, including the Digital Services Act, which is discussed further below. Secondly, the normality criterion in the DSD can sometimes conflict with the criterion of reasonable expectations.[121]

The notion of reasonableness in EU law is inspired by a similar concept in common law, with several adjustments.[122] Recital 46 DSD clarifies that the standard "should be objectively ascertained, having regard to the nature and purpose of the digital content or digital service, the circumstances of the case and to the usages and practices of the parties involved". According to Troiano, references to reasonableness as a model of conduct in EU law relate to the balancing of conflicting interests and as such cannot be examined in isolation.[123] Similarly, Osmola identifies different grounds for reasonable expectations: from mandatory rules to indicative rules and (unregulated) practices.[124] In the case of the DSD, attention must be drawn to the rationale of a "high level" of consumer protection, permeating the consumer *acquis*, which is stressed in the Directive itself as well as in primary law. When choosing the right conduct, traders can thus be required to pay careful attention to consumer interests, and not only prioritise their commercial gain.

Overall, by requiring that digital services comply with objective requirements and enabling their consumer-oriented reading through the notion of reasonable expectations, the DSD aligns well with the need ethic. Nevertheless, the extent to which the Directive can mitigate consumer problems in online travel platforms can be called into doubt. The paradigm of digital services that the DSD appears to have in mind is different from services observed in the travel sector. As mentioned, the definition in Article 2(2) DSD relates to "services that allow the sharing of or any other interaction with data in digital form uploaded or created by the consumer or other users of that service". The focus thus remains on interactions contained to the digital sphere, as in the case of social media, video and audio sharing, or online games.[125] While services enabling "interactions with data in digital form" are also part of the picture in online travel platforms, they are not the only services provided

---

[119] The following analysis in this section is based on my discussion in Jabłonowska (2023), p. 174.

[120] Namysłowska and Jabłonowska (2022), p. 221.

[121] See Schulze (2024), para. 23.

[122] Staudenmayer (2022), p. 219.

[123] Troiano (2009), p. 773.

[124] Osmola (2023), p. 136.

[125] See recital 19 of Directive 2019/770 on digital services.

in that context. Naturally, the Directive also does not apply to contracts between consumers and travel service providers, e.g. hosts and drivers. The extent to which a progressive interpretation of the DSD can improve consumer protection in online travel platforms will be addressed in Chap. 8.

#### 4.3.2.2 Beyond Status-Based Protection: E-Commerce Directive

While status-based instruments are the most prominent part of the EU consumer *acquis*, consumer protection in digital markets has also been achieved through other means. This is notably the case for Directive 2000/31/EC on electronic commerce, which was one of the first EU acts specifically concerned with digital markets. Besides the liberalisation framework discussed earlier, the Directive laid down several protections for service recipients. These include, in particular, a general information duty for all providers of information society services (Article 5), rules on transparency of commercial communications and unsolicited commercial communications (Articles 6 and 7) as well as on formation and transparency of electronic contracts (Articles 10 and 11).[126]

Unlike Directive 97/7/EC, and subsequently Directive 2011/83/EU on consumer rights, the E-Commerce Directive has not been limited to relationships between "consumers" and "traders", understood according to the well-established status-based definitions.[127] As a general rule, it applies to all information society services, irrespective of the professional or non-professional status of the parties involved. Key notions, which determine the Directive's personal scope, are those of a "service provider" and a "recipient of the service". The former is defined as any natural or legal person providing an information society service, while the latter refers to any natural or legal person who, for professional ends or otherwise, uses an information society service.

Pre-contractual information duties and rules related to the placing of an order are not mandatory in B2B relations; the default rule, however, does not apply to peer-to-peer exchange. The instrument also encourages the development of codes of conduct and out-of-court dispute settlement.[128] As such, the act appears well-placed to establish a common baseline of consumer protection in the platform economy, provided that its scope is construed broadly. Such a broad reading, which extends the scope of the ECD to digital components of different economic activities, finds support in the *Ker-Optika* case.[129] The act thus remains relevant to both platform operators and sellers and service providers who make use of their services. At the same

---

[126] Nordhausen (2005), p. 103–106.

[127] See Articles 2(2) and 2(3) of Directive 97/7/EC on distance contracts.

[128] Articles 16 and 17 of Directive 2000/31/EC on electronic commerce.

[129] For a discussion of the *Ker-Optika* case, see Sect. 4.3.1.1 above. See also Wendehorst (2016), pp. 31–32.

time, the *Uber* case law may have the unintended consequence of bringing certain platforms outside the scope of protective e-commerce rules.[130]

While protections laid down in the E-Commerce Directive are not particularly strong, personal scope of the act illustrates an alternative regulatory approach to the digital economy, one extending beyond the B2C dimension. However, so far the path taken by the ECD remains an exception. This has not changed following the adoption of the Digital Services Act, which is the most recent EU legislation explicitly targeting online platforms.

#### 4.3.2.3 Mixed Approach of Digital Services Act

Actions against Abuse

The previously discussed, targeted amendments to the consumer *acquis* demonstrated the growing EU interest in the platform economy. At the same time, the EU legislature recognized that the issues raised by online platforms require a more detailed response. Thus, important safeguards for the participants of the digital economy can also be found in the Digital Services Act.

The DSA is an extensive act of a complex nature. On the one hand, it removes barriers to the growth of the platform economy, by maintaining and adjusting some of the liability limitations, as discussed before. On the other hand, it sets out obligations for the participants of the platform economy, including the providers of online platforms. Notably, the scope of the protection addressees is heterogeneous and includes both broadly construed "service recipients" and more narrowly defined "consumers".

Several provisions of the DSA are particularly relevant to the travel sector. Firstly, Article 14 DSA requires the providers of intermediary services—which includes online platforms—to specify, in their terms and conditions, what restrictions they impose in relation to the use of their service and to act in a diligent, objective and proportionate manner in applying and enforcing them. Secondly, pursuant to Article 15, providers of intermediary services shall make publicly available, at least once a year, clear, easily comprehensible reports on any content moderation that they engaged in during the relevant period. The reporting duties are even more extensive for providers of very large online platforms.[131] Such reports seem to address a major gap in the private governance frameworks identified in Chap. 3. Indeed, the first reports published, among others, by Booking.com shed light on the scale and nature of content moderation practices in online platforms.[132]

[130] Schaub (2018), pp. 111–115.

[131] Article 42 of Regulation 2022/2065 (Digital Services Act).

[132] European Commission, 'How the Digital Services Act enhances transparency online'. Available at: <https://digital-strategy.ec.europa.eu/en/policies/dsa-brings-transparency>.

The DSA further establishes a notice-and-action mechanism for removing illegal content. Notably, the definition of illegal content in the DSA refers to information that breaches applicable law not only by itself but also in relation to an activity, including the sale of products or the provision of services.[133] The providers of hosting services should put reporting tools in place and act upon reports in a timely, diligent, non-arbitrary and objective manner.[134] Providers of online platforms are moreover required to suspend the provision of their services to service recipients that frequently provide manifestly illegal content and report the number of suspensions.[135] In addition, where a provider of hosting services becomes aware of any information giving rise to a suspicion that a criminal offence involving a threat to the life or safety of a person or persons has taken place, is taking place or is likely to take place, it shall promptly inform the relevant law enforcement or judicial authorities.[136]

The provisions discussed above can meaningfully contribute to the protection of travellers in the platform economy, as they specify how providers should police their platforms and ensure transparency reporting. While the focus of this analysis remains on the position of consumers in the travel sector, who will typically benefit from more robust platform policing, it is worth noting that the DSA also contains procedural safeguards for content providers. Notably, as well, the commented provisions do not seem to apply to operators who do not qualify as information society service providers. This, once again, shows an unintended consequence of the *Uber* case law and the decision to leave the regulation of some composite services to the Member States.

#### Traceability of Traders

The safeguards mentioned earlier apply regardless of the status of the service recipient. However, this does not mean that the status-based approach is entirely absent from the DSA. On the contrary, a notable group of DSA provisions only applies to online platforms allowing "consumers" to conclude distance contracts with "traders".

Firstly, Article 30 DSA seeks to improve the traceability of traders concluding contracts with consumers via online platforms. It requires platform operators to ensure that traders can only use their platforms after the operators receive certain information. More specifically, the traders should communicate the following: (i) their name, address, telephone number, and email address, (ii) a copy of their identification document or electronic identification, (iii) payment account details, (iv) the trade register in which the trader is registered and a means of identification in

---

[133] Article 3(h) of Regulation 2022/2065 (Digital Services Act).

[134] Ibid, Article 16.

[135] Ibid, Articles 23 and 24.

[136] Ibid, Article 18.

that register, where applicable, and (v) a commitment to only offer products or services that comply with the EU law. Platform operators should further make best efforts to assess whether the information they obtained is reliable and complete. What is more, where the platform provider obtains sufficient indications or has reason to believe that information it obtained from the trader is inaccurate, incomplete or not up-to-date, that provider should request that the trader remedy that situation and, failing that, suspend the provision of its service to that trader.

Not all information communicated to the operator should be made publicly accessible.[137] The DSA only requires this in relation to the trader's name, address and contact details, the registration number and the commitment made. By contrast, the identification document and payment account details should only be disclosed to third parties under strict conditions, e.g. based on an order issued by competent authorities. Consumers can nonetheless rely on the fact that the identity of the trader has been verified by the platform operator and that authorities can take action when needed.

The requirement to confirm one's identity before offering goods or services to consumers via online platforms departs from the initial perception of the internet as an anonymous space, allowing individuals to express themselves without the fear of being recognized. However, this idea seems to be moving to the background for quite some time already, as users become more easily identifiable and are required to take responsibility for what they do online. As noted in Chap. 3, identity verification tools are also a notable feature of private governance systems deployed in online travel platforms. Indeed, it may be difficult to engender the trust needed for online contracting, if the consumer does not know who he or she is dealing with.

The EU legislature made a deliberate choice to limit the scope of Article 30 DSA to formally defined "traders". The relation of the provision with the recent reform of the Consumer Rights Directive is nonetheless unclear. As noted earlier, the newly added Article 6a CRD requires online marketplace providers to inform consumers "whether the third party offering the goods, services or digital content is a trader or not, on the basis of the declaration of that third party". The CRD does not require operators to make best efforts to assess whether the information they obtained is accurate or act upon the indications to the contrary. It is therefore not clear whether the duty in Article 30 DSA is limited to sellers and suppliers who have declared themselves as traders or is independent from that declaration. The goal of consumer protection would support the latter reading, extending the "completeness" assessment to the question whether the trader's status was accurately revealed.

Finally, Article 30 DSA fails to recognize the risks associated with peer-to-peer transactions, at least in certain areas of the platform economy. This is prominently the case in the travel sector, in which the traveller is suffering from distinct weaknesses, independent of the status of his or her counterparty. Moreover, as noted earlier, the ECD requires the providers of information society services—including parties offering goods and services online—to provide service recipients with

---

[137] Referring to the DSA proposal, see Cauffman and Goanta (2021), p. 763.

certain information, irrespective of both parties' status. This includes information about the name of the service provider as well as his or her address and contact details. A similar disclosure duty can also be found in the Services Directive, touched upon in the next chapter.

In light of the above, there is no convincing reason why the obligation of the platform provider to ensure that sellers and service providers can only use their platforms after the operators receive information about the service provider's name, address and contact details is limited to traders. Moreover, at least with respect to online travel platforms, an argument can be made for extending the duty about identity documents to the peer providers. After all, identity verification tools have proven to be an important trust-building factor in the travel sector. However, the scale of their deployment appears to differ across platforms.[138]

### Compliance by Design

Another notable DSA provision directed at providers of online platforms for B2C contracting concerns compliance by design. Pursuant to Article 31(1) DSA, providers of such platforms should ensure that their online interfaces are designed and organised in a way that enables traders to comply with their obligations regarding pre-contractual information, compliance and product safety information under EU law. In addition, Article 31(3) DSA requires platform operators to make best efforts to assess whether traders have provided relevant information before allowing them to offer products or services on those platforms. Finally, the providers should make reasonable efforts to randomly check in any official, freely accessible and machine-readable online database or online interface whether the products or services offered have been identified as illegal.

The obligation to enable legal compliance through platform design is not a novelty under EU law. As discussed in Chap. 7, such a duty has already been derived from the Unfair Commercial Practices Directive with respect to consumer law.[139] An added value is offered by Article 31(3) DSA which requires platform operators to pre-assess the information. The provision shows similarity to the previously discussed requirement on traders' traceability—this time with a focus on products and services. However, unlike Article 30(2) DSA, the duty of by-design compliance does not involve an assessment of reliability. Rather, platform providers should merely make best efforts to assess "whether" the information was provided, and is thus limited to completeness.[140] To illustrate, when a trader uploads a listing on an accommodation rental platform, the operator is not required to verify the user indeed has a title to a property at the location indicated. The same is true for drivers offering rides to passengers in specific cars. However, at least in the travel sector,

[138] Consider e.g. the voluntary identity verification in BlaBlaCar.

[139] See Chap. 7.

[140] Recital 74 of Regulation 2022/2065 (Digital Services Act).

such an assessment before offering services on the platform could be deemed justified by the severity of consumer weaknesses. Moreover, the duty in Article 31 DSA could easily be extended to the peer providers, considering that certain obligations, e.g. under the E-Commerce and Services Directives, may not be linked to the supplier's status.

As noted, Article 31(3) *in fine* DSA requires platform operators to make reasonable efforts to randomly check in any official, freely accessible and machine-readable online database or online interface whether the products or services offered have been identified as illegal. The provision does not specify the relevant benchmark and, in particular, whether it covers both EU and national law. On the one hand, Article 31(1) DSA refers exclusively to EU law. On the other hand, the notion of "illegal content", referred to elsewhere in the Regulation, includes both harmonised provisions and national law which complies with EU law.[141] In either case, the duty in Article 31(3) *in fine* DSA seems to be more oriented towards goods than services, as illustrated by the reference to product safety law in Article 31(1) DSA and long-standing EU efforts to promote common databases in the context.[142] The same is true for a related obligation in Article 32 DSA to inform consumers who purchased illegal products or services of this fact. Such databases, however, could also be of value in the field of services, most notably in the travel sector, possibly limiting the scale of violations within and across platforms.

### Additional Obligations of Very Large Online Platforms

While the previously discussed provisions apply, in principle, to all online platforms,[143] the DSA also sets out additional obligations applicable to very online large platforms (VLOPs). Pursuant to Article 33(1) DSA, very large platforms are platforms with a number of average monthly active recipients of the service in the Union equal to or higher than 45 million, which have been adequately designated. At the time of writing, the Commission has designated 20 such platforms, including one online travel platform, namely Booking.com.[144]

One of the central duties of the providers of very large online platforms is to perform a risk assessment and put in place mitigation measures. Pursuant to Article 34(1) DSA, providers of VLOPs should diligently identify, analyse and assess any systemic risks in the Union stemming from the design or functioning of their service

---

[141] Ibid, Article 3(h).

[142] Consider, for example, the Information and Communication System on Market Surveillance (ICSMS). Available at: <https://webgate.ec.europa.eu/icsms>.

[143] Some exceptions apply to providers of online platforms allowing consumers to conclude distance contracts with traders that qualify as micro or small enterprises. See e.g. Article 29 of Regulation 2022/2065 (Digital Services Act).

[144] For an up-to-date list see European Commission, 'Supervision of the designated very large online platforms and search engines under DSA'. Available at: <https://digital-strategy.ec.europa.eu/en/policies/list-designated-vlops-and-vloses>.

and its related systems, including algorithmic systems, or from the use made of their services. The relevant risks include, among others: (i) the dissemination of illegal content through the platform services, (ii) any actual or foreseeable negative effects for the exercise of fundamental rights, including the right to a high level of consumer protection enshrined in Article 38 of the Charter, (iii) any actual or foreseeable negative effects on public security, (iv) any actual or foreseeable negative effects in relation to gender-based violence, the protection of public health and minors and serious negative consequences to the person's physical and mental well-being.

In addition, Article 35(1) DSA requires VLOPs providers to put in place reasonable, proportionate and effective mitigation measures, tailored to the specific systemic risks they identified. Such measures may include: (i) adapting the design, features or functioning of their services, (ii) adapting their terms and conditions and their enforcement, (iii) adapting content moderation processes as well as any relevant decision-making processes and resources, (iv) testing and adapting the algorithmic systems used, (v) reinforcing the internal processes, resources, testing, documentation, or supervision of any of their activities in particular as regards detection of systemic risk, (vi) initiating or adjusting cooperation with trusted flaggers and the implementation of the decisions of out-of-court dispute settlement bodies, (vii) initiating or adjusting cooperation with other providers of online platforms through the codes of conduct and the crisis protocols, (viii) taking awareness-raising measures and providing service recipients with more information, (ix) taking targeted measures to protect the rights of the child, or (x) taking measures against inauthentic content (e.g. manipulated images). Reports on the undertaken risk assessment and risk mitigation should be communicated to the competent authorities as well as, in principle, to the general public.[145]

Both the risk groups and mitigation listed above are also very relevant for online travel platforms. At present, however, only one online travel platform falls under those provisions. Due to the distinct nature of risks associated with the travel sector, it is worth considering whether similar duties could not apply also to other platforms active in this area.

## 4.4 Conclusions

The analysis revealed a long-standing EU involvement in digital markets under the internal market policy. This is true not only for the measures that directly aim at deregulation of the so-called information society services but also for the re-regulatory steps taken at the EU level.

The liberalisation framework of the E-Commerce Directive and safe harbour provisions, now set out in the Digital Services Act, underline the importance of

[145] Article 42(4) of Regulation 2022/2065 (Digital Services Act).

removing barriers to trade as a goal of the internal market policy. National efforts to regulate the provision of information society services do not sit easily with the European ambition to support the development of the digital economy.[146] Clearly, rules of this kind may be necessary and justified and the E-Commerce Directive explicitly makes room for this case. At the same time, notification requirements have been established to monitor the effects of domestic measures on the internal market. The goals of such requirements—among others, to avoid re-fragmentation of the internal market[147]—are still highly relevant today. At the same time, regulatory tendencies in the Member States may ultimately strengthen a case for an EU-wide harmonisation of the rules protecting different market actors, including consumers.

Although traditional rationales for recourse to Article 114 TFEU, like removing barriers to trade, continue to be highlighted in the consumer protection *acquis*, a growing emphasis is also being placed on the consumers' role in the internal market project. In particular, the role of "consumer confidence" in improving the functioning of the internal market is being recognized. The need to ensure a high level of consumer protection pursuant to Article 114(3) TFEU, as well as the consumer's position as a weaker party, feature prominently in both legislation and case law. Even though recent legislation mostly pursues full harmonisation, exceptions from this trend can also be observed, as in the case of additional disclosure duties for online marketplaces.[148]

European Union rules on consumer protection continue to be focused on two-party relationships, particularly between formally defined "traders" and "consumers". However, the commitment to establish a high level of consumer protection, referred to in Article 114(3) TFEU, is arguably not limited to the parties of B2C transactions. Consequently, the status-based approach can be criticised for obscuring the position of consumers in the internal market. Rather than using references to consumer protection as part of the generic vocabulary, more efforts are needed to understand the conditions under which consumer protection can become a self-standing or leading motive for taking EU action. Such a more thorough understanding is necessary for lawmakers to navigate the increasingly complex market reality, such as the one currently observed in electronic trade.

The goal of promoting consumer confidence should not treat consumers as a pretext for internal market building and be associated with less robust rules, following the self-reliance ethic. Indeed, the idea of consumer confidence is arguably more universal and can go hand in hand with the different "images" of weaker parties. Such weaknesses can be caused by several factors, not all of which can be captured by status-based positions, especially in the field of services. For a long time, however, the focus of the EU legislature remained on B2C sale contracts. This changed

[146] For a recent illustration, see judgment of the Court of Justice of 9.22.2023 in case C-376/22 *Google Ireland and Others*, ECLI:EU:C:2023:835.

[147] Judgment of the Court of Justice of 12.9.2019 in case C-299/17 *VG Media*, para. 37.

[148] Article 6a(2) of Directive 2011/83/EU, as amended.

more recently with the adoption of the Digital Services Directive and the Digital Services Act, with the latter even partially transcending the status-based divide. Still, recent reforms are far from addressing all consumer weaknesses in online travel platforms. Indeed, notable gaps in protection can be identified across three central themes: (i) consumer information, (ii) choice enhancement, and (iii) safety and performance.

Focusing on consumer information, the previous analysis underlined the important role of disclosure in EU regulation of digital markets. Duties of this kind are the epitome of the self-reliance ethic and can be described as a rather light-touch form of regulation. Thus, it is not surprising that some information requirements found in existing EU law cover not only B2C transactions but also B2B and even peer-to-peer relationships. An extension to peer-to-peer relationships is visible e.g. in the E-Commerce Directive, which could prove particularly relevant to the platform age. However, even though prescribed information may not always be visible on online travel platforms, this does not seem to trigger considerable debate. Possibly, the broader norms in the field of services have been eclipsed by the narrowly perceived consumer *acquis*, to the extent that we forgot about their added value. As a result, peer-to-peer information sharing appears as something foreign to consumer law and the associated role of platform operators is not conceptualised.

Indeed, the EU legislature appears to overlook the fact that EU law already covers some dimensions of peer-to-peer relationships. This impression can be additionally reinforced by the new information duties in Directive 2011/83/EU on consumer rights.[149] In particular, the warning duty in Article 6a CRD, while well-intended, could do more harm than good. As we will see in the following chapter, a similar warning makes sense in Directive 2015/2302, as the sphere of applicable and non-applicable norms is well-delineated in that context. By contrast, a consumer using an online marketplace finds out that consumer rights stemming from Union consumer protection law do not apply to a non-B2C contract. This raises two distinct sets of issues. Firstly, it obscures the fact that some provisions on broadly understood consumer protection do apply to peer-to-peer relationships. Secondly, it may create an impression that consumers in B2C relationships are always offered a higher level of protection than consumers in peer-to-peer transactions while this depends on the type of transaction. For example, a consumer who concludes a contract for a single travel service may not be able to rely on the right to withdraw or the objective conformity requirements, regardless of who his or her counterparty is.

In addition, the focus on B2C relationships means that the role of platform operators facilitating peer-to-peer transactions is moved to the background. Indeed, besides the warning duty mentioned earlier, recent involvement of the EU law in the platform economy is limited to three-party relationships involving a consumer and

[149] Article 4(5) of Directive (EU) 2019/2161 as regards the better enforcement and modernisation of Union consumer protection rules, introducing additional specific information requirements for contracts concluded on online marketplaces in Article 6a of Directive 2011/83/EU.

two professional providers. While this is not surprising for the *Tiketa* judgment,[150] which remained tied to the case at hand, the same cannot be said about the DSA provisions on traceability and compliance by design. Indeed, there is no convincing reason why similar obligations should not apply when services are offered by peer providers, especially if the latter are already subject to disclosure duties.

A further layer of protection is afforded by norms enhancing consumer choice after contract conclusion. A prominent example is the right to withdraw from a distance contract without a penalty, laid down in Directive 2011/83/EC on consumer rights. The right appears to be the strongest form of consumer choice enhancement, tending towards the need ethic.[151] This extra flexibility is enjoyed, first and foremost, by the formally defined "consumers" in B2C transactions.

However, due to exceptions from the scope of Directive 2011/83/EC or its main provisions, the right to withdraw does not apply to the key domains of the travel sector.[152] This might be explained by the specific functions of that right when it comes to services.[153] Unlike in the case of goods, the information asymmetry regarding the quality of services exists irrespective of the means of contract conclusion and a universal right to "test" relevant services would seem to be excessive. Nevertheless, choice-enhancing instruments, which provide consumers with a "cooling-off period" or allow them to respond to a subsequent change of personal circumstances, may still be very useful in promoting confidence.[154] Such instruments, if well-designed, do not need to come at a significant cost to service providers.

Given the above, a different approach to travel services in the CRD should not be taken to imply that choice-enhancing instruments are not generally suitable for this field. On the contrary, the EU legislature seems to recognize that specific conditions of the travel sector call for tailored solutions. The nature of these solutions as well as their scope are further discussed in Chap. 5.

Finally, existing EU law contains important rules on contractual performance, usually tending towards the need ethic. Crucially, also in this respect, digital markets were among the first areas for EU-level action. Indeed, a modest set of rules on performance was already introduced in Directive 97/7/EC for B2C distance contracts. However, further development of performance rules at the EU level has been faced with tensions. On the one hand, the case for harmonisation was particularly strong in the case of transactions with cross-border potential.[155] On the other hand, the development of parallel legal frameworks in core areas of national private law

[150] Judgment of the Court of Justice of 24.2.2022 in case C-536/20 *Tiketa*.

[151] Willett (2018), p. 209.

[152] Articles 3(3)(k) and 16(l) of Directive 2011/83/EC on consumer rights.

[153] Bech Serrat (2012), pp. 103, 111–112.

[154] On the promotion of consumer confidence as a function of the right to withdraw, see Twigg-Flesner et al. (2018), pp. 125–126.

[155] Twigg-Flesner (2013), pp. 322–324.

for cross-border[156] or online[157] contracts only has attracted criticism.[158] The resulting resistance has been difficult to overcome, at times rendering the legislative efforts fruitless or putting them on hold.[159]

One notable consequence of these conceptual and legislative struggles is the widening gap between the standard of consumer protection in sales and service contracts. Some early safeguards for service recipients have even been rolled back, as illustrated by the replacement of Article 7 of Directive 97/7/EC with Article 18 of Directive 2011/83/EU, applicable only to the sale of goods.[160] Limited EU action in the field of services also weakens the impact of the Digital Services Act. As noted, under Article 31(3) *in fine* DSA, the platform provider shall make reasonable efforts to randomly check in any official, freely accessible and machine-readable online database or online interface whether the products or services offered have been identified as illegal. However, if a framework for rendering services illegal (e.g. on grounds of safety) has not been developed, the norm will offer limited protection. With this in mind, the following chapter considers what travel-specific requirements add to the discussion.

## References

Adamski D (2018) Lost on the digital platform: Europe's legal travails with the digital single market. Common Mark Law Rev 55(3):719–751

Bartl M (2020) Socio-economic imaginaries and European private law. In: Kjaer PF (ed) The law of political economy: transformation in the function of law. Cambridge University Press, pp 228–253

Bech Serrat JM (2012) Selling tourism services at a distance: an analysis of the EU consumer acquis. Springer

Bełdowski J, Zachariasiewicz M (2012) Nowy etap harmonizacji prawa umów w UE (cz. I). EPS 8(6):4–11

Busch C (2018) The sharing economy at the CJEU: does Airbnb pass the Uber test? Some observations on the pending case C-390/18 – Airbnb Ireland. J Eur Consum Mark Law 7(4):172–174

Cafaggi F (2013) From a status to a transaction-based approach? Institutional design in European contract law. Common Mark Law Rev 50:311–329

---

[156] For a case in favour of such an approach, see Twigg-Flesner (2012).

[157] For an illustration of an unsuccessful attempt of this kind, see European Commission, 'Proposal for a Directive of the European Parliament and of the Council on Certain Aspects Concerning Contracts for the Online and Other Distance Sales of Goods' (2015) COM(2015) 635 final. In this specific case, however, the criticism of the idea of a parallel framework eventually led to the extension of the original proposal to all B2C sales and its successful adoption as Directive 2019/771.

[158] For an overview of the debate, see Twigg-Flesner (2013), Twigg-Flesner and Metcalfe (2009), pp. 375–376, Bełdowski and Zachariasiewicz (2012), pp. 9–10. Note that the authors eventually consider a limitation to cross-border transactions justified.

[159] Consider the example of the Common European Sales Law, withdrawn by the Commission in 2014, see European Commission, 'Proposal for a Regulation of the European Parliament and of the Council on a Common European Sales Law' (2011) COM(2011) 635 final.

[160] See also Cauffman (2016), p. 240.

Cauffman C (2016) The Commission's European agenda for the collaborative economy—(too) platform and service provider friendly? J Eur Consum Mark Law 5(6):235–243
Cauffman C, Goanta C (2021) A new order: the digital services act and consumer protection. Eur J Risk Regul 12(4):758–774
Cseres K (2016) The regulatory consumer in EU and national law? Case study of the normative concept of the consumer in Hungary and Poland. Yearb Antitrust Regul Stud 9(13):9–41
Dąbrowski D (2017) Uprawnienie podróżnego do odstąpienia od umowy przewozu oraz do jednostronnej zmiany umowy. iKAR 3(6):61–70
de Vries A, Jabłonowska A (2019) Article 11: duty to inform about platform operator and supplier. In: Busch C, Dannemann G, Schulte-Nölke H, Wiewiórowska-Domagalska A, Zoll F (eds) Discussion draft of a directive on online intermediary platforms. Commentary. Jagiellonian University Press, pp 105–119
Delimatsis P (2018) From Sacchi to Uber: 60 years of services liberalization, ten years of the services directive in the EU. Yearb Eur Law 37:188–250
Enchelmaier E (2005) Consumer interests and contract law in the draft directive on services in the internal market. ERA Forum 6(2):232–244
Gnela B (2008) Zakres podmiotowy przepisów ustawy o usługach turystycznych dotyczących ochrony klienta (konsumenta) a zakres podmiotowy umowy o imprezę turystyczną. In: Cybula P, Raciborski J (eds) Turystyka a prawo: aktualne problemy legislacyjne i konstrukcyjne. Wyższa Szkoła Turystyki i Ekologii, pp 48–65
Hacker P (2018) UberPop, UberBlack, and the regulation of digital platforms after the Asociación Profesional elite taxi judgment of the CJEU. Eur Rev Contr Law 14(1):80–96
Helberger N, Sax M, Strycharz J, Micklitz H-W (2022) Choice architectures in the digital economy: towards a new understanding of digital vulnerability. J Consum Policy 45(2):175–200
Hesselink MW (2016) European private law in the division of moral responsibility between the EU, its member states and their citizens. Yearb Eut Law 35(1):410–452
Iamiceli P (2019) Online platforms and the digital turn in EU contract law: unfair practices, transparency and the (pierced) veil of digital immunity. Eur Rev Contr Law 15(4):392–420
Jabłonowska A (2023) EU consumer law and technology. In: Brożek B, Kanevskaia O, Pałka P (eds) Research handbook on law and technology. Edward Elgar, pp 174–189
Jagielska M (2016) Wpływ prawa europejskiego na krajowe prawo prywatne na przykładzie prawa konsumenckiego. In: Wudarski A (ed) Prawo obce w doktrynie prawa polskiego. Stowarzyszenie Notariuszy Rzeczypospolitej Polskiej, pp 159–175
Jagielska M, Jagielski M (2012) Are consumer rights human rights? In: Devenney J, Kenny M (eds) European consumer protection: theory and practice. Cambridge University Press, pp 336–353
Johnston A (2016) Seeking the EU "consumer" in services of general economic interest. In: Leczykiewicz D, Weatherill S (eds) The images of the consumer in EU law: legislation, free movement and competition law. Hart Publishing, pp 93–138
Karsten J (2007) Passengers, consumers, and travellers: the rise of passenger rights in EC transport law and its repercussions for community consumer law and policy. J Consum Policy 30(2):117–136
Krämer L (2021) The origins of consumer law and policy at EU level. In: Micklitz H-W (ed) The making of consumer law and policy in Europe. Hart Publishing, pp 13–30
Loos M (2009) Rights of withdrawal. In: Schulze R (ed) Howells G. Modernising and harmonising consumer contract law, Sellier, pp 237–277
Micklitz H-W (2018) The politics of justice in European private law: social justice, access justice, societal justice. Cambridge University Press
Namysłowska M, Jabłonowska A (2022) Artificial intelligence and platform services: EU consumer (contract) law and new regulatory developments. In: Poncibò C, Zou M (eds) Ebers M. Hart Publishing, Contracting and contract law in the age of artificial intelligence, pp 221–247
Nijenhuis A (2013) Electronic communications and the EU consumer. In: Benyon F (ed) Services and the EU citizen. Hart Publishing, pp 47–74

Nordhausen A (2005) Information requirements in the E-commerce directive and the proposed directive on unfair commercial practices. In: Janssen A, Howells G (eds) Information rights and obligations: a challenge for party autonomy and transactional fairness. Routledge, pp 93–114

Orti Vallejo A (2019) Contractual relationships in collaborative economy platforms. Eur Rev Priv Law 27(5):995–1022

Osmola S (2023) Fixing reasonable expectations in European contract law. Eur Rev Priv Law 19(2):136–155

Pearce G, Platten M (2000) Promoting the information society: the EU directive on electronic commerce. Eur Law J 6(4):363–378

Południak-Gierz K (2016) Konsument czy klient? Zmiana sposobu wyznaczania podmiotów wymagających ochrony w kontekście wybranych rynków regulowanych. TPP 2:61–74

Prastitou Merdi T (2020) The 2018 new Deal on better enforcement and modernisation of EU consumer law: an actually good digital deal? In: Synodinou TE, Jougleux P, Markou C, Prastitou T (eds) EU internet law in the digital era: regulation and enforcement. Springer, pp 347–365

Reich N (2008) Crisis or future of European consumer law? In: Parry D, Nordhausen A, Howells G, Twigg-Flesner C (eds) The yearbook of consumer law 2009. Routledge, pp 3–68

Reich N (2012) From minimal to full to "half" harmonisation. In: Devenney J, Kenny M (eds) European consumer protection: theory and practice. Cambridge University Press, pp 3–5

Reich N, Micklitz H-W (2008) Vollharmonisierung durch die Hintertür?—zur Kritk der Schlussanträge der Generalanwältin Trestenjak in der Rs. Gysbrechts, C-205/07, v. 17.07.2008. VuR 23(9):349–351

Reich N, Micklitz H-W (2014) Economic law, consumer interests, and EU integration. In: Reich N, Micklitz H-W, Rott P, Tonner K (eds) European consumer law. Intersentia, pp 1–66

Roppo V (2009) From consumer contracts to asymmetric contracts: a trend in European contract law? Eur Rev Contr Law 5(3):304–349

Roth W-H (2003) Case C-168/00, Simone Leitner v. TUI Deutschland GmbH & Co. KG, judgment of 12 March 2002 (sixth chamber), ECR 2002, I-2631. Common Mark Law Rev 40(4):937–951

Sanches Lima MG (2018) Traveller vulnerability in the context of travel and tourism contracts: a comparison of Brazilian and EU law. Springer

Schaub MY (2018) Why Uber is an information society service: case note to CJEU 20 December 2017 C-434/15 (Asociación Profesional Élite taxi). J Eur Consum Mark Law 7(3):109–115

Schüller B (2012) The definition of consumers in EU consumer law. In: Devenney J, Kenny M (eds) European consumer protection: theory and practice. Cambridge University Press, pp 123–142

Schulze R (2024) § 327e BGB. In: Schulze R (ed) Bürgerliches Gesetzbuch: Handkommentar, 12th edn. Nomos

Schütze R (2015) EU competences: existence and exercise. In: Arnull A, Chalmers D (eds) The Oxford handbook of European Union law. Oxford University Press, pp 75–102

Sørensen MJ (2022) Is the 'new Deal' for consumers a big deal? Consumer protection and the new information duties for online marketplaces. Eur Rev Priv Law 30(6):1019–1038

Staudenmayer D (2022) The directives on digital contracts: first steps towards the private law of the digital economy. Eur Rev Priv Law 28(2):219–250

Stuyck J (2013) The transformation of consumer law in the EU in the last 20 years. Maastricht J Eur Comp Law 20(3):385–402

Stuyck J (2014) Do we need "consumer protection" for small businesses at the EU level? In: Purnhagen K, Rott P (eds) Varieties of European economic law and regulation: liber amicorum for Hans Micklitz. Springer, pp 359–370

Tonner K (2014) From the Kennedy message to full harmonising consumer law directives: a retrospect. In: Purnhagen K, Rott P (eds) Varieties of European economic law and regulation: liber amicorum for Hans Micklitz. Springer, pp 693–707

Troiano S (2009) To what extent can the notion of 'reasonableness' help to harmonize European contract law? Problems and prospects from a civil law perspective. Eur Rev Priv Law 17(5):749–787

Twigg-Flesner C (2012) A cross-border-only regulation for consumer transactions in the EU: a fresh approach to EU consumer law. Springer

Twigg-Flesner C (2013) EU law and consumer transactions without an internal market dimension. In: Weatherill S (ed) Leczykiewicz D. Hart Publishing, The involvement of EU law in private law relationships, pp 317–331

Twigg-Flesner C (2016) The importance of law and harmonisation for the EU's confident consumer. In: Leczykiewicz D, Weatherill S (eds) The images of the consumer in EU law: legislation, free movement and competition law. Hart Publishing, pp 183–202

Twigg-Flesner C, Metcalfe D (2009) The proposed consumer rights directive—less haste, more thought? Eur Rev Contr Law 5(3):368–391

Twigg-Flesner C, Schulze R, Watson J (2018) Protecting rational choice: information and the right of withdrawal. In: Howells G, Ramsay I, Wilhelmsson T (eds) Handbook of research on international consumer law, 2nd edn. Edward Elgar, pp 111–138

Unberath H, Johnston A (2007) The double-headed approach of the ECJ concerning consumer protection. Common Mark Law Rev 44(5):1237–1284

Van Acker L (2020) C-390/18—the CJEU finally clears the air(bnb) regarding information society services: case note to CJEU, C-390/18 Airbnb Ireland. J Eur Consum Mark Law 9(2):77–80

Weatherill S (2002) The Commission's options for developing EC consumer protection and contract law: assessing the constitutional basis. Eur Bus Law Rev 13(6):497–515

Weatherill S (2012) The consumer rights directive: how and why a quest for coherence has (largely) failed. Common Mark Law Rev 49(4):1279–1317

Weatherill S (2016a) Consumer protection. In: Patterson D, Södersten A (eds) A companion to European Union law and international law. Wiley, pp 285–295

Weatherill S (2016b) Contract law of the internal market. Intersentia

Wendehorst C (2016) Platform intermediary services and duties under the E-commerce directive and the consumer rights directive. J Eur Consum Mark Law 5(1):30–33

Wilhelmsson T (2004) The abuse of the "confident consumer" as a justification for EC consumer law. J Consum Policy 27(3):317–337

Willett C (2018) Re-theorising consumer law. Cambridge Law J 77(1):179–210

Willett C, Morgan-Taylor M (2012) Recognising the limits of transparency in EU consumer law. In: Devenney J, Kenny M (eds) European consumer protection: theory and practice. Cambridge University Press, pp 143–163

# Chapter 5
# Internal Market Policy and Consumer Protection in Travel Sector

## 5.1 Development of EU Travel Law

Like many other areas of the EU economy, the travel sector has been the scene of negative and positive integration over the past decades.[1] A notable feature of this process is the gradual expansion of rules protecting travellers, in addition to the otherwise applicable consumer *acquis*. While both groups of provisions are concerned with the weaker parties, they also show important differences.

Crucially, personal scope of EU travel law tends to be broader than that of consumer law in the narrow sense, as it covers not only business-to-consumer relationships in the status-based understanding. This has notably been the case for Directive 90/314/EEC on package travel, more recently replaced with Directive 2015/2302, as well as regulations on passenger rights, discussed in the next chapter. An exception applies to timeshare contracts, currently regulated in Directive 2008/122/EC,[2] which nonetheless remain of limited importance to the travel sector. Furthermore, while EU travel law is mostly aimed at protecting travellers, it also deals in part with their obligations. Taking both elements into account, travel law emerges as a useful lens for assessing the position of travellers under EU law, before and after the emergence of online travel platforms.

[1] On national licensing requirements for tourist guides, see judgment of the Court of Justice of 26.2.1991 in case C-154/89 *Commission v France*, ECLI:EU:C:1991:76.

[2] Directive 2008/122/EC of the European Parliament and of the Council of 14.1.2009 on the protection of consumers in respect of certain aspects of timeshare, long-term holiday product, resale and exchange contracts [2009] OJ L33/10.

 
A. Jabłonowska, *Consumer Protection and Online Travel Platforms*, Law, Governance and Technology Series 73, https://doi.org/10.1007/978-3-031-90170-6_5

## 5.2 Package Travel: Directives 90/314/EEC and 2015/2302

### *5.2.1 Rationale*

One of the first major instruments of EU travel law was Directive 90/314/EEC on package travel, package holidays and package tours. This framework was recently updated and replaced by Directive 2015/2302 on package travel and linked travel arrangements. Unlike its predecessor, the updated framework provides for a full level of harmonisation. It addresses a similar set of matters as Directive 90/314/EEC but in a more extensive way. To provide a broader historical overview, the following discussion refers to both Directives 90/314/EEC and 2015/2302.

Directive 90/314/EEC was based on Article 100a of the Treaty establishing the European Economic Community (currently Article 114 TFEU). Its preamble observed that the tourist sector formed an "essential part" of the internal market, whose completion was one of the main objectives of the European Economic Community (currently the EU).[3] Attention was drawn to the disparities in national laws concerning package travel, which arguably created obstacles to the freedom to provide services and distortions of competition as well as discouraged consumers from buying packages from other Member States. It was argued that adopting at least a minimum set of common rules would stimulate the growth and productivity of the package travel industry, produce benefits for EU citizens and attract tourists from outside the Community. The need for such minimum protection was explained by the special nature of services supplied in packages which "generally involve the expenditure of substantial amounts of money in advance and the supply of the services in a [Member] State other than that in which the consumer is resident".[4] The focus on the package holiday was further explained by its fundamental role in the tourism sector.[5]

The choice of minimum harmonisation in the 1990 Package Travel Directive highlights the consumer protection perspective. Subject to restrictions under free movement law, Member States could continue to set a higher standard of protection, thus creating "obstacles" to the freedom to provide services and distortions of competition, subject only to the control under free movement law. Despite this fact, the harmonisation of selected baseline provisions was seen as beneficial to the common market, as it allowed consumers to transact with more confidence. Besides the confidence narrative, a perception of the internal market as an area in which a high level of consumer protection should be safeguarded is also noticeable. Crucially, this perspective was applied not only to B2C contracts in a narrow, status-based understanding. The importance of a high level of consumer protection – here interpreted

[3] Recital 1 of Directive 90/314/EEC on package travel.

[4] Ibid, recital 9.

[5] Ibid, recital 7.

broadly as also covering business travellers—found support from the Court of Justice, including in the *Leitner* case[6] discussed further below.

Key arguments invoked in Directive 90/314/EEC continue to be present in Directive 2015/2302. The important role of packages in the travel sector is recognized, despite the acknowledged changes in the market practice. The preamble observes that the internet has become an important medium through which travel services are offered or sold – increasingly not in the form of pre-arranged packages, but in a more customised way.[7] At the same time, the cross-border potential of the package travel market is seen as "not fully exploited" due to disparities in travellers' protection, among other things.[8] Following a broader tendency in consumer law, Directive 2015/2302 thus introduces full harmonisation. Emphasis is also placed on achieving a high level of consumer protection in line with Article 114(3) TFEU.[9] Overall, further harmonisation is considered necessary to "enable travellers and traders to benefit fully from the internal market, while ensuring a high level of consumer protection across the Union".[10] The narrative of consumer confidence is used, not without controversy, to support full harmonisation.

### 5.2.2 Scope of Application

The scope of Directive 90/314/EEC was first and foremost determined by the notion of a "package", understood as the pre-arranged combination of not fewer than two of the listed types of travel services, subject to additional conditions.[11] Harmonised rules were to apply to packages "sold or offered for sale" in the territory of the EU without regard to the traveller's nationality or country of residence. No relevance was also attached to the status of the traveller. The focus was on the relationships between broadly defined consumers,[12] on the one hand, and "organizers" or "retailers", on the other hand. While the Directive did not explicitly require the suppliers to act for purposes related to their trade, business, craft or profession, a connection with such activities—and therefore a "trader" status—appeared to be implicit.

In both respects, Directive 2015/2302 generally maintains the approach of Directive 90/314/EEC while adjusting it slightly. Although market changes are invoked to support the reform, the updated framework continues to be focused on the "package" notion. The concept similarly describes a combination of at least two different types of travel services for the purpose of the same trip or holiday, while

[6] Judgment of the Court of Justice of 12.3.2002 in case C-168/00 *Leitner*, ECLI:EU:C:2002:163.

[7] Recital 2 of Directive 2015/2302 on package travel and linked travel arrangements.

[8] Ibid, recital 6.

[9] Ibid, recital 3.

[10] Ibid, recital 6.

[11] Article 2(1) of Directive 90/314/EEC on package travel.

[12] Ibid, Article 2(4).

travel services refer to: (i) carriage of passengers, (ii) accommodation which is not intrinsically part of carriage of passengers and is not for residential purposes, (iii) rental of cars, other motor vehicles, or motorcycles as well as (iv) any other tourist services not intrinsically part of the travel services mentioned before (subject to further conditions).[13] Following Directive 90/314/EEC, the act does not apply to packages covering a period of less than 24 h, unless overnight accommodation is included.[14]

In addition, the definition of a package in Directive 2015/2302 elaborates on that known from Directive 90/314/EEC, considering the case law of the Court of Justice, among other things.[15] Accordingly, Article 3(2) lists alternative conditions related to the transaction which must be fulfilled for a combination to qualify as a package. Unsurprisingly, the first criterion describes the most established model, namely "when the services are combined by one trader, including at the request of or in accordance with the selection of the traveller, before a single contract on all services is concluded". Equally important, however, are the following five criteria, which apply irrespective of whether separate contracts are concluded with individual travel service providers. This is the case when services are: (i) purchased from a single point of sale and those services have been selected before the traveller agrees to pay, (ii) offered, sold or charged at an inclusive or total price, (iii) advertised or sold under the term "package" or under a similar term, (iv) combined after the conclusion of a contract by which a trader entitles the traveller to choose among a selection of different types of travel services, or (v) purchased from separate traders through linked online booking processes where the traveller's name, payment details and e-mail address are transmitted from the trader with whom the first contract is concluded to another trader and a contract with the latter trader is concluded at the latest 24 hours after the confirmation of the booking of the first travel service. As accurately noted by Tereszkiewicz, the Directive "lays down an objective test as to whether a travel package is sold to a traveller".[16] If conditions of the test are fulfilled, a supplier who combines relevant services, such as an agent or an intermediary, becomes liable as an organiser.

Considering the transformation of the travel sector, the category set out above under (v) appears to be particularly interesting. Of relevance is, firstly, the existence of a "linked online booking process" of separate providers, and secondly, the temporal proximity between the conclusion of particular contracts. In practice, packages of this kind may be difficult to distinguish from a further group of transactions, which are partially brought within the Directive's scope. These are captured by the

---

[13] Articles 3(1) and 3(2) of Directive 2015/2302 on package travel and linked travel arrangements.

[14] Ibid, Article 2(2)(a).

[15] See especially judgment of the Court of Justice of 30.4.2002 in case C-400/00 *Club-Tour*, ECLI:EU:C:2002:272, finding that terms "package" and "pre-organised combination" also include holidays organised by travel agents, at the request of and in accordance with the specifications of a consumer or limited group of consumers as well as combinations of tourist services put together at the time when the contract is concluded between the travel agency and the consumer.

[16] Tereszkiewicz (2018), p. 917.

notion of "linked travel arrangements", defined in Article 3(5) as at least two different types of travel services purchased for the purpose of the same trip or holiday, not constituting a package, resulting in the conclusion of separate contracts with the individual travel service providers, if a trader facilitates: (i) on the occasion of a single visit or contact with his or her point of sale, the separate selection and separate payment of each travel service by travellers, or (ii) in a targeted manner, the procurement of at least one additional travel service from another trader where a contract with such other trader is concluded at the latest 24 h after the confirmation of the booking of the first travel service. The scope of safeguards afforded to travellers purchasing linked travel arrangements is significantly more limited compared to those enjoyed by package travellers. The purchase of a travel service on a standalone basis as a single travel service constitutes neither a package nor a linked travel arrangement and remains outside the scope of Directive 2015/2302.[17]

As regards personal scope, Directive 2015/2302 continues to transcend the status-based approach, albeit to a more limited extent. As explained in recital 7, although the majority of travellers buying packages or linked travel arrangements are "consumers" in the narrow sense of the word, it is not always easy to distinguish between consumers so defined and representatives of small businesses or professionals who book trips related to their business or profession through the same booking channels. What is more, such travellers, the preamble goes, often require a similar level of protection. While reasons for this finding are not explained, one may assume that they relate to the two dimensions of consumer (traveller) weaknesses, elaborated by Willett: weaker position as loss bearers and difficulties in exercising self-reliance.[18] Of relevance is therefore not only the asymmetry of knowledge, bargaining power and experience but also particular types of negative effects, to which service providers are not exposed, such as loss of time, distress, and inconvenience in personal lives. It is worth noting, however, that the personal scope of Directive 2015/2302 is slightly narrowed down compared to Directive 90/314/EEC. Specifically, under Article 2(2)(c), packages and linked travel arrangements purchased on the basis of a general agreement for the arrangement of business travel between two traders, remain outside the scope of the act. The EU legislature thus seems to assume that parties of this kind can negotiate on travellers' protection. To avoid confusion with the definition of the term "consumer" in other EU acts, persons protected under Directive 2015/2302 are referred to as "travellers". A similar quest for clarity has led the EU legislature to explicitly embrace the notion of the "trader" on the supply side, thus moving in the status-based direction.[19] In addition, Article 2(2)(b) further excludes the packages offered, and linked travel arrangements facilitated, occasionally and on a not-for-profit basis and only to a limited group of travellers, such as trips organised by sports clubs for their members.[20] It is

[17] Recital 15 of Directive 2015/2302 on package travel and linked travel arrangements.

[18] Willett (2018), p. 187.

[19] Article 3(7) of Directive 2015/2302 on package travel and linked travel arrangements.

[20] Ibid, recital 19.

important to stress, however, that the status-based limitation on the supply side introduced by Directive 2015/2302 only refers to its core addressees, namely organisers[21], retailers,[22] and traders facilitating linked travel arrangements, and not direct providers of the combined travel services.

## 5.2.3 *Protection Standard*

The majority of the provisions laid down originally in Directive 90/314/EEC, and today in Directive 2015/2302, are protective of travellers' interests. Protection of this kind is afforded, in particular, through rules on information and choice, remedies in case of non-performance of the traveller's counterparty, assistance to the traveller in difficulty and insolvency safeguards. The focus of the following discussion remains on the currently applicable norms of Directive 2015/2302, which elaborate on the protection standard previously provided under Directive 90/314/EEC. The underlying principle of full harmonisation should be borne in mind throughout the analysis.

### 5.2.3.1 Information at Different Stages of Contracting

Disclosure rules are among the most prevalent safeguards afforded to EU market actors. Directive 90/314/EEC introduced them at both the pre-contractual and the contractual stage and the same approach continues to be followed in Directive 2015/2302. Article 5 of the new Package Travel Directive lists numerous items of information that the organiser and, where relevant, the retailer shall provide the traveller before the latter is bound by the contract or offer. These include information about key rights under Directive 2015/2302, communicated through a standard form, as well as additional information regarding the trader and detailed conditions of the contract. The traveller should be informed, among others, about "the means, characteristics and categories of transport" (Article 5(a)(ii)) along with "the location, main features and, where applicable, tourist category of the accommodation under the rules of the country of destination" (Article 5(a)(iii)). Differently from Directive 90/314/EEC, no explicit reference is made to the "approval" of relevant accommodation under the rules of the host Member State concerned.[23] Pursuant to Articles 6 and 7 of Directive 2015/2302, pre-contractual information forms an integral part of the package travel contract and the burden of proof as regards compliance with information is placed upon the trader.[24] The act further defines the content

---

[21] Ibid, Article 3(8).

[22] Ibid, Article 3(9).

[23] Cf. Article 5(1)(a)(iii) of Directive 2015/2302 and Article 3(2)(b) of Directive 90/314/EEC and point c) to its Annex.

[24] Cf. Articles 6(5) and 6(9) of Directive 2011/83/EU on consumer rights.

of the package travel contract and establishes form requirements, which allow the traveller to consult the contract at a later time.[25] Information about key rights under Directive 2015/2302 plays a prominent role, showing a double function of disclosure rules, linked to both the facilitation of consumer choice and the effectiveness of EU law.

A separate set of disclosure duties applies to traders facilitating linked travel arrangements. Crucially, this newly introduced category of service providers can, under certain conditions, include platform operators. This is especially the case when the provider facilitates the conclusion of contracts for different travel services, thus allowing the traveller to purchase at least two different types of travel services for the same trip or holiday via a single platform.[26] Pursuant to Article 19(2) of Directive 2015/2302, before the traveller is bound by any contract leading to the creation of a linked travel arrangement or any corresponding offer, the trader facilitating such arrangement, shall state in a clear, comprehensible and prominent manner that the traveller: (i) will not benefit from any of the rights applying exclusively to packages under the Directive and that each service provider will be solely responsible for the proper contractual performance of his service, and (ii) will benefit from insolvency protection in accordance with Article 19(1). In doing so, Directive 2015/2302 recognizes the variety of business models in the travel sector, while seeking to improve legal clarity so that travellers can make "informed choices" as to the different services on offer and the corresponding level of protection.[27] The solution, therefore, resembles the newly added information duties for online marketplaces in Directive 2011/83/EU on consumer rights, concerning the lack of application of consumer law to peer-to-peer transactions.[28] Differently from the CRD, the Package Travel Directive also takes a small step to substantively improve consumer protection in linked travel arrangements, focused on cases of insolvency. Finally, and equally importantly, the failure to comply with requirements to disclose information and provide insolvency protection brings services included in the linked travel arrangement within the scope of the Directive's key provisions.[29]

#### 5.2.3.2 Choice-Enhancing Instruments Following Contract Conclusion

Information duties are not the only instruments facilitating travellers' choice in Directive 2015/2302. A certain level of protection is also provided after the contract conclusion, not unlike the right of withdrawal in the Consumer Rights Directive.[30] The approach taken in package travel law, however, is more elaborate and seeks to strike a balance between the interests of both parties. Firstly, pursuant to Article 9 of

[25] Article 7 of Directive 2015/2302 on package travel and linked travel arrangements.

[26] Cf. ibid, recitals 12 and 13.

[27] Ibid, recital 16.

[28] See Sect. 4.3.2.1.

[29] Article 19(3) of Directive 2015/2302 on package travel and linked travel arrangements.

[30] Article 9 of Directive 2011/83/EU on consumer rights.

Directive 2015/2302, upon reasonable notice on a durable medium, a traveller may transfer his or her package travel contract to another person satisfying the applicable conditions. A notice given at the latest seven days before the start of the package is deemed to be reasonable in any event, which constitutes a helpful clarification compared to the broad wording of Article 4(3) of Directive 90/314/EEC. Importantly, the analysed provision does not set out only the travellers' rights but also their obligations. Specifically, under Article 9(2) the transferor and transferee are jointly and severally liable for the payment of the balance due and for any additional fees, charges or other costs arising from the transfer. The latter should neither be unreasonable nor exceed the actual cost incurred by the organiser and should be communicated to the transferor by the organiser, along with relevant proof.[31]

Another important instrument aimed at facilitating travellers' choice, introduced in Article 12(1) of Directive 2015/2302 (without a direct counterpart in Directive 90/314/EEC), is the right to terminate the package travel contract at any time before the start of the package. Differently from the right to withdraw known from the other legal acts,[32] the exercise of this right is not subject to time constraints other than the start of the package. The traveller may, nonetheless, be required to pay an appropriate and justifiable termination fee to the organiser. The provision further specifies that reasonable standardised termination fees may be determined in the package travel contract based on the time of the termination of the contract and the expected cost savings and income from alternative deployment of the travel services. In the absence of standardised termination fees, the amount shall correspond to the price of the package minus the cost savings and income from alternative deployment of the travel services. Justification for the calculation of the fee should be provided at the traveller's request. Due to the full harmonisation principle, Member States cannot generally provide the travellers with an additional right to withdraw from the package travel contract. Pursuant to Article 12(5) such a possibility has nonetheless been granted, by way of an exception, for off-premises contracts. Importantly, the provisions on contract transfer and its termination also apply in relation to the travel services included in the linked travel arrangement if the trader facilitating such an arrangement had failed to fulfil his or her duties under Articles 19(1) and 19(2). Consequently, the traveller can transfer or terminate the contracts concluded with respective service providers, who may be directly exposed to these effects due to a failure of a third-party trader. No references to joint and several liability, similar to the one concerning travellers transferring the package travel contract, are made in this regard.

It is worth noting that EU package travel law grants certain flexibility not only to the travellers but also to the organisers. Most importantly, Directive 2015/2302 defines under which conditions the organiser may exceptionally adjust the contract terms *ex post*. Article 10 refers to price, while the following provision concerns the other contract terms. In both cases, changes to contract terms are only allowed if the

---

[31] Article 9(3) of Directive 2015/2302 on package travel and linked travel arrangements.

[32] In addition to the Consumer Rights Directive, consider Article 6 of Directive 2008/122/EC on timeshare.

contract expressly reserved that possibility. In addition, variations in prices are possible exclusively as a direct consequence of changes in certain cost categories, e.g. fuel or taxes, and the possibility of price increase should go hand in hand with a corresponding possibility of price reduction.[33] The traveller should furthermore be notified of the changes, along with a justification, at the latest 20 days before the start of the package.[34] As far as other terms are concerned, only insignificant changes can be made unilaterally, provided that notification requirements are complied with. In case of significant changes to any main characteristics of the travel services, Directive 2015/2302 provides the traveller with the possibility to decide, within a reasonable period, either to accept the proposed changes or to terminate the contract without paying a termination fee.[35] If the traveller accepts the changes to the package travel contract, and as a result receives a package of lower quality or cost, he or she is further entitled to an appropriate price reduction.[36] In the latter case, the organiser should refund all payments made by or on behalf of the traveller without undue delay and in any event not later than 14 days after the contract is terminated. The provision lays down a balanced solution, remains conceptually connected to the rule on the inability to perform originally found in Directive 97/7/EC,[37] and shows a potential for broader application.

Under Article 12(2) of Directive 2015/2302 termination without a fee is also possible in the event of unavoidable and extraordinary circumstances occurring at the place of destination or its immediate vicinity and significantly affecting the performance of the package or significantly affecting the carriage of passengers to the destination. As signalled before in Chapter 3, the possibility of cancelling confirmed reservations in exceptional circumstances is also provided in certain platform models. The importance of Article 12(2) of Directive 2015/2302 manifested itself during the global outbreak of coronavirus disease (COVID-19) in 2020, resulting in a protective line of the CJEU case law.[38]

#### 5.2.3.3 Non-Performance: General Framework

A crucial part of Directive 2015/2302, and previously Directive 90/314/EEC, concerns liability for non-performance of the package travel contract. First and foremost, Article 13(1) of Directive 2015/2302 requires Member States to ensure that

---

[33] Articles 10(1), 10(4) and 10(5) of Directive 2015/2302 on package travel and linked travel arrangements.

[34] Ibid, Article 10(3).

[35] The same applies to an increase of price by more than 8%, Article 10(2) in connection with Article 11(2) of Directive 2015/2302 on package travel and linked travel arrangements.

[36] Ibid, Article 11(4).

[37] Article 7(2) of Directive 97/7/EC on distance contracts.

[38] See e.g. judgment of the Court of Justice of 8.6.2023 in case *UFC – Que choisir and CLCV*, ECLI:EU:C:2023:449 and judgment of the Court of Justice of 8.6.2023 in case *Commission v Slovakia*, ECLI:EU:C:2023:450.

the organiser is responsible for the performance of the travel services included in the package travel contract, irrespective of whether those services are to be performed by the organiser or by other travel service providers. As was indicated before, the notion of "service provider" used in this context bears no relation to the status of a "trader" and should rather be considered analogous to the one in Directive 2006/123/EC on services in the internal market, and not far from the approach of Directive 2000/31/EC on electronic commerce. The term "service" in Article 4(1) of the Services Directive refers to its established definition from primary law and describes "any self-employed economic activity, normally provided for remuneration, as referred to in Article 50 of the Treaty" (current Article 57 TFEU). In line with the relevant case law, the decisive factor in the classification of a given activity as a service is its economic character, meaning that it must not be provided for nothing.[39] This, however, does not mean that a service provider needs to act "for purposes relating to his or her trade, business, craft or profession" or that he or she should necessarily seek to make a profit.[40]

It is worth noting that the liability framework in the new Package Travel Directive is focused on the organiser and does not address comprehensively the contractual position of other suppliers.[41] Under the second paragraph of Article 13(1), Member States are allowed to maintain or introduce national provisions under which the retailer is also responsible for the performance of the package. Should national lawmakers exercise this regulatory choice, multiple provisions of Directive 2015/2302, including those related to the liability of the organiser, also apply *mutatis mutandis* to the retailer. In addition, the entire framework for the liability for non-performance, as well as complementing rules on assistance to travellers in difficulty, also apply to the travel services included in the linked travel arrangement if the trader facilitating such an arrangement has violated Articles 19(1) and 19(2). Reservations expressed before, as regards the providers' exposure to the associated consequences, apply with even more force in the present context.

Regardless of Member States' decisions, under Article 15 of Directive 2015/2302, the traveller who bought a package through a retailer may address messages, requests or complaints about the performance of the package directly to that retailer, who in turn should forward them to the organiser without undue delay. For the purpose of compliance with time-limits or limitation periods, receipt of relevant messages, requests or complaints by the retailer is considered as receipt by the organiser. This applies, among others, to the traveller's duty to inform the organiser without undue delay, taking into account the circumstances of the case, of any lack of conformity perceived during the performance of a travel service included in the

[39] Judgment of the Court of Justice of 18.12.2007 in case C-281/06 *Jundt*, ECLI:EU:C:2007:816, para. 32.

[40] Judgment of the Court of Justice of 12.7.2001 in case C-157/99 *Smits and Peerbooms*, ECLI:EU:C:2001:404, para. 50 and 52, judgment of the Court of Justice of 18.12.2007 in case C-281/06 *Jundt*, para. 33.

[41] de Vries (2016), p. 124.

package travel contract.[42] Interestingly, an obligation concerning the transfer of communications is not imposed on traders facilitating linked travel arrangements. At least for linked travel arrangements purchased from a single point of sale, such as an online platform, a corresponding rule would not be unimaginable.

Under Article 13(3) of Directive 2015/2302, if any of the travel services are not performed according to the contract, the organiser shall remedy the lack of conformity, unless that: (i) is impossible, or (ii) entails disproportionate costs, taking into account the extent of the lack of conformity and the value of the travel services affected. If one of the above conditions is fulfilled, the traveller is entitled to an appropriate price reduction and compensation for the damage sustained under Article 14 (subject to exceptions mentioned therein). If, in turn, neither condition applies, but the organiser refuses or fails to remedy the lack of conformity within a reasonable period set by the traveller, or an immediate remedy is necessary, the traveller may do so himself or herself and request reimbursement of the necessary expenses.[43] The provision attempts to strike a balance between the interests of both parties and, as such, shows a potential for broader application.

Article 13(5) of Directive 2015/2302 applies to situations where a "significant proportion of the travel services cannot be provided as agreed", in which case the organiser is obliged to offer, at no extra cost to the traveller, suitable alternative arrangements of, where possible, equivalent or higher quality.[44] Should alternative arrangements result in a package of a lower quality, the traveller is entitled to an appropriate price reduction. It is worth noting that, under Article 13(5) *in fine*, the traveller may reject the proposed alternative arrangements "only if they are not comparable to what was agreed in the package travel contract or the price reduction granted is inadequate", which is another attempt to balance the protection granted. If alternative arrangements are impossible or the traveller exercises his or her right to reject the proposed arrangement, the traveller is, where appropriate, entitled to a price reduction and/or compensation for damages under Article 14 without terminating the package travel contract. In both cases, the traveller is also entitled to a repatriation, provided that the package purchased includes the carriage of passengers.[45]

Finally, if the lack of conformity "substantially affects the performance of the package" and the organiser has failed to remedy it within a reasonable period set by the traveller, the traveller may terminate the package travel contract without paying a termination fee and, where appropriate, request the price to be reduced and/or damages to be compensated.[46] If the package includes the carriage of passengers, the organiser shall also provide repatriation of the traveller with equivalent transport without undue delay and at no extra cost to the traveller.

---

[42] Article 13(2) of Directive 2015/2302 on package travel and linked travel arrangements.

[43] Ibid, Article 13(4).

[44] Ibid, Article 13(5).

[45] Ibid, Article 13(6).

[46] Ibid.

As seen above, Directive 2015/2302 provides travellers with a number of remedies in case of non-performance while at the same time maintaining a certain hierarchy between them, aimed, in the first place, to allow non-performance to be cured. This, once again, resembles the solution for which Directive 97/7/EC on distance contracts left space.[47] The hierarchy was also present to a certain degree in the original Directive 90/314/EEC on package travel. The new Directive not only expands upon this logic but also affords it with the rigidity of full harmonisation. The resulting framework delineates the range of choices available to the traveller across different scenarios and may strike the reader as too complicated. It is through that level of detail, however, that the EU lawmaker attempts to balance the interests of both parties while providing them with a level of confidence needed to bring the internal market forward. The fact that equally detailed terms are now being developed by leading platform companies, such as Airbnb, suggests that the approach of Directive 2015/2302 is not entirely misplaced. Furthermore, the fact that Directive 2015/2302 allows for liability rules to be triggered in case of non-compliance of the trader facilitating linked travel arrangements with his or her duties, shows that rules of this kind can generally apply to individual travel services. The provision of a level of protection equal to the one afforded in the package travel model may in this case appear particularly generous to the traveller. This should nonetheless be considered an exceptional measure, meant to account for the traveller's reasonable expectations regarding the purchase of a package. At the same time, one could imagine a differentiation of the protection level between the different models of travel services distribution, taking account of all suppliers involved, beyond the package travel model. For the time being, however, Directive 2015/2302 is not an instrument of this kind.

#### 5.2.3.4 Compensation for Damages

The remedy that received particular attention under Directive 90/314/EEC, and has generally been maintained in Directive 2015/2302,[48] is the compensation for damages. Under Article 14(2) of the new Directive, the traveller shall be entitled to receive appropriate compensation from the organiser for any damage which the traveller sustains as a result of any lack of conformity unless one of the exceptions applies. Specifically, no compensation is due if the organiser proves that the lack of conformity is (i) attributable to the traveller, (ii) attributable to a third party unconnected with the provision of the travel services included in the package travel contract and is unforeseeable or unavoidable, or (iii) due to unavoidable and extraordinary circumstances. The above wording resembles the previously applicable Article 5(2) of Directive 90/314/EEC. Over the past two decades, the provision has led to two important judgments of the Court of Justice. Firstly, the landmark

[47] Article 7(3) of Directive 97/7/EC on distance contracts.

[48] See Articles 14(2) and 14(3) of Directive 2015/2302 on package travel and linked travel arrangements.

*Leitner* case explored whether or not the consumer should also be entitled to seek compensation for non-material damage in the case of loss of enjoyment of a holiday, or similar circumstances.[49] Secondly, in the more recent case *Kuoni Travel*, the Court considered whether the organiser's liability extended to the improper performance resulting from the actions of an employee of the service provider.[50]

The *Leitner* case involved an Austrian consumer who, in 1997, booked a two-week all-inclusive stay in a holiday resort on the Turkish coast with TUI Deutschland, through an Austrian travel agent. About eight days after the arrival, the consumer showed symptoms of salmonella poisoning caused by the food offered in the resort. The illness had comparably severe symptoms, such as a fever of up to 40 degrees over several days, and lasted beyond the end of the holiday. Upon return, the plaintiff sued the organiser for compensation for pain and suffering as well as non-material damage in respect of loss of enjoyment of her holiday. The latter type of damage was not covered under Austrian civil law, yet the question was raised whether such legislation remained in line with Article 5 of Directive 90/314/EEC. A reference was therefore made to the Court of Justice.

In its very concise judgment, the Court found that Article 5 of Directive 90/314/EEC on package travel indeed conferred on consumers a right to compensation for non-material damage resulting from the non-performance or improper performance of the services constituting a package holiday. Following the Advocate General, the Court observed that Article 5(2) merely referred in a general manner to the concept of damage. Moreover, according to the Court, the Directive implicitly recognised the existence of a right to compensation for damage other than personal injury, including non-material damage, by envisaging that damage of this kind could be limited under the contract.[51] The Court supported this conclusion with a teleological argument, according to which the existence in some Member States but not in others of an obligation to provide compensation for non-material damage in the field of package holiday would cause "significant distortions of competition, given that (…) non-material damage is a frequent occurrence in that field".[52] The reading was further explained by the fact that Directive 90/314/EEC "was designed to offer protection to consumers and, in connection with tourist holidays, compensation for non-material damage arising from the loss of enjoyment of the holiday is of particular importance to consumers".[53] Even though the matters of competence have remained peripheral to the case, the judgment has been criticised for establishing

---

[49] Judgment of the Court of Justice of 12.3.2002 in case C-168/00 *Leitner*, operative part.

[50] Judgment of the Court of Justice of 18.3.2021 in case C-578/19 *Kuoni Travel Ltd*, ECLI:EU:C:2021:213.

[51] Note that the boundaries of contractual limitations of the organiser's liability are defined more clearly in Article 14(4) of Directive 2015/2302, according to which the package travel contract may limit compensation to be paid by the organiser as long as that limitation does not apply to personal injury or damage caused intentionally or with negligence and does not amount to less than three times the total price of the package.

[52] Judgment of the Court of Justice of 12.3.2002 in case C-168/00 *Leitner*, para. 21.

[53] Ibid, para. 22.

the connection between significant distortions of competition and consumer protection too hastily.[54] Instead of reasoning along traditional lines—one can argue—the Court could have recognized the self-standing role of consumer protection in the internal market policy, most notably via the notion of consumer confidence.

While the *Leitner* case focused on damages, the more recent judgment in *Kuoni Travel* considered under which conditions the organiser's liability is incurred in the first place. The case involved a rape and assault of a traveller by an electrician employed at the hotel, who was on duty and wore a uniform. The question was raised whether the liability of the organiser extended to the actions of that employee. The Court observed that the liability of organisers, without doubt, covers the proper performance of the obligations arising under the package travel contract by service suppliers. The latter notion was understood to cover natural and legal persons providing services for remuneration and not their employees.[55] Such an interpretation, however, did not preclude an employee's acts or omissions from being treated, for the purposes of EU travel law, in the same way as those of the supplier of services employing him or her.[56] In this respect, the Court found, firstly, that for the organiser's liability to be incurred there must be a link between the act or omission which caused damage to that consumer and the organiser's obligations arising from the package travel contract, which themselves cannot be interpreted restrictively.[57] Secondly, the Court accepted that the performance or failure to perform certain actions by the employees of service providers may constitute non-performance or improper performance of the obligations arising from the package travel contract, and in consequence, render the organiser liable.[58] Finally, the Court held that the third indent of Article 5(2) of Directive 90/314/EEC could not be relied on to exempt organisers from liability as the event at issue did not lie beyond the sphere of control of the service supplier. Despite the adjusted wording of Article 14(3)(c) of Directive 2015/2302, the above interpretation is likely to hold under existing rules, thus providing the traveller with a high level of protection.

#### 5.2.3.5 Assistance

An element of travellers' protection, whose importance is hard to overstate, pertains to practical assistance in case of difficulty. As was already stressed, an essential part of the weaker position of service recipients concerns their position as loss bearers.[59] Indeed, any potential complications experienced during the journey can be additionally challenging for the traveller who is, by definition, geographically removed from

[54] Wyatt (2009), p. 129.

[55] Judgment of the Court of Justice of 18.3.2021 in case C-578/19 *Kuoni Travel Ltd*, para. 38 and 41.

[56] Ibid, para. 43.

[57] Ibid, para. 45–46.

[58] Ibid, para. 47–48.

[59] Willett (2018), p. 187.

his or her place of residence. To deal with emerging problems and fulfil even basic needs, such as finding a shelter, a traveller may often need to navigate an unknown environment. Recipients of travel services are therefore more likely to experience negative effects such as distress, loss of time, and inconvenience in personal lives than service providers. The suppliers, moreover, may often be much better placed to mitigate these negative effects.

It is for these reasons that the EU package travel law, aside from organisers' liability for non-performance, has also addressed the travellers' need for assistance. Under Article 16 of Directive 2015/2302, Member States are obliged to ensure that the organiser gives appropriate assistance without undue delay to the traveller in difficulty, including when the difficulties are caused by unavoidable and extraordinary circumstances, in particular by: (i) providing appropriate information on health services, local authorities and consular assistance, and (ii) assisting the traveller to make distance communications and helping the traveller to find alternative travel arrangements. The organiser shall be able to charge a reasonable fee for such assistance—not exceeding the actual costs incurred by the organiser—if the difficulty is caused intentionally by the traveller or through the traveller's negligence.[60] Furthermore, under Article 13(7), if the traveller's return as agreed in the package travel contract is impossible because of unavoidable and extraordinary circumstances, the organiser is required to bear the cost of necessary accommodation, if possible of equivalent category, for a period not exceeding three nights per traveller. The provision aims to provide the traveller with immediate shelter and the possibility to consider the available options. Temporal limitation of the obligation to provide accommodation constitutes another attempt at balancing the interests of both parties. It is worthy of note, however, that longer periods of assistance may also apply under Union passenger rights legislation, which is discussed more extensively in the following chapter. As already signalled before, the provisions on assistance to the traveller in difficulty also apply to the travel services included in the linked travel arrangement if the trader facilitating such an arrangement has violated Articles 19(1) and 19(2).

#### 5.2.3.6 Insolvency Protection

The final part of the protection framework established by Directive 2015/2302, and previously Directive 90/314/EEC, relates to the possible insolvency of the traveller's counterparty. Pursuant to Article 17(1) of Directive 2015/2302, Member States are obliged to ensure that organisers established in their territory, as well as organisers not established in a Member State which sell or offer for sale packages within their jurisdiction, provide security for the refund of all payments made by or on behalf of travellers insofar as the relevant services are not performed as a

[60] Cf. Article 5(2) of Directive 90/314/EEC on package travel under which the organiser and/or retailer were required to give prompt assistance to a consumer in difficulty liability, except in cases when the difficulty was attributable to the consumer himself or herself.

consequence of the organiser's insolvency. The security shall be available free of charge to ensure repatriations and, if necessary, the financing of accommodation before the repatriation. The focus thus remains on reimbursing payments already made and bringing travellers to the point of departure, although continuation of the package may also be offered.[61] The importance of the provision manifested itself during the compulsory liquidation of one of the world's oldest package tour organisers, Thomas Cook, in 2019.[62]

The obligation to provide security is also one of the few requirements—next to a corresponding information duty—that Directive 2015/2302 imposes on traders facilitating linked travel arrangements. Pursuant to Article 19(1), the relevant security should cover a refund of all payments received from the travellers "insofar as a travel service which is part of a linked travel arrangement is not performed as a consequence of (…) insolvency" of those traders. If such traders are the party responsible for the carriage of passengers, the security shall also cover the traveller's repatriation. In the context of the analysed platform markets, the provision appears to provide limited protection, considering that the insolvency of platform operators seems to be the least likely reason for the non-performance of underlying travel services. This does not render the insurance coverage in these types of markets entirely irrelevant. On the contrary, as discussed in Chap. 3, security provided for a range of unexpected events appears to play a growing role in the platform economy.

## 5.3 Tourism Accommodation Beyond Package Travel

While the EU law has introduced harmonised measures in the field of package travel at a comparably early stage, the scope of its harmonisation efforts has been much more limited when it comes to self-standing accommodation services. Private law relationships with providers of travel services who do not qualify as either organisers or retailers are not specifically addressed at the EU level. Relationships of this kind may fall within the scope of existing horizontal rules, most notably of Directive 2006/123/EC on services in the internal market. The Directive operates with the broad notion of "service provider", which also includes peer providers, as long as their activities are of an economic nature.[63] The relevant rules, however, do not deal with the thorniest liability problems, but mainly with disclosure duties.[64] What is

[61] Articles 17(1) *in fine* and 17(4) of Directive 2015/2302 on package travel and linked travel arrangements.

[62] Bunyan (2019) Thomas Cook: The U.K.'s Oldest Travel Company. TIME Magazine, 7 October 2019; Airbnb, 'Airbnb Hosts Share More Than Six Million Listings Around the World' (2019) https://news.airbnb.com/airbnb-hosts-share-more-than-six-million-listings-around-the-world/.

[63] Cf. Articles 4(1) and 4(2) of Directive 2006/123/EC on services in the internal market, judgment of the Court of Justice of 18.12.2007 in case C-281/06 *Jundt*, paras. 32–33.

[64] Article 22 of Directive 2006/123/EC on services in the internal market.

more, the corresponding rules on professional liability insurance and quality of services are framed in very general terms, leaving Member States and the relevant service providers a broad room for discretion.[65] Such state of affairs should not be understood as EU institutions' lack of interest in providing service recipients with a higher degree of protection. In fact, the contrary is true, as illustrated by previous initiatives, such as the proposed directive on the liability of suppliers of services, which met with resistance during negotiations.[66] Even if the criticism of the proposal has not been unfounded,[67] it is remarkable that no attempts have been made to follow up on this discussion, based on the extensive research undertaken.[68]

In contrast to the field of transport, discussed in the subsequent chapter, the EU has also not been able to rely on common rules protecting recipients of tourism accommodation services developed at the international level. The only moderate success in this domain is the Paris convention on the liability of hotel-keepers.[69] The convention lays down minimum liability rules for hotel-keepers concerning the property of their guests. Article 3 of the Annex provides for strict liability, limited only by the three exoneration grounds, covering cases in which the damage, destruction or loss are due to: (i) the guest or any person accompanying him or her or in his or her employment or any person visiting him or her, (ii) an unforeseeable and irresistible act of nature or an act of war, or c) the nature of the article. The convention further lays down a liability cap in the equivalent of 3000 gold francs and provides for unlimited liability where the property has been deposited with hotel-keepers or where they have refused to receive property which they are bound to receive for safe custody.[70] Open to ratification in 1962, the treaty has so far been ratified by 17 Member States of the Council of Europe, including 12 EU Member States, which is far from satisfactory from the internal market perspective.[71]

Besides (regulatory) private law, the public law requirements concerning quality and safety of the travel services are also worth considering. As was signalled before, compliance of tourism accommodation with local laws was indirectly addressed by Directive 90/314/EEC on package travel, which required retailers and organisers to

[65] Ibid, Articles 23, 26 and 27.

[66] European Commission, 'Proposal for a Council Directive on the Liability of Suppliers of Services' (1990) COM(90) 482 final.

[67] European Commission, 'Communication from the Commission on New Directions on the Liability of Suppliers of Services' (1994) COM(94) 260. See also references in Hondius (1995), p. 251.

[68] Magnus and Micklitz (2006). See also Reich (2008), pp. 48–49, Tai (2016), pp. 354–355, 359.

[69] Council of Europe, Convention on the Liability of Hotel-keepers concerning the Property of their Guests, Paris, 17.12.1962.

[70] Article 2 of the Annex to the Convention on the Liability of Hotel-keepers concerning the Property of their Guests.

[71] Council of Europe, 'Chart of Signatures and Ratifications of Treaty 04' www.coe.int/en/web/conventions/full-list/-/conventions/treaty/041/signatures. Following the Agreement on the withdrawal of the United Kingdom of Great Britain and Northern Ireland from the European Union and the European Atomic Energy Community [2019] OJ C144 I/1, the United Kingdom is no longer treated as an EU Member State.

inform consumers about this fact.[72] Interestingly, a requirement of this kind appears to be absent from Directive 2015/2302. This is somewhat surprising, considering that the EU legislature has generally shown interest in the monitoring and, to some extent, approximating safety and quality requirements imposed on tourism accommodation providers. Efforts of this kind date back to the early days of the EU consumer protection *acquis*, as illustrated by the 1986 Council Recommendation on fire safety in existing hotels.[73] Moreover, Article 26 of the Services Directive requires Member States, in cooperation with the Commission, to "take accompanying measures to encourage" a number of actors, including service providers, professional bodies and consumer associations, to ensure the quality of service provision. The provision also promotes the development of "voluntary European standards with the aim of facilitating compatibility between services supplied by providers in different Member States, information to the recipient and the quality of service provision".[74] Although the approximation has borne limited fruit until today,[75] the initiative has not been abandoned by the European Commission. On the contrary, the Green Paper on the safety of tourism accommodation services published in 2014 continued to stress the connection between "adequate and efficient safety levels" and both consumer confidence and the growth of the tourism sector.[76] The focus on safety issues (as opposed to quality) indeed seems justified by the nature of tourism accommodation services, which remain context-specific and diverse. As convincingly argued by van Leeuwen, this desirable diversity potentially weakens the case for the EU-wide standardisation of the quality of services.[77] This argument seems to apply with additional force to services provided by peers in the collaborative economy, in which case the associated consumer expectations may deviate from those applying to services provided in more established models.[78] Van Leeuwen notes, however, that arguments of this kind should not be used as an excuse to refrain from regulating safety aspects.[79] The renewed interest in tourism accommodation safety following the global outbreak of COVID-19 could create new momentum for increased EU involvement in the mentioned domain.[80] Interestingly, even the quality dimension does not appear to be entirely off the EU agenda, as illustrated by a

[72] Article 4(2)(a) of Directive 90/314/EEC on package travel directive in conjunction with point (c) of its Annex.

[73] Council Recommendation 86/666/EEC of 22.12.1986 on fire safety in existing hotels [1986] OJ L384/60.

[74] Article 25(5) of Directive 2006/123/EC on services in the internal market.

[75] van Leeuwen (2017), pp. 143–144.

[76] European Commission, 'Green Paper on the Safety of Tourism Accommodation Services' (2014) COM(2014) 464 final.

[77] van Leeuwen (2017), p. 115.

[78] Kucharska (2019), pp. 32–34.

[79] van Leeuwen (2017), p. 115.

[80] European Commission, 'Communication from the Commission. COVID-19: EU Guidance for the Progressive Resumption of Tourism Services and for Health Protocols in Hospitality Establishments' (2020) C(2020) 3251 final.

study commissioned in 2019 to investigate the feasibility of possible initiatives at the EU level and the establishment of a multi-stakeholder platform on the quality of tourism accommodation.[81] From both safety and quality perspectives, online platforms appear to pose new risks associated with an even more remarkable diversity of service providers involved. Nonetheless, platform operators also have a variety of tools at their disposal, which can be used to mitigate these risks and which certainly should be included in the EU-level debates.

## 5.4 Conclusions

The growing role of consumer protection in the evolution of EU primary law over past decades is beyond doubt. The notion of "consumer" is not defined in the Treaties and requirements of consumer protection, referred to in Article 12 TFEU, can be interpreted broadly as covering a wide range of passive market participants finding themselves in need of such protection due to a position of weakness. Article 169 TFEU further underlines the importance of a "high level" of consumer protection and points to its core aspects, spanning from the protection of health, safety and economic interests of consumers to the promotion of their right to information, education and organisation. It also contains two distinct competence norms, associated more specifically with consumer protection, and extending, respectively, to the measures adopted pursuant to Article 114 TFEU in the context of the completion of the internal market as well as measures which support, supplement and monitor the policy pursued by the Member States. In the latter domain, only a minimum level of harmonisation can be pursued.

The analysis confirms the position of Article 114 TFEU as a powerful norm justifying the involvement of EU law in digital markets and the travel sector. The Court of Justice tends to give a broad reading to the competence norm of Article 114(1) TFEU and is not too restrictive in the assessment of the grounds for taking legislative action. Attention is paid primarily to the justification put forward by the EU legislature, which in practice tends to contain a mixture of established grounds on removing barriers to trade and distortions of competition and more consumer-oriented references to confidence-building. Ultimately, the development of consumer protection in secondary law, including in e-commerce and travel, is a function of important choices made by the EU institutions. Priority is generally given to domains with an internal market dimension, while the competence norm of Article 169(2)(b) remains of marginal importance.

Even though unanimity is no longer required, all three co-legislators—the European Commission, the European Parliament and the Council—continue to play

[81] European Commission, 'Call for Tenders No 773/PP/GRO/PPA/19/11226: Study on the Feasibility of Possible Initiatives at EU Level and Establishment of a Multi-Stakeholder Platform on Quality of Tourism Accommodation' https://etendering.ted.europa.eu/cft/cft-display.html?cftId=4988.

an important role in shaping the internal market policy. The European Commission proposes the measure, while two remaining institutions decide whether to introduce amendments and adopt it based on majority voting. In practice, wide acceptance from the Member States is usually sought as part of trialogue discussions and the original proposals are drafted in a way that makes a successful adoption most likely.[82] The personal and substantive scope of relevant EU measures and the pursued level of harmonisation are the subject of negotiations. This explains why so many instruments of EU law follow a piecemeal approach and address only particular types of problems arising in relationships between particular types of market actors and/or in particular sectors.

While the legislative developments to date do not exhaust the role of consumer protection in EU integration, their analysis provides important insights into how competences and policy priorities are being understood and exercised in practice. Without a doubt, Article 114 TFEU assumes a central role in both de- and re-regulation of the internal market and is overwhelmingly relied upon to introduce measures of consumer protection. The expansion of consumer protection measures generally accompanies the process of bringing down the barriers to cross-border trade. At the same time, the connection between internal market-building and consumer protection is not fully captured by the image of the two consecutive processes. Measures aimed at consumer protection also remain an inherent part of the internal market project. To recall, pursuant to Article 169(2)(a) TFEU, the Union contributes to the attainment of a high level of consumer protection *through* measures adopted pursuant to Article 114 TFEU in the context of the completion of the internal market. The notion of consumer confidence lends additional support to the harmonisation of consumer protection rules on the basis of Article 114 TFEU. While reliance on this narrative is not always uncontroversial,[83] in areas, in which the vision of consumers seeking for counter-parties from other Member States is truly viable, it does appear well-founded. Both digital markets and travel sector can be viewed as prominent examples of such areas and arguments of consumer confidence-building seem all the more convincing when both domains intersect.

Indeed, like in digital markets, EU harmonisation efforts based on Article 114 TFEU are clearly visible in the travel sector. This has been the case primarily for so-called package travel contracts and, to a more limited extent, other models of travel services' distribution, such as linked travel arrangements and stand-alone tourism accommodation services. Individual transport services have not been subject to this process, due to their central role in a distinct policy area—the common transport policy. As will be discussed in the next chapter, however, the development of the common transport policy has remained closely interlinked with the internal market policy and the growing number of EU measures concerned with passenger protection has remained its prominent feature.

[82] Craig (2021), pp. 58–61, 72.

[83] Wilhelmsson (2004), p. 317.

The analysis of package travel law revealed that the traditional, supplier-oriented perspective on legal integration linked to internal market building remains strong.[84] A complementary view on the role of consumers in the internal market, associated with consumer confidence, is also gaining prominence.[85] Importantly, as EU travel law shows, considerations of this kind can equally apply to a broader category of passive market participants, and not just narrowly defined "consumers". Clearly, a move towards full harmonisation underlines the continued importance of the business-oriented perspective on the internal market. Such a move, however, does not necessarily conflict with fostering travellers' confidence, provided that the relevant measures ensure that such confidence is not, in fact, misplaced.[86]

Directive 2015/2302 identifies different dimensions of travellers' weaknesses and, following both self-reliance and need ethics, establishes a rather generous protection framework addressing several aspects listed in Article 169(1) TFEU. By turning organisers into core addressees of travellers' claims, the Directive provides the latter with what Wilhelmsson calls "easy access to a counterparty".[87] The act further acknowledges the importance of the platform-driven transformation of the travel sector from the internal market perspective. One can doubt, however, whether a half-baked category of "linked travel arrangements", coming with a limited protection framework, is what consumers need to contract with more confidence.

A careful reading of Directive 2015/2302 shows that the EU legislature remains aware of not just the new ways of combining multiple services but also other market practices. Recital 21 explicitly indicates that "Member States may maintain or introduce corresponding provisions for certain stand-alone contracts regarding single travel services (such as the rental of holiday homes)". The Directive is right to recognize these business models and its restraint in subjecting them to the same set of rules can be understood. It is doubtful, however, that the normative framework for "linked travel arrangements" sets an example to be followed.

Indeed, Directive 2015/2302 does not go very far in actually protecting travellers purchasing linked travel arrangements. In particular, triangular relationships between the traders facilitating linked travel arrangements, providers of travel services and travellers themselves remain underdeveloped. Key aspects of protection only become available if the trader facilitating linked travel arrangements fails to comply with his or her disclosure duties, and even then, the consequences of such a failure seem to be only borne by service providers. Despite tendencies to this effect

[84] Cf. recital 4 of Directive 2015/2302 on package travel and linked travel arrangements. ("Legal fragmentation leads to higher costs for businesses and obstacles for those wishing to operate cross-border, thus limiting consumers' choice.")

[85] Cf. recital 6 of Directive 2015/2302 on package travel and linked travel arrangements. ("Disparities in the rules protecting travellers in different Member States act as a disincentive for travellers in one Member State from buying packages and linked travel arrangements in another Member State.")

[86] More critically with regard to the move towards full harmonisation: Wilhelmsson (2004), p. 325.

[87] Ibid, p. 329.

in other fields of EU law, manifested recently in the *Wathelet* case,[88] the fact that the traveller would in this case likely expect the trader facilitating linked travel arrangements to be the organiser, is not explicitly accounted for. Although the trader facilitating linked travel arrangements may indeed not always be best placed to remedy non-performance, this argument does not apply with equal force to all market scenarios. For at least a certain group of cases, the introduction of joint and several liability would not only be imaginable but would also better account for the relationship between multiple parties, providing travellers with improved protection.

When it comes to the sharing of responsibility, the focus of Directive 2015/2023 remains almost entirely on the well-established package travel model, under which it is especially the organiser who bears responsibility vis-à-vis the traveller[89] and may subsequently seek redress from relevant third parties.[90] The latter can include retailers who provided wrong information and direct suppliers of travel services in question. The lack of a corresponding rule addressing the position of service suppliers vis-à-vis traders facilitating linked travel arrangements can be considered problematic. Interestingly, joint and several liability is introduced directly only on the traveller's side, in the context of contract transfer.

All in all, the EU legislature can be credited for attempting to clarify the differences between the different models of travel services' distribution, observed especially in online trade, embedding them in appropriate legal frameworks and providing consumers with the ability to choose between particular models according to their preferences. That choice, however, should not be between full protection and (almost) no protection at all. Unfortunately, the EU legislature appears to go in this direction, by focusing primarily on package holidays. The resulting asymmetry of the level of travellers' protection in different models of travel service distribution, may be harmful to the goals of the internal market policy. Most importantly for this inquiry, it appears to fall short of providing consumers with the needed confidence. Despite their current limitations, EU sectoral rules may provide valuable insights on how the protection of travellers could be improved *de lege ferenda*. To complete this sectoral picture, harmonisation of consumer protection rules in the transport sector is discussed below.

[88] Judgment of the Court of Justice of 9.11.2016 in case C-149/15 *Wathelet*, ECLI:EU:C:2016:840, paras. 41 and 45, in which the Court found the intermediary to qualify as a "seller" within the meaning of Article 1(2)(c) of Directive 1999/44/EC on consumer sales. For an analysis, see Devolder (2019), pp. 48–51.

[89] The retailer plays a role primarily with respect to providing information, see de Vries (2016), p. 124, Tereszkiewicz (2018), p. 918.

[90] Article 22 of Directive 2015/2023 on package travel and linked travel arrangements.

## References

Craig P (2021) Institutions, power, and institutional balance. In: Craig P, de Búrca G (eds) The evolution of EU law, 3rd edn. Oxford University Press, pp 46–89

de Vries A (2016) Travel intermediaries and responsibility for compliance with EU travel law: a scattered legal picture. Eur Consum Mark Law 5(3):119–125

Devolder B (2019) Contractual liability of the platform. In: Devolder B (ed) The platform economy: unravelling the legal status of online intermediaries. Intersentia, pp 31–88

Hondius E (1995) The reception of the directive on unfair terms in consumer contracts by Member States. Eur Rev Priv Law 3(2):241–255

Kucharska A (2019) Bezpieczeństwo konsumentów w świecie gospodarki współpracy z perspektywy prawa Unii Europejskiej – analiza wybranych problemów. iKAR 8(8):25–35

Magnus U, Micklitz H-W (2006) Liability for the safety of services. Nomos

Reich N (2008) Crisis or future of European consumer law? In: Parry D, Nordhausen A, Howells G, Twigg-Flesner C (eds) The yearbook of consumer law 2009. Routledge, pp 3–68

Tai ETT (2016) Services, including services of general interest. In: Twigg-Flesner C (ed) Research handbook on EU consumer and contract law. Edward Elgar, pp 336–359

Tereszkiewicz P (2018) Digital platforms: regulation and liability in the EU law. Eur Rev Priv Law 26(6):903–920

van Leeuwen B (2017) European standardisation of services and its impact on private law: paradoxes of convergence. Hart Publishing

Wilhelmsson T (2004) The abuse of the "confident consumer" as a justification for EC consumer law. J Consum Policy 27(3):317–337

Willett C (2018) Re-theorising consumer law. Cambridge Law J 77(1):179–210

Wyatt D (2009) Community competence to regulate the internal market. In: Dougan M, Currie S (eds) 50 years of the European treaties: looking back and thinking forward. Hart Publishing, pp 93–136

# Chapter 6
# Consumer Protection and Common Transport Policy

## 6.1 Preliminary Remarks

The previous chapters have shown how EU competences concerning the establishment and the functioning of the internal market have been interpreted and exercised over time, so as to gradually extend the scope and variety of rules on consumer protection. Such an analysis makes it possible to identify the basis for, as well as core aspects and ethics of, the harmonised EU measures of relevance to the travel sector. This, in turn, informs the inquiry of the potential disconnection between the existing legal framework and the transforming market practice as well as the need for, and means of, re-establishing a connection. The present chapter repeats this exercise, focusing on the common transport policy.

Some of the measures mentioned in the previous chapters can also be of relevance to the transport sector. For example, transport services are indirectly covered by Directive 2015/2302 on package travel and linked travel arrangements, insofar as they form part of packages or linked travel arrangements. They also fall within the scope of Directives 2005/29/EC on unfair commercial practices and 93/13/EEC on unfair contract terms,[1] which will be discussed in Chap. 7. Services in the field of transport and contracts for transport services are, nonetheless, excluded from the scope of numerous other measures. This is prominently the case for Directive 2006/123/EC on services in the internal market as well as Directive 2000/31/EC on

[1] Note, however, that pursuant to Article 1(2) of Directive 93/13/EEC, contractual terms, which reflect mandatory statutory or regulatory provisions and the provisions or principles of international conventions, particularly in the transport area, are excluded from the Directive's scope. Clearly, the exclusion only applies to the extent the relevant transport services are covered by those other norms. See also the judgment of the Court of Justice of 7.11.2019 in case C-349/18 *Kanyeba*, ECLI:EU:C:2019:936, paras. 57–63.

 
A. Jabłonowska, *Consumer Protection and Online Travel Platforms*, Law, Governance and Technology Series 73, https://doi.org/10.1007/978-3-031-90170-6_6

electronic commerce, as the *Uber* jurisprudence made clear.[2] Finally, Directive 2011/83/EU on consumer rights applies to contracts for passenger transport services only to a limited extent, particularly as regards the protection against hidden costs.[3]

The emerging, fragmented picture can be linked to the perceived special status of the transport sector, one which had already been recognized in the founding Treaties. Indeed, the EU involvement in the transport sector largely follows a sector-specific approach. Still, the connection between the internal market policy and the common transport policy remains strong, which explains why certain general rules on consumer protection are directly applicable to the transport sector.

## 6.2 Development of Common Transport Policy and Consumer Protection

### *6.2.1 Interplay Between Internal Market and Common Transport Policy*

The development of a common approach to the provision of transport services across the Member States has presented a challenge from the early days of the European integration. On the one hand, the importance of the transport sector to the internal market goals was readily apparent. On the other hand, Member States remained reluctant to open it to competition. Many transport services relied on costly infrastructures and involved comparably high fixed costs, which could only be borne by major companies, in particular the state-owned ones. Societal implications of the availability of transport services offered further support to such public involvement.[4] To the extent necessary, cooperation at the international level was achieved through bilateral or multilateral treaties.[5] Such a system did not sit very easily with the market integration goals of the emerging European Economic Community. At the same time, specific features of the transport sector warranted a

[2] See especially the judgment of the Court of Justice of 20.12.2017 in case C-434/15 *Asociación Profesional Elite Taxi (Uber Spain)*, ECLI:EU:C:2017:981.

[3] The scope of rules, originally laid down in Directive 97/7/EC on distance contracts and currently in Directive 2011/83/EU on consumer rights, applicable to the transport sector has been evolving over time. However, the general conclusion about the limited applicability of relevant norms in the analysed context remains valid and directly affects passenger transport services in the platform economy. Key stages of this evolution include the judgment of the Court of Justice of 10.3.2005 in case C-336/03 *easyCar*, ECLI:EU:C:2005:150, as well as the adoption of Directives 2011/83/EU and 2019/2161.

[4] Hojnik (2016), p. 218. See also European Commission, 'Legal Status of Rail, Road and Inland Waterway Transport in the Member States of the European Economic Community. Situation at 1 July 1962' (1963).

[5] See e.g. Convention on the Contract for the International Carriage of Goods by Road (CMR) of 19.5.1956, Convention on International Civil Aviation (Chicago Convention) of 7.12.1944.

careful approach. Already in the Treaty of Rome, therefore, the policy in the sphere of transport—particularly as regards rail, road and inland waterway—was envisaged as a specified common policy, next to agriculture and fisheries and the common commercial policy.[6]

The importance of the transport sector for the common market and its particular status within the integration project found expression in Article 3(e) of the Treaty of Rome. The provision explicitly described the adoption of "a common policy in the sphere of transport" as one of the activities to be taken by the Community in line with its purpose of, among others, establishing a common market. The special status of transport also found support in other parts of the Treaty. In line with Article 61(1), the freedom to provide services in the field of transport was to be governed by the provisions of the Title relating to transport. This notably included Article 75 which prescribed the measures to be taken, covering: (i) common rules applicable to international transport to or from the territory of a Member State or passing across the territory of one or more Member States, (ii) the conditions under which non-resident carriers may operate transport services within a Member State, and (iii) any other appropriate provisions.

In the 1960s, the Commission began to draft policy documents to bring a common transport policy to life. In an extensive memorandum of 1961, the Commission underlined the close interrelationship between the common transport policy and the general development of the common market.[7] The focus remained on the role of transport in the supply chains, whereby transport was seen as a stimulus to the growth of trade and expansion of markets.[8] Its importance for other fundamental freedoms, such as the free movement of people, was also underlined.[9] The document described the Treaty as "an indivisible whole", highlighting that its general rules must be applied in every economic field unless the Treaty itself provides for exceptions.[10] The Commission stressed that proceeding to establish a common transport policy was not only the possibility granted in the Treaty but also an obligation, in which all institutions had a part to play.[11] Gradual liberalisation and approximation of the operating conditions of different forms of transport within the Community were expected to raise the productivity of the entire sector, improving the quality of the relevant services and reducing transport rates.[12] However, despite the Commission's proposals, legislative developments initially were limited.[13]

---

[6] Articles 3(e) and 74 *et seq.* of the EEC Treaty.

[7] European Commission, 'Memorandum on the General Lines of the Common Transport Policy' (1961) COM(61) 50 final, p. I.

[8] Ibid, pp. 4–5.

[9] Ibid, p. 5.

[10] Ibid, p. III, 26.

[11] Ibid, p. V.

[12] Ibid, p. 22.

[13] The main developments included Council Decision 65/271/EEC of 13.5.1965 on the harmonisation of certain provisions affecting competition in transport by rail, road and inland waterway [1965] OJ88/1500, Regulation (EEC) No 1017/68 of the Council of 19.7.1968 applying rules of

The slow pace of the progress towards the common transport policy met with criticism from other European institutions, which decided to take action before the Court of Justice. Two cases are particularly noteworthy in this context. Firstly, *Commission v France*[14] considered the extent to which general Treaty provisions on free movement applied to the transport sector. The Court confirmed that the provisions on the freedom to provide services were not applicable, due to the derogation in Article 61(1), but those on other freedoms were.[15] Secondly, in 1983 the European Parliament decided to bring an action against the Council for failure to act.[16] The Court observed that the Council's obligations in relation to the freedom to provide services in the field of transport were sufficiently elaborated in Article 75 (1)(a) and (b) of the Treaty, and the Council should have taken action referred to therein.[17] Beyond this domain, the Council was at liberty to adopt "such accompanying measures as it consider[ed] necessary and to do so in the order it [held] to be appropriate".[18] Overall, both judgments have pushed the common transport policy forward and confirmed its ties with other EU goals.[19] Action in the field of consumer protection remained within the Council's margin of discretion, yet—like in the case of the internal market policy[20]—its gradual development was to be expected.

---

competition to transport by rail, road and inland waterway [1968] OJ L175/1 and Regulation (EEC) No 543/69 of the Council of 25.3.1969 on the harmonisation of certain social legislation relating to road transport [1969] OJ L77/49.

[14] Judgment of the Court of Justice of 4.4.1974 in case C-167/73 *Commission v France*, ECLI:EU:C:1974:35.

[15] Importantly, the Court later confirmed that despite the inapplicability of the general rules on services, the freedom to provide services is nonetheless highly relevant to the transport sector. Moreover, in *Nouvelles Frontières*, the Court expanded this analysis to competition rules. See judgment of the Court of Justice of 18.1.2001 in case C-361/98 *Italy v Commission*, ECLI:EU:C:2001:29, para. 32, judgment of the Court of Justice of 6.2.2003 in case C-92/01 *Stylianakis*, ECLI:EU:C:2003:72, para. 23 and judgment of the Court of Justice of 30.4.1986 in case C-209/84 *Ministère public v Asjes (Nouvelles Frontières)*, ECLI:EU:C:1986:188, paras. 42, 50–52.

[16] Huttunen (2013), p. 12.

[17] Judgment of the Court of 22.5.1985 in case C-13/83 *Parliament v Council*, ECLI:EU:C:1985:220, para. 68–70.

[18] Ibid, para. 61.

[19] European Commission, 'Competing the Internal Market. White Paper from the Commission to the European Council' (1985) COM(85) 310. See also Ehlermann (1987), p. 361, Karsten (2007), pp. 124–125.

[20] See especially Council resolution of 14.4.1975 on a preliminary programme of the European Economic Community for a consumer protection and information policy [1975] OJ C92/1 and Council Resolution of 19.5.1981 on a second programme of the European Economic Community for a consumer protection and information policy [1981] OJ C133/1.

### 6.2.2 Development of Articles 91 and 100 TFEU as Legal Bases for Passenger Protection Measures

As noted earlier, the judgments delivered throughout the 1970s and 1980s provided a stimulus for the common transport policy. The primary law framework, which the Court interpreted, is still relevant today. Article 58(1) TFEU on the freedom to provide services further refers to the common transport policy. Article 90 TFUE, in turn, reiterates that the Treaty objectives in matters related to transport shall be pursued within the common transport policy while the subsequent provisions engage with rail, road, and inland waterways. Sea and air transport is, in turn, separately addressed in Article 100(2) TFEU.

While the common transport policy maintained its special status, the allocation of relevant competences has evolved. Most notably, the involvement of the European Parliament under what is now Article 91 TFEU has increased. In addition, the specified categories of measures implementing the common transport policy have been expanded to include transport safety. Interestingly, Article 100(2) TFEU, which relates to sea and air transport, does not include a similar particularization. However, also in these domains legislative action on transport safety, and passenger protection generally, has been extensive.

Overall, despite the original tensions, the EU legislative activity in the transport sector has strongly accelerated since the 1980s.[21] The relevant legislation follows a characteristic pattern. The focus at the early stage remained on opening freight and, increasingly, passenger transport markets to competition. Increased competition was expected to bring benefits to passengers in the form of greater choice, reduced prices and more innovation.[22] Gradually as well, common rules related to passenger safety and, subsequently, direct passenger rights, began to emerge. The beneficiaries of these protections are usually not limited to formally defined "consumers", but extend to a broader category of transport users (passengers).[23] Despite differences in terms of pace and scope, this overall direction can be observed for all modes of transport.[24] The following discussion begins with air transport, where passenger protections appear to be particularly well-developed, and concludes with road transport, which is the primary subject of the platform-driven transformation. Attention

---

[21] European Commission, 'The Future Development of the Common Transport Policy: A Global Approach to the Construction of a Community Framework for Sustainable Mobility. White Paper' (1992) Bulletin of the European Communities Supplement 3/93.

[22] Karsten (2007), p. 125.

[23] Ibid, pp. 126–129.

[24] See especially European Commission, 'White Paper. European Transport Policy for 2010: Time to Decide' (2001) COM(2001) 370 final, p. 64, European Commission, 'White Paper. Roadmap to a Single European Transport Area – Towards a Competitive and Resource Efficient Transport System' (2011) COM(2011) 144 final, pp. 21–24 and European Commission, 'Communication from the Commission to the European Parliament and the Council. A European Vision for Passengers: Communication on Passenger Rights in All Transport Modes' (2011) COM(2011) 898 final.

is also drawn to the most recent legislative proposals on improving passenger rights. The analysis of existing and ongoing harmonisation efforts makes it possible to identify the basis for, as well as the core aspects and ethics of, the passenger protection measures in the common transport policy. As such, it not only supports the investigation of the protection gaps emerging in the platform age but also serves as an inspiration for the proposals *de lege ferenda*.

## 6.3 Common Transport Policy and Passenger Protection

### *6.3.1 Air Transport*

#### 6.3.1.1 From Liberalisation to the Early Measures on Passenger Rights

The involvement of the EU legislature in the air transport sector began with three legislative packages, adopted between 1987 and 1992, which extended the freedom to provide services in the EU to air transport.[25] The measures introduced in that period opened air transport to new providers, including low-cost carriers.[26]

In parallel to the liberalisation policy, legislation on passenger interests has gradually been adopted. Improving safety (i.e. the prevention of accidents capable of causing harm to person or property damage) as well as security (i.e. the prevention of acts of unlawful interference against civil aviation) belonged to their central themes.[27] Both aspects had previously been addressed at national and international levels,[28] yet the EU sought to establish a common level of protection.[29]

As air transport developed, the EU began to touch upon private law relationships between carriers and passengers. The initial rules adopted at the international level, shielding air carriers from far-reaching liability in the event of accidents, were

[25] See generally Komorek (2014), p. 19.

[26] Core measures on licensing of air carriers, access to air routes and fares and rates for air services, introduced in that period, were subsequently consolidated in a single instrument, namely Regulation (EC) No 1008/2008 of the European Parliament and of the Council of 24.9.2008 on common rules for the operation of air services in the Community (Recast) [2008] OJ L293/3. See also Huttunen (2013), p. 17.

[27] On the distinction, see e.g. European Commission, 'Communication from the Commission to the European Parliament, the Council, the European Economic and Social Committee and the Committee of the Regions. An Aviation Strategy for Europe' (2015) COM(2015) 598 final, pp. 9–10.

[28] Rossi Dal Pozzo (2015), pp. 11, 55.

[29] This was especially the case after the tragic events of 11 September 2001. For the currently applicable framework see Regulation (EC) No 300/2008 of the European Parliament and of the Council of 11.3.2008 on common rules in the field of civil aviation security and repealing Regulation (EC) No 2320/2002 [2008] OJ L97/72. The establishment of the European Aviation Safety Agency (EASA) constitutes an important milestone as far as safety is concerned. See also Komorek (2014), p. 21.

deemed inadequate for the EU passengers. This prompted the renegotiation of the previously applicable Warsaw Convention,[30] and eventually the adoption of the Montreal Convention,[31] which both the EU and its Member States have become parties to.[32] The conventions were complemented at the EU level with Regulation 2027/97 on air carrier liability in the event of accidents.[33] Complemented with insurance requirements,[34] the overall framework bears witness to the role of air passenger rights perceived at the transnational level.

#### 6.3.1.2 Regulation 261/2004 on Compensation and Assistance to Air Passengers

Montreal Convention and Regulation 2027/97 have without doubt improved the legal position of air passengers experiencing a range of issues—from major tragedies to more ordinary complications during their journeys. The next important EU milestone was the adoption of Regulation 261/2004 establishing common rules on compensation and assistance to passengers in the event of denied boarding and of cancellation or long delay of flights.[35] According to Weatherill, the act belongs to the "most high profile of all the EU's legislative measures".[36] The instrument replaces contractual negotiations between passengers and air carriers with a framework of regulatory contract law and establishes common safeguards not only for passengers who were denied boarding against their will but also for passengers whose flights were cancelled or delayed.

Similarly to other instruments of EU law, Regulation 261/2004 combines prevention and behaviour-steering functions with compensatory measures more

[30] Convention for the Unification of Certain Rules Relating to International Carriage by Air, Signed at Warsaw on 12.10.1929. See also Karsten (2013), p. 31.

[31] Convention for the Unification of Certain Rules for International Carriage by Air, opened for Signature at Montreal on 28.5.1999 (ICAO Doc No 4698).

[32] Council Decision 2001/539/EC of 5.4.2001 on the conclusion by the European Community of the Convention for the Unification of Certain Rules for International Carriage by Air (the Montreal Convention) [2001] OJ L194/38.

[33] Council Regulation (EC) No 2027/97 of 9.10.1997 on air carrier liability in the event of accidents [1997] OJ L285/1, as amended by Regulation (EC) No 889/2002.

[34] See Article 50 of the Montreal Convention. The minimum insurance requirements in respect of liability for passengers, baggage and cargo ensuring that air carriers are adequately insured to cover their liability under the Montreal Convention are laid down in Regulation (EC) No 785/2004 of the European Parliament and of the Council of 21.4.2004 on insurance requirements for air carriers and aircraft operators [2004] OJ L138/1, as amended by Regulation 285/2010 [2010] OJ L87/19.

[35] Regulation (EC) No 261/2004 of the European Parliament and of the Council of 11.2.2004 establishing common rules on compensation and assistance to passengers in the event of denied boarding and of cancellation or long delay of flights, and repealing Regulation (EEC) No 295/91 [2004] OJ L 46/1 (Regulation 261/2004 on air passenger rights).

[36] Weatherill (2016), p. 141.

traditionally associated with private law.[37] One of its goals is to "induce" air carriers to inform passengers of travel complications before the scheduled time of departure and, in case of cancellations or overbooking, to offer them reimbursement or reasonable re-routing, so that passengers can make alternative arrangements.[38] Failing that, air carriers are obliged to pay standardised compensation, the amount of which is linked to the distance covered by the flight, except when denied boarding or cancellation were caused by extraordinary circumstances. As explained further below, the right to standardised compensation has, over time, been extended to other groups of air passengers as a result of judicial activism. On top of standardised compensation, Regulation 261/2004 sets out other compensatory measures for passengers affected by overbooking, cancellations and delays, such as immediate assistance and care, which air carriers are required to provide even in case of complications resulting from extraordinary circumstances.

Unsurprisingly, Regulation 261/2004 met with dissatisfaction from airline representatives. However, the Court did not find reasons that would affect the act's validity. Instead, it confirmed the broad mandate of the EU legislature and laid the ground for expanded passenger protection.[39]

Notably, in *IATA and ELFAA* the Court distinguished between two types of damage occasioned by delays in the carriage of passengers. Firstly, according to the Court, excessive delays cause damage that is almost identical for every passenger, which may be redressed through standardised and immediate assistance or care for everybody concerned, constituted by the inconvenience suffered. Secondly, passengers can further be exposed to individualised damage, inherent in the reason for travelling, which has to be assessed on a case-by-case basis. In the Court's view, while the latter is the domain of the Montreal Convention, the same is not true for the former. Consequently, other forms of intervention, such as standardised and immediate redress for the damage constituted by the inconvenience, are not precluded by international law.[40] Moreover, according to the Court, the EU action was also proportionate to the objective pursued.[41] Finally, the Court rejected the arguments of unequal treatment, noting that passenger rights in case of delays and cancellations may differ according to the mode of transport.[42]

The distinction established by the Court has been subject to a critical debate.[43] The target of this criticism has not been the standardised redress *per se*, but rather the conceptual distinction between the different types of damages and the ensuing relationship between EU and international law.[44] Despite this criticism, the reading

[37] For an in-depth analysis of those *prima facie* contradictory functions, see Wagner (2006), pp. 422–426.

[38] See recital 12 of Regulation 261/2004 on air passenger rights.

[39] Judgment of the Court of Justice of 10.1.2006 in case C-344/04 *IATA and ELFAA*, ECLI:EU:C:2006:10.

[40] Ibid, paras. 45–46.

[41] Ibid, paras. 78–92.

[42] Ibid, paras. 93–99.

[43] McClean (2016), p. 61.

[44] Balfour (2016), p. 73. For a different critique see McClean (2016), p. 62.

in *IATA and ELFAA* has been consistently reaffirmed in subsequent case law.[45] Overall, one can conclude that considerations of passenger protection are not only reflected in the legal framework but also largely guide the development of the common transport policy, as interpreted by the Court of Justice.

Indeed, a strong focus on passenger protection is visible in the more recent case law, in which the Court tends to read Regulation 261/2004 broadly. Most notably, in *Sturgeon*,[46] the Court established that passengers who suffer a delay of at least 3 h must be treated in the same way as passengers whose flights are cancelled as far as compensation is concerned.[47] Moreover, in *České aerolinie*, the Court found that in the case of connecting flights subject to a single reservation, a passenger who suffers a delay of 3 h or more may bring an action for compensation against the air carrier who performed the first flight, even if the cause of the delay arose in the second flight.[48] In doing so, the Court appears to promote "easy access to the counterparty" as an important aspect of consumer confidence-building.

A tendency to further improve passenger protection can also be observed at the legislative level. For example, the most recent legislative proposals provide that the air carrier may make the reimbursement through an intermediary if the ticket was bought in this way, in which case the passenger should be informed accordingly.[49] Importantly, the reimbursement through an intermediary should not prolong the process or involve extra costs. In addition, the proposal requires air carriers shall establish service quality standards and implement a quality management system to maintain service quality. Thus, provisions on safety and security are gradually complemented with quality requirements.

### 6.3.2 *Rail and Waterborne Transport*

As noted earlier, the Court lent far-reaching support to the EU action on air passenger rights, as it previously did for package travel. In addition, the *Sturgeon* ruling offered notable insights into the legislative treatment of different carriers. The Court refused the arguments about unequal treatment between the different types of carriers using the same transport mode, such as low-cost and other airlines, arguing that

---

[45] See, in particular, judgment of the Court of Justice of 23.10.2012 in case C-581/10 *Nelson and Others*, ECLI:EU:C:2012:657, paras. 46–55. On the deduction of compensation, see judgment of the Court of Justice of 29.7.2019 in case C-354/18 *Rusu*, ECLI:EU:C:2019:637, para. 47.

[46] Judgment of the Court of Justice of 19.11.2009 in case C-402/07 *Sturgeon*, ECLI:EU:C:2009:716, para. 69.

[47] For a critique, see Dempsey and Johansson (2010), p. 207.

[48] Judgment of the Court of Justice of 11.7.2019 in case C-502/18 *České aerolinie*, ECLI:EU:C:2019:604.

[49] European Commission, Proposal for a Regulation of the European Parliament and of the Council amending Regulations (EC) No 261/2004, (EC) No 1107/2006, (EU) No 1177/2010, (EU) No 181/2011 and (EU) 2021/782 as regards enforcement of passenger rights in the Union, COM(2023) 753 final, Article 1(2).

the damage suffered by passengers is similar regardless of the specific carrier.[50] The focus thus remained on the comparability of passengers' experience, which notably may differ *between* the transport modes. In particular, the Court observed that the inconvenience suffered by air passengers is affected by specific airport locations and procedures. In doing so, the Court appears to accept that the instruments of passenger protection may differ according to the mode of transport, while at the same time encouraging the EU legislature to further develop the relevant framework. This, indeed, has been the process observable in all other modes, starting with rail and waterborne transport.

Like in air transport, the protection of rail passengers began with safety aspects,[51] followed by rules affecting private law relationships. In 2007, Regulation 1371/2007 on rail passengers' rights and obligations was adopted.[52] The act similarly complemented the pre-existing international laws[53] with passenger rights to immediate assistance, reimbursement or re-routing as well as standardised compensation in case of delays. A similar trajectory is also visible in the case of waterborne transport.[54] In 2021, the original framework of rail passenger rights was replaced with Regulation 2021/782, which is the most recent EU act on passenger rights at the time of writing.[55]

An important difference between Regulation 2021/782 (as well as its predecessor) and Regulation 261/2004 on air transport concerns the standardised compensation. In particular, the former act links the amount of compensation not to the distance covered, but to the ticket price.[56] Consumer detriment is therefore not about the inconvenience suffered; rather, the focus is on the consideration provided for a service not supplied as promised.[57] A similar approach is found in Regulation 1177/2010 concerning the rights of passengers when travelling by sea and inland waterway.[58] Both acts confirm the importance of compensation for delays, in addi-

---

[50] Ibid, paras. 96–97.

[51] For the currently applicable framework see Directive (EU) 2016/798 of the European Parliament and of the Council of 11.5.2016 on railway safety [2016] OJ L138/102. See also Directive 2007/59/EC of the European Parliament and of the Council of 23.10.2007 on the certification of train drivers operating locomotives and trains on the railway system in the Community [2007] OJ L315/51.

[52] Regulation (EC) No 1371/2007 of the European Parliament and of the Council of 23.10.2007 on rail passengers' rights and obligations [2007] OJ L315/14.

[53] See, in particular, the Uniform Rules concerning the contract for international carriage of passengers and luggage by rail (CIV) constituting an appendix to the Convention concerning International Carriage by Rail (COTIF), as modified by the 1999 Protocol.

[54] See generally Petit Lavall (2013), p. 65.

[55] Regulation (EU) 2021/782 of the European Parliament and of the Council of 29 April 2021 on rail passengers' rights and obligations (recast) [2021] OJ L172/1.

[56] See Article 19 of Regulation 2021/782 on rail passengers' rights and obligations.

[57] Judgment of the Court of Justice of 26.9.2013 in case C-509/11 *ÖBB-Personenverkehr*, ECLI:EU:C:2013:613, para. 38.

[58] Regulation (EU) No 1177/2010 of the European Parliament and of the Council of 24.11.2010 concerning the rights of passengers when travelling by sea and inland waterway and amending Regulation (EC) No 2006/2004 [2010] OJ L334/1.

tion to reimbursement, re-routing and assistance. Moreover, Regulation 2021/782 already requires railway undertakings to establish service quality standards and implement a quality management system, while a corresponding amendment to Regulation 1177/2010 is envisaged by a recent proposal.[59]

## 6.3.3 *Road Transport*

### 6.3.3.1 EU Freight and Passenger Transport by Road

The prominent role of road transport among the different transport modes is beyond doubt. As of 2018, transport by road amounted to 75.4% of the total inland freight transport in EU-27 (based on tonne-kilometres performed), compared to 18.7% attributable to rail and 6% to inland waterways.[60] A high share of road transport is also visible in total inland passenger transport. As of 2017, a share of 82.9% of passenger-kilometres was attributable to passenger cars, 9.4% to motor coaches, buses and trolley buses and 7.8% to rail.[61] The strong position of road transport in the modal split is also visible in other data. In 2021, the share of passenger cars in the EU passenger transport was estimated at 78.3%, while buses and coaches accounted for a further 6.8%.[62] In freight, by contrast, the share of transport by sea has remained significant over the years, amounting to more than a quarter of all tonne-kilometres performed.[63]

The strong position of road transport can be explained by its flexibility, door-to-door convenience and comparably low costs, also due to their only partial internalisation.[64] This has led to the growing personal use of passenger cars, at the expense of transport services provided by third parties, except for air transport whose benefits in terms of speed are beyond question. Road transport has also managed to establish itself as a major mode of carrying freight. This has been linked, among others, to the changing structure of goods in the industrial sectors and the increasing share of time-sensitive, high-value goods in overall output.[65] Road transport is furthermore characterized by comparably low barriers to entry leading to a relatively

---

[59] European Commission, Proposal for a Regulation of the European Parliament and of the Council amending Regulations (EC) No 261/2004, (EC) No 1107/2006, (EU) No 1177/2010, (EU) No 181/2011 and (EU) 2021/782 as regards enforcement of passenger rights in the Union, COM(2023) 753 final, Article 3(5).

[60] Eurostat, 'Energy, Transport and Environment Statistics. 2020 Edition' (2020) 52 https://ec.europa.eu/eurostat/web/products-statistical-books/-/ks-dk-20-001.

[61] Ibid, p. 69.

[62] European Commission, 'EU Transport in Figures: Statistical Pocket Book 2023' (2023) 48 https://op.europa.eu/s/zIy9.

[63] Ibid, p. 36.

[64] Schroten et al. (2019), p. 64.

[65] European Conference of Ministers of Transport, 'Transport and Economic Development' (2002), p. 16.

large number of smaller providers operating alongside larger ones. The opening of the EU road transport market to competition was therefore easier to achieve compared to other transport modes. The focus has remained on the opening of international (intra-EU) freight and passenger services, which by now has largely been achieved.[66] In particular, common rules for access to the international market for coach and bus services are currently laid down in Regulation 1073/2009,[67] which replaced the original Regulation 684/92.[68] Liberalisation of passenger transport services with smaller vehicles has not been viewed as a priority, considering that these were generally not regulated. An exception applied to taxi services, yet their cross-border importance has been considered too small to merit dedicated action.[69] Perspectives on the EU-wide relevance of passenger transport services by car may nonetheless soon change in view of the current development of platform-based mobility patterns. What is more, similarly to other transport modes, the opening of the road transport market to competition has been accompanied by an EU-level action on road safety and passenger protection, for which cross-border aspects have remained of secondary importance.

#### 6.3.3.2 Harmonised Regulation and the Role of Passenger Protection

Safety in General Road Traffic and Passenger Transport

Aside from opening road transport markets to competition, and opening borders to facilitate mobility more generally, road transport has also been subject to significant (re-)regulation. Already in the early phase of European integration, common basic standards were established to ensure, for example, that road passenger transport operators had the necessary qualifications[70] and were not working excessively long

[66] European Commission, 'Transport in the European Union: Current Trends and Issues' (2019) 7.

[67] Regulation (EC) No 1073/2009 of the European Parliament and of the Council of 21.10.2009 on common rules for access to the international market for coach and bus services, and amending Regulation (EC) No 561/2006 [2009] OJ L300/88.

[68] Council Regulation (EEC) No 684/92 of 16.3.1992 on common rules for the international carriage of passengers by coach and bus [1992] OJ L74/1.

[69] See especially questions raised by the Members of the European Parliament, Jorgo Chatzimarkakis and Marie-Thérèse Sanchez-Schmid, for written answer to the Commission as regards cross-border transport by taxi between Germany and France and France and Spain, respectively, as well as answers given by Mr. Kallas on behalf of the Commission [2011] OJ C249 E, [2013] OJ C166 E.

[70] Council Directive 74/562/EEC of 12.11.1974 on admission to the occupation of road passenger transport operator in national and international transport operations [1974] OJ L308/23, currently: Regulation (EC) No 1071/2009 [2009] OJ L 300/51. See also Council Directive 76/914/EEC of 16.12.1976 on the minimum level of training for some road transport drivers [1976] OJ L357/36, currently: Directive (EU) 2022/2561 [2022] OJ L 330/46.

hours.[71] Mirroring the approach to market access rules, however, the focus in this area remained on larger vehicles.[72] Further actions—with a much broader scope of application—aimed to increase safety in the process of vehicle construction and testing, to the benefit of all users of the EU roads.[73] The process of harmonisation was also not without effects for those travelling on their own account, as illustrated by the rules on standardised driving licences,[74] or the compulsory use of seat belts.[75] Direct reference to safety in road transport introduced in the Maastricht Treaty—currently found in Article 91(1)(c) of the TFEU—further clarified the legal means available to the EU in this domain.[76] Overall, both an increase in road transport safety over past decades and a further potential for improvement are beyond question. Between 2008 and 2018, EU fatalities in road traffic accidents fell by 37%, yet in 2018 a total of 23,339 people still lost their lives on EU roads.[77] Improving road transport safety thus remains a priority of the common transport policy. Safety implications of the novel mobility patterns, including in the so-called collaborative economy, are part of this discussion, even if their analysis is still at an early stage.[78] In parallel, the discussion continues on other areas of protection, such as motor insurance and more direct passenger rights.

---

[71] Regulation (EEC) No 543/69 of the Council of 25.3.1969 on the harmonisation of certain social legislation relating to road transport [1969] OJ L77/49, currently: Regulation (EC) No 561/2006 [2006] OJ L102/1.

[72] Requirements for drivers and vehicles additionally formed part of markets access rules, referred to in the previous section.

[73] See e.g. Council Directive 70/156/EEC of 6.2.1970 on the approximation of the laws of the Member States relating to the type-approval of motor vehicles and their trailers [1970] OJ L42/1 and Directive 2001/85/EC of the European Parliament and of the Council of 20.11.2001 relating to special provisions for vehicles used for the carriage of passengers comprising more than eight seats in addition to the driver's seat, and amending Directives 70/156/EEC and 97/27/EC [2002] OJ L42/1. More recently: Regulation (EU) 2018/858 [2018] OJ L151/1 and Regulation (EU) 2019/2144 [2019] OJ L325/1.

[74] Currently Directive 2006/126/EC of the European Parliament and of the Council of 20.12.2006 on driving licences (Recast) [2006] OJ L403/18.

[75] Council Directive 91/671/EEC of 16.12.1991 on the approximation of the laws of the Member States relating to compulsory use of safety belts in vehicles of less than 3,5 tonnes [1991] OJ L373/26, as amended.

[76] In a number of areas Member States have remained reluctant to a common action, leading the EU institutions to adopt a softer approach, see e.g. Commission Recommendation of 17.1.2001 on the maximum permitted blood alcohol content (BAC) for drivers of motorised vehicles [2001] OJ L43/31, Commission Recommendation of 6.4.2004 on enforcement in the field of road safety [2004] OJ L111/75.

[77] Eurostat, 'Energy, Transport and Environment Statistics. 2020 Edition' (2020), p. 86.

[78] European Commission, 'Commission Staff Working Document: EU Road Safety Policy Framework 2021–2030 - Next Steps towards "Vision Zero"' (2019) SWD(2019) 283 final 3, p. 17.

### Directive 2009/103/EC on Motor Insurance

The EU framework on motor vehicle insurance dates back to the 1970s[79] and is currently laid down in Directive 2009/103/EC.[80] Unlike other instruments discussed throughout this chapter, the Directive derives its legal basis from the competence norm in Article 114 TFEU, reflecting—once again—a strong connection between the internal market and the common transport policy and the associated role of weaker party protection.[81] Under Directive 2009/103/EC, Member States are required to ensure that civil liability in respect of the use of vehicles normally based in their territory is covered by insurance. Article 3 further provides that the extent of the liability covered and the terms and conditions of the cover are determined based on national law. Indeed, liability for accidents in road transport has not been harmonised in the EU[82] and the efforts taken to that effect at the international level have yielded limited results.[83] Nonetheless, the underlying liability rules have, in fact, been indirectly affected by the EU law, as interpreted by the Court of Justice, in favour of maximising liability.[84] This remains interlinked with a significant measure of harmonisation concerning conditions of the cover, which the Directive has introduced.

First of all, Article 3 of Directive 2009/103/EC provides that the insurance should cover compulsorily both damage to property and personal injuries, caused not only in the relevant Member State but also in other EU countries. Moreover, minimum amounts of the compulsory insurance cover are prescribed for cases of personal injury and damage to property.[85] Thirdly, the party injured as a result of an accident should not be required to bear any excess as far as compulsory insurance is con-

---

[79] Council Directive 72/166/EEC of 24.4.1972 on the approximation of the laws of Member States relating to insurance against civil liability in respect of the use of motor vehicles, and to the enforcement of the obligation to insure against such liability [1972] OJ L103/1.

[80] Directive 2009/103/EC of the European Parliament and of the Council of 16.9.2009 relating to insurance against civil liability in respect of the use of motor vehicles, and the enforcement of the obligation to insure against such liability [2009] OJ L263/11.

[81] Recital 2 of Directive 2009/103/EC relating to insurance against civil liability in respect of the use of motor vehicles, which notes that motor insurance remains "of special importance for European citizens, whether they are policyholders or victims of an accident", also having an impact "on the free movement of persons and vehicles". See also judgment of the Court of Justice of 4.9.2014 in case C-162/13 *Vnuk*, ECLI:EU:C:2014:2146, para. 49, referring to a "dual objective of protecting the victims of accidents caused by motor vehicles and of liberalising the movement of persons and goods with a view to achieving the internal market pursued by those directives".

[82] Note the controversy surrounding liability norms contained in the proposal for the act ultimately adopted as Regulation 181/2011 on the rights of passengers in bus and coach transport.

[83] The principle of strict liability was foreseen in the European Convention on Civil Liability for Damage caused by Motor Vehicles of 14.5.1973, which, however, has not entered into force due to the lack of a sufficient number of ratifications.

[84] Davey (2017), p. 240. See e.g. judgment of the Court of Justice of 30.6.2005 in case C-537/03 *Candolin and Others*, ECLI:EU:C:2005:417, paras. 24–28.

[85] Pursuant to Article 9(1) of Directive 2009/103/EC, the minimum amount of cover in the case of personal injury amounts to EUR 1000000 per victim or EUR 5000000 per claim, whatever the

cerned.[86] Fourthly, the act defines the scope of damage suffered by special categories of victims which should be covered by relevant insurance, including liability for personal injuries to all passengers, other than the driver, arising out of the use of a vehicle.[87] Article 13(1) further prevents the exclusion from insurance, by law or by contract, of the use or driving of vehicles by: (i) persons who do not have express or implied authorisation to do so, (ii) persons who do not hold a licence permitting them to drive the vehicle concerned, and (iii) persons who are in breach of the statutory technical requirements concerning the condition and safety of the vehicle concerned. A possible exception may be provided for the persons who voluntarily entered the vehicle which caused the damage or injury when the insurer can prove that they knew the vehicle was stolen. This, however, appears to be a rare instance, in which irresponsible behaviour of the passenger may deprive him or her of the insurance coverage.[88] The situation of passengers travelling with drunk drivers provides a prominent illustration: under Article 13(3), an injured party should not be denied coverage on the basis that he or she knew or should have known that the driver of the vehicle was under the influence of alcohol or of any other intoxicating agent at the time of an accident.[89]

To complete the protection framework, Directive 2009/103/EC provides the parties injured with a direct right of action against the insurance undertaking covering the person responsible against civil liability, which provides for easy access to a counterparty and, together with harmonised procedures for the settlement of claims, facilitates effective redress.[90] On top of that, a scheme is put in place to ensure compensation for damage caused by an unidentified vehicle or a vehicle for which the insurance obligation has not been satisfied, in which case easy access to a counterparty and swift compensation are also ensured.[91]

### Regulation 181/2011 on the Rights of Passengers Travelling by Bus and Coach

Turning even more directly to passenger protection, a gradual expansion of passenger rights can also be observed in the field of road transport. This remains in line with the general trend identified in other transport modes. Unlike those other modes, however, passenger rights in the road transport market had not been previously

number of victims, while in the case of damage to property, EUR 1000000 per claim, whatever the number of victims.

[86] Article 17 of Directive 2009/103/EC on motor insurance.

[87] Ibid, Article 12.

[88] See judgment of the Court of Justice of 30.6.2005 in case C-537/03 *Candolin and Others*, para. 21, in which the Court of Justice recalls that the analysed provision establishes a derogation from a general rule, and as such must be interpreted strictly.

[89] The provision builds upon the judgment of the Court of Justice of 30.6.2005 in case C-537/03 *Candolin and Others*.

[90] Articles 18–27 of Directive 2009/103/EC on motor insurance.

[91] Ibid, Article 11.

subject to extensive regulation at an international level. Hence, the relevant provisions—for now limited to Regulation 181/2011 on the rights of passengers travelling by bus and coach[92]—potentially reflect a model more specific to the EU. Still, as the subsequent analysis shows, experiences from other modes of transport have influenced legislative works on road passenger rights. To what extent this could inform further debates on passenger protection remains an open question.

At the moment, Regulation 181/2011 remains limited to passengers travelling by larger vehicles, with additional differentiation between regular and occasional and long-distance and short-distance services.[93] This gradation is an outcome of the complex legislative negotiations on the Commission's proposal[94] and, without doubt, reduces the clarity of the framework. In particular, the rationale behind different regimes according to the distance covered is not immediately apparent.[95]

Overall, the most extensive passenger protection framework established by Regulation 181/2011 applies to regular services for non-specified categories of passengers, where the scheduled distance of the service is 250 km or more. In this respect, the Regulation lays down, among others, detailed rules on compensation and assistance in the event of accidents, passenger rights in the event of cancellation or delay and general rules on information and complaints. Importantly, the instrument not only addresses the relationship between carriers and passengers but also stipulates certain obligations of terminal managing bodies, travel agents and tour operators.[96] The latter two are, however, only subject to a more limited set of rules defining the rights of disabled persons and persons with reduced mobility, particularly as regards reservations, information and notifications. Due to the special role and immense societal importance, analysis of these norms deserves a dedicated study and cannot be done justice in the present book.

The focus will, therefore, remain on the provisions addressing carriers and terminal managing bodies, which—as will be argued below—might, at times, be

[92] Regulation (EU) No 181/2011 of the European Parliament and of the Council of 16.2.2011 concerning the rights of passengers in bus and coach transport and amending Regulation (EC) No 2006/2004 [2011] OJ L55/1.

[93] A further distinction was drawn between domestic and international transport but lost weight over time. Pursuant to Article 2(4) of Regulation 181/2011, Member States may exempt domestic regular services from the application of Regulation 181/2011 for the maximum period of 8 years beginning from the date of application of the regulation, that is 1.3.2013.

[94] European Commission, 'Proposal for a Regulation of the European Parliament and of the Council on the Rights of Passengers in Bus and Coach Transport and Amending Regulation (EC) No 2006/2004 on Cooperation between National Authorities Responsible for the Enforcement of Consumer Protection Laws' (2008) COM(2008) 817 final.

[95] The reasoning could be linked to the interests of smaller carriers. Recital 3 of Regulation 181/2011 notes that "Union measures to improve passengers' rights in the bus and coach transport sector should take account of the specific characteristics of this sector, which consists largely of small- and medium-sized undertakings".

[96] For a discussion of these issues across particular passenger rights regulations, see de Vries (2016), pp. 122–123. The author observes that, despite certain inconsistencies in the allocation of responsibility for compliance with respective rules, most recent instruments on waterborne and road transport, are a step towards more coherence.

compared to platform operators. Notably, Article 5 sets out a general rule for the allocation of responsibility between different performing parties. On the one hand, the parties who are subject to the obligations under Regulation 181/2011 (carriers, travel agents, tour operators, terminal managing bodies) remain liable for acts and omissions of other performing parties (such as performing carriers or ticket vendors). On the other hand, other performing parties, to whom the performance of respective obligations has been entrusted, are brought within the scope of Regulation 181/2011 with regard to those obligations. Both provisions touch upon a broader issue of passenger protection in multi-party settings and, as such, show a potential for broader application.[97]

The first notable set of passenger protection rights, laid down in Regulation 181/2011, concerns compensation and assistance in the event of accidents. One cannot fail to note that this part of the framework had significantly evolved during legislative negotiations. The initial proposal defined the scope of the carrier's liability, following the model of other transport modes. The act eventually adopted instead provides, in Article 7, that passengers and, as a minimum, persons whom the passenger would have had a legal duty to maintain, shall be entitled to compensation for death, including reasonable funeral expenses, or personal injury, as well as loss or damage to luggage due to accidents arising out of the use of the bus or coach. The details of the liability framework are not subject to harmonisation but remain a domestic matter. Regulation 181/2011 only provides that any maximum limit to the relevant compensation should not be less than EUR 220,000 per passenger and EUR 1200 per item of luggage.

Replacement of a common, consumer-oriented liability norm with a reference to national law does not immediately imply that the EU co-legislators underestimate the importance of passenger protection in the event of accidents. Harmonisation of liability norms—as the core of national private laws—has long belonged to the most controversial areas of EU integration. Still, the protection of passengers in the event of accidents does play a prominent role in Regulation 181/2011. Firstly, Article 7 reaffirms that a compensation scheme covering death, personal injury and loss or damage to luggage should be established. Secondly, the establishment of a minimum compensation cap distinguishes Regulation 181/2011 from international conventions in other modes of transport, highlighting its protection-oriented approach. Thirdly, the provision on compensation is accompanied by further important norms: Article 8 of Regulation 181/2011 on assistance following the accident and insurance requirements, laid down in Directive 2009/103/EC. As a matter of fact, the former has been introduced to the analysed instrument in the course of legislative negotiations in lieu of the Commission's proposal on advance payments.[98] The provision

---

[97] Coherence of the broader framework for the allocation and sharing of responsibility is also underlined by de Vries (2016), p. 123.

[98] More specifically, advanced payments were addressed in Article 8 of the original proposal, see European Commission, 'Proposal for a Regulation of the European Parliament and of the Council on the Rights of Passengers in Bus and Coach Transport and Amending Regulation (EC) No 2006/2004 on Cooperation between National Authorities Responsible for the Enforcement of Consumer Protection Laws' (2008).

requires the carrier to provide reasonable and proportionate assistance with regard to the passengers' immediate practical needs following the accident, which should include, where necessary, accommodation, food, clothes, transport and the facilitation of first aid. To ensure the balance between the interest of both parties, Article 8 further clarifies that the total cost of accommodation, for each passenger, may be limited to EUR 80 per night and for a maximum of 2 nights and that any assistance provided shall not constitute recognition of liability. What is more, Article 19(3) additionally refers to a situation whereby a bus or coach becomes inoperable during the journey, in which case the carrier shall provide either the continuation of the service with another vehicle from the location of the inoperable vehicle, or transport from the location of the inoperable vehicle to a suitable waiting point or terminal from where continuation of the journey becomes possible. Both provisions follow a highly pragmatic approach, known from instruments on other transport modes, and apply it not only to cancellations or delays but also to accidents and breakdowns.

Indeed, aside from accidents, the obligation to provide assistance under Regulation 181/2011 also applies to cancellations and delays in departure from a terminal of more than 90 minutes. The obligation, set out in Article 21, resembles those known from other transport modes and covers free of charge: (i) snacks, meals or refreshments in reasonable relation to the waiting time or delay, provided they are available on the bus or in the terminal, or can reasonably be supplied, and (ii) accommodation and assistance to arrange transport between the terminal and the place of accommodation in cases where a stay of 1 or more nights becomes necessary, with an analogous quantitative limitation. Under Article 23(2), the obligation to provide accommodation under Article 21(b) does not apply where the carrier proves that the cancellation or delay is caused by severe weather conditions or major natural disasters endangering the safe operation of bus or coach services. Logically, the above limitation does not apply in case of accidents.

The obligation to provide assistance is not the only element of the passenger protection framework in case of cancelled or delayed departure. Like in instruments on other transport modes, the entire scheme is designed to ensure that the need for such assistance is limited in the first place. First of all, under Article 20, passengers departing from terminals and, where feasible, bus stops should be informed as soon as possible of the relevant cancellation or delay and the estimated departure time. Notably, the above obligation is shared by the carrier and terminal managing body. Secondly, pursuant to Article 19(1), as soon as the carrier reasonably expects a regular service to be cancelled or delayed in departure from a terminal for more than 120 minutes or in the case of overbooking, the passenger shall immediately be offered the choice between: (i) continuation or re-routing to the final destination, at no additional cost and under comparable conditions, as set out in the transport contract, at the earliest opportunity, or (ii) reimbursement of the ticket price, and, where relevant, a return service by bus or coach free of charge to the first point of departure, as set out in the transport contract, at the earliest opportunity.[99] Notably, how-

[99] Article 19(4) of Regulation 181/2011 provides for a similar right for passengers departing from bus stops.

ever, unlike in other transport modes, cancellation or delay of a certain duration does not automatically entail the right to compensation, at least in the form of a partial refund of the ticket price. To recall, under Article 19(1) of Regulation 2021/782 on rail passenger rights, passengers are entitled to request compensation of between 25% and 50% of the ticket price, depending on the duration of the delay, without losing their right of transport. Following the Court of Justice, compensation of this kind reflects the consideration provided for a service, which was not ultimately supplied in accordance with the transport contract.[100] By contrast, compensation laid down in Article 19(2) of Regulation 181/2011 is essentially a sanction for the carrier's failure to offer the passenger the choice between continuation, re-routing or reimbursement. In such a case, the passenger shall have the right to compensation amounting to 50% of the ticket price, in addition to the reimbursement referred to in the previous provision. The regulation further defines the modalities of compensation pay-out, following the approach of other transport modes.[101]

The final building block of the passenger protection framework established by Regulation 181/2011 encompasses general rules on information and complaints. Specifically, Article 24 imposes a broadly framed obligation on both carriers and terminal managing bodies to provide passengers with adequate information throughout their travel, within their respective areas of competence. Under Article 25, both actors are also required to ensure that passengers are provided with appropriate and comprehensible information regarding their rights under analysed regulation at the latest on departure. This information should be provided at terminals and, where applicable, online and should include contact details of the relevant enforcement bodies. The provision serves a similar effectiveness-oriented function as analogous norms known, among others, from package travel rules. The same is true for the following provisions on complaints and dispute settlement.

Rules on information and complaints equally apply to all regular services, regardless of the distance.[102] The reasons for their non-applicability to occasional services are not immediately apparent. For the time being, passengers travelling with occasional services are covered by the scope of harmonised rules on compensation and assistance in the event of accidents.[103] The relevant norms are, in turn, not applicable to short-distance services, the reasons for which—once again—are not duly explained.[104] However, the extension of the common rules on compensation and assistance in the event of accidents to shorter-distance journeys is not envisaged in the recent proposals for reform.

---

[100] Judgment of the Court of Justice of 26.9.2013 in case C-509/11 *ÖBB-Personenverkehr*, para. 38.

[101] Article 19(5) of Regulation 181/2011 on the rights of passengers in bus and coach transport.

[102] Ibid, Articles 2(1), 2(2) and 2(4).

[103] Ibid, Article 2(3).

[104] Ibid, Article 2(2).

### 6.3.4 Interim Conclusions

The expansion of EU action on passenger rights as an aspect of the common transport policy is beyond doubt. This general direction has found active support from the Court of Justice, as has the potential diversity of the measures taken by EU legislature depending on the transport mode. Variations of this kind can be attributed to several factors, most notably the manner of the operation of different transport modes and conditions governing their accessibility and network distribution.[105] Other elements can be linked to differences in the pre-existing rules of international law, even though EU institutions have shown a record of influencing and even sidelining them if the afforded level of passenger protection was viewed as insufficient.[106] By contrast, the differences in the constitutional embeddedness of given transport modes in EU Treaties appear to be less relevant for passenger protection. To recall, the expansion of passenger rights in the event of cancellations and delays began with the air transport sector, which is subject to a separate legal basis in Article 100(2) TFEU. Over time, similar measures have been adopted for other modes as well. Most illustratively, Regulation 1177/2010 derives its legal basis from both Article 91(1) and Article 100(2) TFEU and lays down a common set of rules for passengers travelling by sea and inland waterway. By the same token, the fact that safety is not expressly included in Article 100(2) TFEU does not imply that it is less important for air and maritime transport. On the contrary, it constitutes a vital common thread of the common transport policy in all transport modes. Its explicit mention in Article 91(1)(c) TFEU serves to underline that improving the safety of, among others, road transport represents a task not only of the Member States but also the EU.

While the overview of the common transport policy in all transport modes provides a useful background on passenger protection measures, the developments in the road transport market are especially relevant for this book. Prior measures on road transport safety and motor insurance set out universal basic safeguards, applicable also to passenger transport arranged via online platforms. The role of Regulation 181/2011 on the rights of passengers in bus and coach transport appears to be more difficult to assess. Clearly, the focus of the instrument remains on the carriage of passengers by larger vehicles, namely by bus and coach, in particular offered on a regular basis. As was said, platform-based mobility patterns rather involve transport by cars, usually on flexible routes. Nonetheless, the protection scheme of Regulation 181/2011 may also provide a useful reference point for the platform economy. Firstly, unlike general rules on safety and insurance, the instrument is specifically concerned with the rights of passengers, whom the EU legislature considers worthy of additional protection. As observed in the previous chapters, ride-sharing and rides-on-demand are more often than not activities of an economic nature and so are, without doubt, the activities of platform operators. At the same

---

[105] See e.g. judgment of the Court of Justice of 26.9.2013 in case C-509/11 *ÖBB-Personenverkehr*, para. 47.

[106] See e.g. judgment of the Court of Justice of 10.1.2006 in case C-344/04 *IATA and ELFAA*, para. 46.

time, unlike in the narrowly defined EU consumer *acquis*, the protection of passengers in Regulation 181/2011 does not depend on the status of relevant counterparties.[107] Attention is paid to the specific detriment to which passengers are exposed, not the status-oriented criteria. Transport services contracted for via online platforms may involve similar risks as transport by bus and coach, most notably related to accidents, cancellations and delays. Furthermore, Regulation 181/2011 underlines the importance of a holistic framework, taking into account the variety of actors involved (carriers, terminal managing bodies, etc), which remains conceptually aligned with the multi-party nature of the platform economy.

Finally, as a comparably recent act, adopted in the field not covered by the pre-existing international rules, Regulation 181/2011 reflects a truly EU approach to passenger protection, built upon the experiences from other transport modes. Therefore, its analysis in light of the broader development of the common transport policy provides important insights into the latter's goals and instruments. In all analysed modes, the expansion of passenger rights has generally gone hand in hand with the process of removing barriers to trade. Aside from safety, which assumes a particularly prominent role in the examined field, informed decision-making and protection in case of non-performance appear as common themes. The level of protection differs depending on the transport mode but is overall rather high and tends towards the need ethic. The distinctly EU nature of the emerging body of rules is underlined by the use of regulations instead of directives and openness towards pragmatic solutions, like standardised compensation and assistance. The latter not only increase the effectiveness of passenger protection, but also provide a constructive alternative to the more controversial harmonisation of liability rules. Clearly, specific passenger protection measures may vary depending on the mode of transport. Yet, even between the modes so different from each other like air and road transport, several common threads can be established. These general lessons may, therefore, equally hold true for novel services contracted for via online platforms, potentially even beyond the transport sector. For the time being, however, the protections enjoyed by the passengers in the platform economy, for the most part, do not seem to derive from EU law.

## 6.4 Passenger Protection and Online Travel Platforms: Identifying Gaps

### *6.4.1 Information at Different Stages of Contracting*

As was signalled before, contracts for passenger transport services are often excluded from the scope of information duties—generally associated with self-reliance ethics—laid down in horizontal instruments, like Directive 2011/83/EU on

[107] Karsten (2007), p. 135.

consumer rights[108] or Directive 2006/123/EC on services in the internal market.[109] This is explained not by the fact that disclosure is less important for this type of contracts, but rather by the existence of sector-specific rules addressing these matters at EU or national level.[110] It may thus be considered surprising that applicable measures on passenger rights do not provide for particularly detailed rules on disclosure. This discrepancy is especially visible at the pre-contractual stage, where—aside from the more specific case of information provided to disabled persons and persons with reduced mobility—the focus remains on information about statutory passenger rights.[111] To recall, a similar information duty about the existence of statutory rights is found in Directive 2015/2302 on package travel and linked travel arrangements, although in that case it is also complemented by a set of additional disclosure norms.[112]

Considering the criticism of the growing information overload[113] and the extent of the relevant mandatory rights in transport regulations, a more moderate approach to pre-contractual disclosure in this field may seem understandable. However, insofar as no similar statutory rights exist for certain types of contracts, such as those concluded via analysed online platforms, a potential for protection gaps arises. The same is also true in respect of important information duties set out in EU transport law at other stages of contracting. Here, again, the piecemeal approach of passenger rights regulation, together with an *en bloc* exclusion of the transport services from horizontal norms on consumer protection, result in protection gaps. Information related to cancellations and delays, set out in all analysed regulations, provides an illustrative example. Passengers affected by such complications seem equally worthy of protection, at least through information, regardless of the transport mode. Regulation 181/2011 on the rights of passengers travelling by bus and coach furthermore contains a brief, yet important, reference to "adequate information" to be provided to the passengers "throughout their travel", which again shows a potential for broader application.[114] Notably, the relevant duty is shared by carriers and terminal managing bodies, which reflects the emerging pattern of harmonisation concerning shared responsibility for information disclosure.

At the pre-contractual stage, a more tailored exclusion of the transport services from the scope of Directives 2011/83/EU and 2006/123/EC could prevent the protection gaps. Arguably, at least certain items of information laid down in those Directives, such as information on main characteristics of the services and identity of the supplier, could also be relevant to passengers. A lighter information duty for

[108] Article 3(3)(k) of Directive 2011/83/EU on consumer rights.

[109] Article 2(2)(d) of Directive 2006/123/EC on services in the internal market.

[110] Recital 27 of Directive 2011/83/EU on consumer rights.

[111] Cf. Articles 11 and 25 of Regulation 181/2011 on the rights of passengers in bus and coach transport.

[112] Article 5 of Directive 2015/2302 on package travel and linked travel arrangements.

[113] Howells (2005), pp. 356–362, Ben-Shahar and Schneider (2014), pp. 55–118. See also Seizov et al. (2019), pp. 49–50.

[114] Article 24 of Regulation 181/2011 on the rights of passengers in bus and coach transport.

contracts concluded through "means of distance communication which allow limited space or time to display the information", set out in Article 8(4) of Directives 2011/83/EU on consumer rights, could provide a suitable model for mobile applications. Arguably, already *de lege lata* a basis for improved information provision in the platform economy could derive from Directive 2000/31/EC on electronic commerce. For this be achieved, however, the scope of the act should be read in the light of *Ker-Optika* judgment, namely covering the digital component of a variety of economic activities.[115] Even in such a case, however, a potential for further elaboration remains, particularly in respect of information to be provided at other stages of contracting as well as shared responsibility.[116]

As was noted before, the idea of shared responsibility in transport sector finds increasing support in the emerging EU framework on passenger rights.[117] To recall, an obligation to ensure that passengers travelling by bus and coach are provided with appropriate and comprehensible information about their rights, any arising delays or cancellations along with the alternative connections, as well as other adequate information throughout their travel, is imposed on both carriers and terminal managing bodies.[118] It is worthy of note that Regulation 181/2011 on the rights of passengers travelling by bus and coach also provides for a shared responsibility between carriers and terminal managing bodies for this disclosure.[119] On top of that, Article 5 of Regulation 181/2011 ensures that the parties who entrust their relevant obligations to others remain liable for acts and omissions of those other parties. Such shared responsibility could provide a promising starting point for conceptualizing the role of platform operators, particularly when their actual engagement is taken into account. Although platform operators are often described as intermediaries, similar to travel agents, a comparison of their voluntary efforts, elucidated in Chap. 3, with the obligations imposed on different actors under Regulation 181/2011 shows more similarity between their role and that of terminal managers and, in certain cases, even carriers themselves. All analysed platforms in passenger transport market provide, or assist suppliers to provide, extensive information to passengers before and after, and in case of rides-on-demand also during their journeys. The situation is generally no different for short-term accommodation rental, which shows that a horizontal approach, following the model of E-Commerce Directive, could be appropriate for this field.

Finally, the previous analysis has shown that the limited scope of pre-contractual information duties imposed on carriers in passenger rights regulations coincides with extensive statutory protections applicable to these transactions. Other terms of the contracts between passengers and carriers are usually laid down in the latter's

---

[115] Judgment of the Court of Justice of 2.12.2010 in case C-108/09 *Ker-Optika*, ECLI:EU:C:2010:725, paras. 23–28.

[116] Wendehorst (2016), pp. 31–32.

[117] de Vries (2016), pp. 122–123.

[118] Articles 20, 24 and 25 of Regulation 181/2011 on the rights of passengers in bus and coach transport.

[119] Ibid, Article 20.

standard terms. Importantly, also in this respect passengers, at least those qualifying as "consumers" according to the standard definition, are not left without harmonised instruments of protection. Of relevance are especially the norms on transparency and fairness control of standard terms set out in Directive 93/13/EEC on unfair terms in consumer contracts. Unlike in case of Directives 2011/83/EU and 2006/123/EC, recognition of the special status of the travel sector has not led to its *en bloc* exclusion from the scope of relevant safeguards. Such a consequence is limited to contractual clauses which "reflect" mandatory statutory or regulatory provisions and the provisions or principles of international conventions, particularly in the transport area.[120] The extent to which the UCTD could also serve the protection of passengers in the platform economy will be explored in the following chapter. As was mentioned before, the act only applies to business-to-consumer contracts, which may *prima facie* render it unsuitable for the analysed spheres of contracting, especially in the collaborative economy. In fact, however, the opposite is true: in triangular relationships established via online platforms non-individually negotiated terms are usually those set forth by platform operators, who generally qualify as traders. The situation may be more problematic from the perspective of business users of online platforms, whose contracts may be qualified as ones between two businesses. While this aspect does not belong to the core of this book, it is worthy of note that EU law is also increasingly concerned with this group of users.[121]

### 6.4.2 *Choice-Enhancing Instruments Following Contract Conclusion*

Unlike in case of the right to withdraw in Directive 2011/83/EU on consumer rights, or the contract transfer or termination at a fee in Directive 2015/2302 on package travel and linked travel arrangements, increased choice in passenger rights regulations is linked to travel complications, which arise on the part of the carrier. These may transpire already prior to the departure, for example when a cancellation of a previously planned journey becomes necessary. As soon as the carrier "reasonably expects" that a situation of this kind will arise, it should not only inform the passengers of this fact, but also offer them a choice between re-routing or reimbursement of the ticket price.[122] The requirement to inform passengers of the envisaged complications seeks to allow the latter to readjust their plans, including by making entirely new arrangements, which the choice between re-routing and reimbursement makes possible. On top of this, passengers may be granted a right to standardised compensation, provided that conditions set out for particular transport modes are fulfilled. From the

[120] Article 1(2) of Directive 93/13/EEC on unfair terms in consumer contracts. See also judgment of the Court of Justice of 7.11.2019 in case C-349/18 *Kanyeba*, paras. 57–63.

[121] Regulation (EU) 2019/1150 of the European Parliament and of the Council of 20.6.2019 on promoting fairness and transparency for business users of online intermediation services [2019] OJ L186/57. On the limitations of this legal act, see Iamiceli (2019), pp. 409–410.

[122] Article 19(1) of Regulation 181/2011 on the rights of passengers in bus and coach transport.

perspective of choice enhancement, of interest is especially the compensation scheme laid down in Article 19(2) of Regulation 181/2011. The provision essentially sets out a sanction for the carrier's failure to offer the passenger the choice between continuation, re-routing or reimbursement and equips the latter with the right to compensation amounting to 50% of the ticket price, in addition to the reimbursement. As such, it forms part of the choice-enhancement framework, generally tending towards need ethics, but at the same time offering a balanced solution, particularly when compared to the standardised compensation scheme in the air transport sector.[123] It is not entirely clear why Regulation 181/2011 on the rights of passengers travelling by bus and coach does not additionally provide for a solution similar to the one known from regulations on passenger rights in rail and waterborne transport. To recall, under Article 19(1) of Regulation 2021/782 on rail passenger rights, passengers are entitled to request compensation of between 25% and 50% of the ticket price, depending on the duration of delay, without losing their right of transport. Following the Court of Justice, compensation of this kind reflects the consideration provided for a service which was not ultimately supplied in accordance with the transport contract,[124] and therefore fulfils a different function than the aforementioned Article 19(2) of Regulation 181/2011. Nonetheless, the purpose of this book is not to propose adjustments to existing norms of passenger rights in markets, which are already covered by a certain degree of passenger protection. Key observation in respect of present analysis is that none of the instruments of choice enhancement discussed above apply to the areas of travel sector mostly transformed by the platform economy. They could, nevertheless, provide a model to inform future debates about an increased consumer protection—in the passenger transport market and beyond.

### 6.4.3 *Safety and Performance*

Another prominent domain of EU transport law, in which extensive measures have been taken, is linked to safety and performance. In both cases, the established framework is based primarily on the need ethic, reflecting vulnerability of passengers, and partly even broader groups of individuals, to detriment linked to transport activities. Weaknesses of this kind are linked not only to the perception that the relevant parties may struggle to exercise self-reliance, but also to their weaker position as loss bearers.[125] In the context of passenger transport services, the former may especially arise with respect to reimbursement of the price paid for services not performed or performed inadequately or the passengers' claims for alternative performance. The latter concerns, for example, the impact of accidents and other travel complications, such as distress, loss of time, or inconvenience in personal lives,

[123] On the nature of the compensation for delays in air transport, see judgment of the Court of Justice of 10.1.2006 in case C-344/04 *IATA and ELFAA*, paras. 45–46 and judgment of the Court of Justice of 23.10.2012 in case C-581/10 *Nelson and Others*, paras. 46–55.

[124] Judgment of the Court of Justice of 26.9.2013 in case C-509/11 *ÖBB-Personenverkehr*, para. 38.

[125] See Willett (2018), p. 187.

which affect passengers (or other injured parties) particularly intensely, regardless of their formal status.[126]

Similarly to the other aspects of passenger protection, also in respect of safety and performance an overarching pattern of harmonisation can be observed across all transport modes. Focusing on road transport, which remains directly related to the platform economy, measures taken with regard to the construction of cars, requirements for driving licenses and compulsory use of seat belts illustrate the impotence of increasing general traffic safety. However, harmonisation of additional requirements in the field of passenger transport has been limited to larger vehicles. While the applicable national and local rules may be well-placed to fill this gap, the observed developments suggest that requirements for drivers, and in some jurisdictions—platform operators, particularly in the model rides-on-demand, may differ sharply. Considering that the relevant services are often used by recipients from various Member States, which the shift towards mobile applications further promotes, a case could be made for at least a set of minimum common safeguards. Although further measures to bring the number of accidental and non-accidental harms in road transport down are indeed considered by EU institutions, and safety implications of the novel mobility patters are part of this discussion, the analysis appears to be at an early stage. So far the focus has remained on shared vehicles (car-sharing) and not so much on ride-sharing and rides-on-demand.[127] Nonetheless, instances of reckless driving or sexual misconduct, which have been reported to occur in the latter models, illustrate that significant risks also exists in this domain.[128] For the time being, a common level of protection appears to be derived from contract-based and other voluntary efforts of platform operators, which, as was said, may turn out insufficient.

An important aspect of passenger protection, closely interlinked with the safety dimension, concerns liability in respect of the use of vehicles and associated insurance norms. As was mentioned before, Directive 2009/103/EC requires Member States to ensure that civil liability in respect of the use of vehicles normally based in their territory is covered by insurance. Although the extent of the liability covered and the terms of the cover are determined on the basis of national law, Directive 2009/103/EC does, in fact, provide for a significant measure of harmonisation. Worth highlighting is especially Article 12(1), which, while remaining without prejudice to civil liability, provides that the compulsory insurance should cover liability for personal injuries to all passengers, other than the driver, arising out of the use of a vehicle. The importance of protecting passengers, as a particularly vulnerable

---

126 Sanches Lima (2018), pp. 155–173. See also Enchelmaier (2005), pp. 237–238.

127 European Commission, 'Commission Staff Working Document: EU Road Safety Policy Framework 2021–2030 - Next Steps towards "Vision Zero"' (2019), p. 3, 17.

128 Conger (2019) Uber says 3045 sexual assaults were reported in U.S. rides last year. The New York Times, 5 December 2019. See also Gajewska (2023) Interpelacja nr 38,836 do prezesa Rady Ministrów w sprawie zmian w przepisach zwiększających poziom bezpieczeństwa pasażerów zamawiających przejazdy „na aplikację".

category of potential victims, has been underlined by the Court of Justice.[129] The Court also gave a broad interpretation to key elements of the insurance framework, such as the notion of the "use of a vehicle".[130] As was mentioned before, liability for accidents has not been harmonised at either EU or international level, yet the EU motor insurance rules have been described as a form of "shadow tort regime".[131] At the most general level, the principle of strict liability appears to be the dominant direction of national liability norms in the analysed area, even though the scope of relevant exceptions may differ. Some Member States, for example, provide for a lighter liability regime in case of the so-called "courtesy rides", which may *prima facie* seem relevant to the ride-sharing model.[132] The exception itself, however, appears to lose importance in domestic laws, in line with the broader push from the EU to extend liability, and, in any case, does not appear to correspond with remunerated nature of relationships established in the platform economy.[133] Article 13 of Directive 2009/103/EC furthermore prevents the exclusion from insurance, by law or by contract, of the use or driving of vehicles by (a) persons who do not have express or implied authorisation to do so, (b) persons who do not hold a licence permitting them to drive the vehicle concerned, and (c) persons who are in breach of the statutory technical requirements concerning the condition and safety of the vehicle concerned. The extent of permitted exclusion clauses is especially relevant to the model of rides-for-demand, whose legal status is often underdeveloped or remains in flux in a number of Member States.[134] In particular, it is feared that the lack of an insurance required for traditional taxis may endanger passenger interests in case of an accident.[135] In view of Article 13 of Directive 2009/103/EC, and the case law of the Court of Justice which, in general, tends towards increased protection of the injured parties, considerations of this kind appear to be unfounded. Nonetheless, confirmation of the advocated pro-consumer line of reasoning as part of judicial or legislative action would be useful to dispel any doubts.

While Directive 2009/103/EC does provide important protection in case of personal injuries incurred by passengers arising out of the use of a vehicle, further-reaching insurance, for example, offering assistance in case of a breakdown, is not

---

[129] Judgment of the Court of Justice of 1.12.2011 in case C-442/10 *Churchill Insurance Company and Evans*, ECLI:EU:C:2011:799, para. 27.

[130] See, in particular, judgment of the Court of Justice of 4.9.2014 in case C-162/13 *Vnuk*, para. 56 and the judgment of the Court of Justice of 20.6.2019 in case C-100/18 *Línea Directa Aseguradora*, ECLI:EU:C:2019:517. This judicial expansion has triggered a legislative response, see Directive (EU) 2021/2118 of the European Parliament and of the Council of 24.11.2021 amending Directive 2009/103/EC relating to insurance against civil liability in respect of the use of motor vehicles, and the enforcement of the obligation to insure against such liability [2021] OJ L430/1.

[131] Davey (2017), p. 240.

[132] See e.g. Article 436 of the Polish Act of 23.4.1964 – Civil Code (*Kodeks cywilny*), Dz.U. 2024 poz. 1061.

[133] Ludwichowska (2009), pp. 70, 73–75.

[134] Consider, for example, the recent reform of the Polish Act on road transport, Dz.U. 2024 poz. 1539.

[135] Mazur et al. (2018), p. 118.

part of this framework. At the same time, the need for such assistance has been recognized by the EU legislator in the case of passengers travelling by bus and coach. Pursuant to Article 8 of Regulation 181/2011 the carrier is required to provide reasonable and proportionate assistance with regard to the passengers' immediate practical needs following the accident arising out of the use of the bus or coach. The provision applies to regular and occasional long-distance bus and coach transport services, suggesting that the remoteness of the passenger from his or her point of departure may be a factor to consider. It does not apply to passengers travelling by other means of road transport such as passenger cars used in the models of ride-sharing and rides-on-demand. However, Regulation 181/2011 may arguably still be used as a point of reference with respect to the platform economy. As was shown in Chap. 3, platform operators may already take voluntary steps, including related to assistance and insurance, which are normally associated with the position of the carrier. Thus, *de lege ferenda* an extension of existing norms on assistance could be envisaged, taking into account the multi-party nature of the analysed platform settings.

Finally, as far as performance is concerned, key elements of harmonised passenger protection framework concern cancellations or delays. Less emphasis is placed, among others, on the standard of vehicles, which appears to be left to applicable market access requirements for coach and bus services and the general requirements on vehicle construction. However, the recently proposed amendments, including to Regulation 181/2011, also require carriers to establish service quality standards and implement quality management systems.[136] Regarding cancellations and delays, passenger rights are strongly interlinked with the previously discussed instruments of choice enhancement and, in the case of transport by road, are similarly linked to Regulation 181/2011. Logically, therefore, the relevant provisions do not apply to the passenger transport by car, but are limited to bus and coach. The emerging gap is also not filled by the otherwise applicable norms, even though the importance of timely reimbursement for consumer confidence-building, had been recognized already in Directive 97/7/EC.[137] Also in this respect, therefore, protection appears to be based on the self-commitment of platform operators, some of which may even combine the roles of carriers and terminal managing bodies. Firstly, all analysed operators engage in reimbursement in case of cancellations. They appear to do so in their capacity as payment services provides, which I will further address later in the book. Secondly, operators of ride-hailing platforms are additionally well-equipped to provide alternative connections if the driver originally matched does not arrive. Correspondence between these self-assumed roles and the role of carriers under passenger rights regulations is least pronounced in respect of compensation on top of reimbursement, which may only be provided at the operator's full discretion. Even though the applicable norms on passenger rights provide for a range of

[136] European Commission, Proposal for a Regulation of the European Parliament and of the Council amending Regulations (EC) No 261/2004, (EC) No 1107/2006, (EU) No 1177/2010, (EU) No 181/2011 and (EU) 2021/782 as regards enforcement of passenger rights in the Union, COM(2023) 753 final, Article 4(7).

[137] Articles 7(2) and 7(3) of Directive 97/7/EC on distance contracts.

models, neither of them appears to be reflected in the market practice. The analysed private governance frameworks appear to be particularly robust in the case of reimbursement and, to a more limited degree, re-rerouting (alternative performance). As a matter of fact, a similar conclusion can also be reached in respect of operators active in the market for tourism accommodation. This shows that platform providers are increasingly able to assume or support the responsibilities traditionally associated with direct contractors. They are able to do so because of their specific matchmaking (and often market-making) role as well as their significant size and resources, fuelled by the network effects and winner-takes-all market dynamic. Legislators wishing to provide a stronger legal basis for the current practices in analysed markets or extend the level of consumer protection so as to include, for example, standardised compensation could do so in either a regulatory or co-regulatory fashion, which I further explore in the next part of the book.

## 6.5 Conclusions

To conclude, even though the transport sector has traditionally been treated as a separate field, the development of a harmonised framework for passenger protection tends to follow the patterns of the internal market policy. Unlike in the latter domain, the role of consumer (passenger) protection in the EU measures in the transport sector does not trigger heated debates from a primary law perspective. Broadly framed competence norms of Article 91 and 100(2) TFEU appear to make notions such as "consumer confidence" less relevant. Ensuring a high level of passenger protection, taking account of the requirements of consumer protection in general, seems more readily accepted as a self-standing goal to be pursued. Paraphrasing Hesselink, both norms could potentially justify the vision of the EU transport market as a market that is equipped with institutions, which provide at least a minimal level of protection against unjust market conduct, not merely against consumers in formally defined B2C relations, but also against professionals and peers.[138] Still, a connection between the internal market and common transport policy remains strong and many of the safeguards put in place in the latter field appear to be well-suited to increase passengers' confidence in the EU transport sector and incentivize overall mobility. To recall, as argued by Wilhelmsson[139] and Twigg-Flesner,[140] what a confident consumer really needs is easy access to a counterparty as well as direct regulation of products and services. Paradoxically, the types of legal interventions envisaged by both authors seem more common in EU transport law than in the general consumer protection *acquis*. What is more, the norms adopted in the transport sector are generally not limited to formal B2C relationships.

[138] Hesselink (2016), pp. 450–451.

[139] Wilhelmsson (2004), pp. 329–332.

[140] Twigg-Flesner (2016), p. 200.

Indeed, the notion of consumer, in the narrow, status-based understanding, appears to be of marginal importance to the common transport policy. Instead, a broader concept of a "passenger" assumes a central role. A general tendency to expand the scope of passenger protection across its different aspects is visible in all transport modes. Already in the early days of EU integration attention has been paid to the measures improving transport safety and security. These, have gradually been complemented with further important safeguards of passenger rights, partly developed against the background of existing international norms, partly reflecting a more genuinely EU approach.[141] In 2011, the White Paper on the Roadmap to a Single European Transport Area noted that the EU has already established a comprehensive set of passengers' rights, which need to be consolidated further.[142] The relevant safeguards are indeed rather extensive and follow a characteristic pattern, with specific adaptations according to the transport mode, as endorsed by the Court of Justice.[143] Besides safety and mandatory insurance requirements, rules on delays and cancellations belong to common themes. In some areas, harmonisation also extends to liability rules for personal injury and damage to baggage, even though approximation of these aspects of private law has traditionally remained controversial. Equally important are passenger rights to information and care as well as special categories of rights of persons with disabilities or with reduced mobility. The harmonised framework is generally applicable irrespective of whether a passenger is travelling domestically or across borders, although certain limitations may apply and the types of transport services subject to EU regulation are primarily those of more than local relevance. Still, as Regulation 2021/782 on rail passenger rights shows, key passenger protections can be provided even for urban transport.

While existing norms of transport law do provide a certain level of protection also in the platform economy, an asymmetry between the legal safeguards of passenger interests in traditional and platform-driven mobility patterns remains significant. Importantly, this finding equally applies to instruments based on self-reliance and need ethics. As regards the former, it is not unlikely that the identified asymmetry is unintended and follows from the lack of synchronization between the scope of different norms. Most illustratively, the non-applicability of the provisions of the Services Directive on information and complaints to services in the field of transport seems to rely on the assumption that necessary safeguards are afforded in sectoral norms. As the previous analysis has shown, however, the latter fail to address all areas of passenger transport. With the growing role of services provided in the model of ride-sharing and rides-on-demand, available all over the EU from a single platform, the identified protection gap may be assessed as both non-negligible and unjustified.

In respect of the provisions more akin to the need ethic, the asymmetry between traditional and new mobility patterns is more difficult to assess. As far as vehicle

---

[141] Petit Lavall (2013), p. 65.

[142] European Commission, 'White Paper. Roadmap to a Single European Transport Area - Towards a Competitive and Resource Efficient Transport System' (2011) COM(2011) 144 final, p. 12.

[143] Karsten (2013), p. 36.

safety and insurance covering personal injuries arising out of the use of vehicles (and, indirectly, the associated liability) are concerned, a baseline level of protection appears to be in place for all road passengers. However, more specific safety risks associated with passenger transport in the platform economy may potentially remain unaddressed. In respect of performance, the level of protection provided by applicable norms in traditional models of passenger transport appears to deviate strongly from the one available in the models of ride-sharing and rides-on-demand. This is primarily the case for standardised protection instruments, such as assistance in case of accidents, delays or cancellations, re-routing or reimbursement and potentially compensation. As the previous analysis of private governance frameworks has shown, platform operators are often well-placed to provide protections of this kind. However, considering the latter's discretionary nature, one can doubt whether operators alone can ensure a "high level" of consumer protection. In my view, private governance frameworks can rather serve as a valuable reference point for a common (co-)regulatory approach, taking the operators' role into account. A tendency of this kind can already be observed in certain EU countries as well as jurisdictions outside of Europe, most notably in the United States.[144]

Overall, while the platform-driven transformation of the transport sector has been noticed by both EU institutions and the Member States, the ongoing discussion is yet to bring tangible results.[145] The main problem, which has been considered so far, is whether operators of passenger transport platforms qualify as providers of information society services or services in the field of transport.[146] As was noted in Chap. 4, an answer to this question defines the scope of Member States' discretion in the regulation of relevant operators. What attracts somewhat less attention is that the same finding also determines the relevant policy and competence norms available to the EU legislature, should a common approach be sought. Ultimately, the conclusion reached on this point may be less pertinent than it seems at first sight. This is because, as far as the protection of consumers concluding, or seeking to conclude, standalone contracts for single transport services is concerned, a case for a corresponding EU action can potentially be made on grounds of both internal market and common transport policy. All of this calls for the reflection whether the platform-driven transformation of the travel sector should not meet with a clearer response from the European Union law and if so, what shape such a response could take.

---

[144] See generally Moran and Lasley (2017), p. 163, Wyman (2018), p. 129.

[145] See e.g. European Commission, 'Commission Staff Working Document. The Implementation of the 2011 White Paper on Transport "Roadmap to a Single European Transport Area—towards a Competitive and Resource-Efficient Transport System" Five Years after Its Publication: Achievements and Challenges' (2016) SWD(2016) 226 final. See also European Commission, 'Communication from the Commission to the European Parliament, the Council, the European Economic and Social Committee and the Committee of the Regions. A European Agenda for the Collaborative Economy' (2016) COM(2016) 356 final. For Germany, see e.g. Domurath (2017), pp. 106–107.

[146] Judgment of the Court of Justice of 20.12.2017 in case C-434/15 *Asociación Profesional Elite Taxi (Uber Spain)*, operative part.

## References

Balfour J (2016) Luxembourg v Montreal: time for the Hague to intervene. In: Bobek M, Prassl J (eds) Air passenger rights: ten years on. Hart Publishing, pp 65–73

Ben-Shahar O, Schneider CE (2014) More than you wanted to know the failure of mandated disclosure. Princeton University Press

Davey J (2017) A compulsory diet of chickens and eggs: the EU motor insurance directives as a shadow tort regime. In: Giliker P (ed) Research handbook on EU tort law. Edward Elgar, pp 239–272

de Vries A (2016) Travel intermediaries and responsibility for compliance with EU travel law: a scattered legal picture. J Eur Consum Mark Law 5(3):119–125

Dempsey PS, Johansson SO (2010) *Montreal v. Brussels*: the conflict of laws on the issue of delay in international air carriage. Air Space Law 35(3):207–224

Domurath I (2017) Verbraucherrecht in der Plattformökonomie. In: Micklitz H-W, Reisch LA, Joost G, Zander-Hayat H (eds) Verbraucherrecht 2.0—Verbraucher in der digitalen Welt. Nomos, pp 103–134

Ehlermann CD (1987) The internal market following the single European act. Common Mark Law Rev 24(3):361–409

Enchelmaier E (2005) Consumer interests and contract law in the draft directive on services in the internal market. ERA Forum 6(2):232–244

Hesselink MW (2016) European private law in the division of moral responsibility between the EU, its member states and their citizens. Yearb Eur Law 35(1):410–452

Hojnik J (2016) Legal challenges of the railway liberalisation in the EU. In: Bodiroga-Vukobrat N, Rodin S, Sander G (eds) New Europe—old values? Springer, Reform and perseverance, pp 215–234

Howells G (2005) The potential and limits of consumer empowerment by information. J Law Soc 32(3):349–370

Huttunen M (2013) The development of the air transport policy of the European Union from the point of view of the consumer: from the creation of the internal market to the regulation of consumer rights proper. In: Benyon F (ed) Services and the EU citizen. Hart Publishing, pp 9–24

Iamiceli P (2019) Online platforms and the digital turn in EU contract law: unfair practices, transparency and the (pierced) veil of digital immunity. Eur Rev Contr Law 15(4):392–420

Karsten J (2007) Passengers, consumers, and travellers: the rise of passenger rights in EC transport law and its repercussions for community consumer law and policy. J Consum Policy 30(2):117–136

Karsten J (2013) Travel and tourism. In: Benyon F (ed) Services and the EU citizen. Hart Publishing, pp 25–46

Komorek E (2014) From protected national markets to networked governance? Regulatory revolution in the EU aviation sector. In: Fenwick M, Van Uytsel S, Wrbka S (eds) Networked governance, transnational business and the law. Springer, pp 13–38

Ludwichowska K (2009) Odpowiedzialność cywilna posiadacza samochodu przy przewozie z grzeczności (zasada winy czy ryzyka). PiP 2:68–77

Mazur J, Włoch R, Śledziewska K (2018) Taksówkarz – cyfrowy przedsiębiorca. DELab UW

McClean D (2016) EU law and the Montreal convention of 1999. In: Bobek M, Prassl J (eds) Air passenger rights: ten years on. Hart Publishing, pp 57–64

Moran M, Lasley P (2017) Legislating transportation network companies. Transp Res Rec 2650(1):163–171

Petit Lavall V (2013) Regulation (EU) No 1177/2010 and protection of passengers in sea and inland waterway transport. Eur J Commer Contr Law 5(3):65–72

Rossi Dal Pozzo F (2015) EU legal framework for safeguarding air passenger rights. Springer

Sanches Lima MG (2018) Traveller vulnerability in the context of travel and tourism contracts: a comparison of Brazilian and EU law. Springer

Schroten A, van Essen H, van Wijngaarden L, Sutter D, Andrew E (2019) Sustainable transport infrastructure charging and internalisation of transport externalities: main findings. European Commission

Seizov O, Wulf AJ, Luzak J (2019) The transparent trap: a multidisciplinary perspective on the design of transparent online disclosures in the EU. J Consum Policy 42(1):149–173

Twigg-Flesner C (2016) The importance of law and harmonisation for the EU's confident consumer. In: Leczykiewicz D, Weatherill S (eds) The images of the consumer in EU law: legislation, free movement and competition law. Hart Publishing, pp 183–202

Wagner G (2006) Prävention und Verhaltenssteuerung durch Privatrecht – Anmaßung oder legitime Aufgabe? AcP 206(2–3):352–476

Weatherill S (2016) Contract law of the internal market. Intersentia

Wendehorst C (2016) Platform intermediary services and duties under the E-commerce directive and the consumer rights directive. J Eur Consum Mark Law 5(1):30–33

Wilhelmsson T (2004) The abuse of the "confident consumer" as a justification for EC consumer law. J Consum Policy 27(3):317–337

Willett C (2018) Re-theorising consumer law. Common Law J 77(1):179–210

Wyman KM (2018) The novelty of TNC regulation. In: Davidson NM, Finck M, Infranca JJ (eds) The Cambridge handbook of the law of the sharing economy. Cambridge University Press, pp 129–140

# Part III
# Horizontal Norms and Future Outlook

# Chapter 7
# Horizontal Norms on Unfair Commercial Practices and Unfair Contract Terms

## 7.1 Preliminary Remarks

As seen from the previous analysis, the scope of consumer protection in EU law remains uneven and important gaps in EU sectoral rules can be identified. Consumer protection measures are often limited by the status-based approach which appears to overemphasise just one facet of the weaker position. The situation is different for certain EU measures protecting consumers as service recipients, including in the travel sector.[1] Still, due to the fragmentation of the overall framework, further exacerbated by the partial separation of the internal market and common transport policies, the reality of online travel platforms is largely missed by the studied provisions. This raises the question of whether existing horizontal norms could fill the gaps in consumer protection. Before addressing this question, a few more general remarks about status-based rules are in order.

## 7.2 Potential and Limits of Status-Based Regulation

One of the key claims of this book is that the business-to-consumer distinction, focusing on the purposes for which both parties are acting, is an imperfect proxy of consumers' weaker position vis-à-vis the seller or service provider.[2] In addition, the status-based approach to consumer protection in EU law renders the applicable legal framework less responsive to the transformation of the market practice and contributes

[1] Most prominently in Directive 2006/123/EC on services in the internal market. For an illustration of the tendency to extend the scope of protective rules to B2B relationships, see Karsten (2007), p. 135. See also Nihoul (2008), p. 72; Nijenhuis (2013), pp. 55–60; Johnston (2016), pp. 96–97.

[2] Cafaggi (2013), p. 327.

 
A. Jabłonowska, *Consumer Protection and Online Travel Platforms*, Law, Governance and Technology Series 73, https://doi.org/10.1007/978-3-031-90170-6_7

to identified protection gaps. Such a consequence is especially observable in relation to the measures offering a higher level of protection, associated with need ethics.

Despite this criticism, standard rules of consumer law, limited to business-to-consumer relationships, should not be immediately discarded as unfit to increase the level of consumer protection in the transforming travel sector. To appreciate their role in the filling of protection gaps, a comprehensive view on the investigated phenomena must be taken. As noted in Chap. 2, a prominent characteristic of relationships established in the platform economy is their triangular character.[3] Consequently, even if the underlying contracts for short-term accommodation rental or passenger transport escape the B2C qualification, the same is not necessarily the case for the relationships between users and platform operators. Considering the essential role played by the latter, identification and interpretation of the legal norms applicable to their practices can be highly relevant.

The qualification of platform-user relationship is relatively unproblematic in a number of cases. First and foremost, platform operators generally act for purposes relating to their trade, business, craft or profession and therefore qualify as "traders".[4] On the other hand, individuals making use of online platforms in view of seeking access to services offered by the suppliers for reasons unrelated to their business, trade, craft or profession, generally do so in their capacity of formally defined "consumers". Consequently, horizontal EU rules on consumer protection—such as those laid down in Directives 93/13/EEC on unfair terms and 2005/29/EC on unfair commercial practices—can potentially be relied upon to improve the protection of consumers in their relationship with platform operators and, indirectly, with suppliers.

Further-reaching solutions, including a near automatic re-qualification of underlying relationships from peer-to-peer to B2C due to the involvement of a professional intermediary, are currently not represented under EU law.[5] A possible reclassification of the underlying contract as, in fact, a platform-user contract may be more imaginable in the light of the Court's case law in *Wathelet*[6] or *Uber Spain*.[7]

---

[3] Tereszkiewicz (2019), p. 143. Petersen et al. (2018), pp. 43–44.

[4] For further elaboration, see Commission Notice, Guidance on the interpretation and application of Directive 2005/29/EC of the European Parliament and of the Council concerning unfair business-to-consumer commercial practices in the internal market [2021] OJ C526/1, sec. 4.2.1. Similarly Narciso (2019), p. 567.

[5] A solution of this kind was reportedly adopted in Denmark. See Sørensen (2016), p. 17. The European Commission considered a similar proposal in prior policy debates, but currently appears to focus on the clarification of existing statuses. Cf. European Commission, 'Green Paper on the Review of the Consumer Acquis' (2007) COM(2006) 744 final, pp. 17–18 and European Commission, 'Communication from the Commission to the European Parliament, the Council, the European Economic and Social Committee and the Committee of the Regions. A European Agenda for the Collaborative Economy' (2016) COM(2016) 356 final, pp. 9–10. New information duties imposed on the providers of online marketplaces further support this finding. See also Devolder (2019), p. 52.

[6] Judgment of the Court of Justice of 9.11.2016 in case C-149/15 *Wathelet*, ECLI:EU:C:2016:840, paras. 41 and 45.

[7] Judgment of the Court of Justice of 20.12.2017 in case C-434/15 *Asociación Profesional Elite Taxi (Uber Spain)*, ECLI:EU:C:2017:981, paras. 37–41. The relevance of this interpretation for EU

To what extent the reasoning adopted in both judgments could become more universally relevant has been a matter of debate.[8] Most importantly from the present perspective, none of the further-reaching proposals signalled above would directly benefit consumers in the travel sector, considering the lack of harmonised provisions addressing the underlying relationships.

As seen from above, even without broadening of personal scope, horizontal EU rules on consumer protection can potentially be relied upon to improve the protection of consumers in their relationships with platform operators. The situation is less clear from the perspective of other groups of users. In particular, a question can be raised about the importance of the parties' formal status in the underlying relationships for their qualification in relationships with platform operators. Regulation 2019/1150 on promoting fairness and transparency for business users of online intermediation services (P2B Regulation)[9] attempted to resolve this question. The instrument refers to the "business users" of online intermediation services, defined as private individuals acting in a commercial or professional capacity who, or legal persons which, through online intermediation services offer goods or services to consumers for purposes relating to its trade, business, craft or profession. In doing so, the Regulation reaffirms that parties of this kind do not qualify as "consumers" in the narrow sense of the EU consumer protection *acquis*. At the same time, reference to the notion of a "user" underlines their passive position in the analysed relationship, one which—due to a specific type of asymmetry—deserves tailored protection. The advocated line of interpretation further implies that peer suppliers maintain their formal "consumer" status in relation to platform operators. If the purpose of the P2B Regulation is to reduce the asymmetry between platform operators and a specific category of platform service recipients, the exclusion of peer suppliers from the relevant safeguards would not seem justified, unless they already enjoy protection under the applicable rules. This finding is further supported by the fact that even professional suppliers offering goods or services to other businesses are not left entirely unprotected by the P2B Regulation. Indeed, on a closer look, the instrument is not really concerned with underlying relationships perceived on an individual basis. Hence, suppliers may still qualify as "business users" if at least some of their customers qualify as narrowly defined "consumers".

A final question concerns the qualification of the relationship between the platform operator and buyers and service recipients acting outside their personal capacity in underlying relationships, including business travellers. While sellers and service providers active on the platform may gradually progress from a "consumer"

contract law could have been tested by the Court in case C-311/15 *TrustBuddy*, concerning the potential qualification of the platform operator as a "creditor" under Directive 2008/48/EC on consumer credit, had the preliminary reference not been withdrawn by the referring court. See order of the President of the Court of Justice of 23.10.2015 in case C-311/15 *TrustBuddy*, ECLI:EU:C:2015:759.

[8] Tereszkiewicz (2018), pp. 907–911.

[9] Regulation (EU) 2019/1150 of the European Parliament and of the Council of 20.6.2019 on promoting fairness and transparency for business users of online intermediation services [2019] OJ L186/57.

(peer supplier) to a "business user" status,[10] the same is not true for buyers or service recipients. On the contrary, the purposes for which consumers act in underlying relationships may differ from one transaction to another. Qualification of their relationship with platform operators based on the nature of underlying relationships therefore is not the right way forward. Instead, a holistic view on the relationship between the platform operator and passive users should be endorsed. Consumers who use the platform for various purposes should therefore rather be assessed as parties to mixed-purpose relationships, referred to in recital 17 of Directive 2011/83/EU.[11] This opens the way to the qualification as B2C relationships also of those relationships in which consumers, at times, are using the platform for purposes related to their business, trade, craft or profession, but the trade purpose cannot be considered predominant in the overall context of the contract. Axiologically, an argument in favour of an even more extensive scope of protection can be made if the passive market position in each case also implies a position of weakness, as seems to be the case for consumers in the travel sector. For the time being, the fact remains that many EU legal instruments refer to "business" and "consumer" statuses. This is the case for the horizontal provisions on unfair commercial practices and unfair contract terms, which are discussed in more detail below.

## 7.3 Directive 2005/29/EC on Unfair Commercial Practices as a Safety Net in Relation to Private Governance by Code

### *7.3.1 Main Elements of the Framework and Its Role in Digital Markets*

The spectacular rise of online travel platforms would not have been possible without the private governance frameworks detailed in Chap. 3. Notably, mechanisms of this kind do not operate in the legal void. This is not only true for standard contract terms, to which we will turn later, but also for the means of governance embedded in the "code". In this regard, particular attention should turn to Directive 2005/29/EC on unfair commercial practices.[12] The Directive establishes an important safety net, as it contains a horizontal prohibition of unfair business-to-consumer commercial practices. As such, it remains of direct importance to relationships between consumers and platform operators.

---

[10] See e.g. the factors relevant to the qualification of a party as a "trader", including regular or frequent activity, laid out in the judgment of the Court of Justice of 4.10.2018 in case C-105/17 *Kamenova*, ECLI:EU:C:2018:808, para. 38.

[11] Similarly Loos and Luzak (2016), pp. 66–67.

[12] Wielsch (2019), p. 211.

Directive 2005/29/EC operates with a broad notion of "business-to-consumer commercial practices", defined in Article 2(d) as "any act, omission, course of conduct or representation, commercial communication including advertising and marketing, by a trader, directly connected with the promotion, sale or supply of a product to consumers." Article 3(1) further specifies that the Directive applies to practices, in which traders engage before, during and after a commercial transaction related to a product (covering both goods and services). Accordingly, not only a particular commercial message, but also the more general design of an online service, can potentially qualify as a commercial practice. The notion has been interpreted broadly by the Court of Justice, which found, among others, that the relevant conduct can also take place only on one occasion and affect only one consumer.[13]

The notion of a "commercial practice" is, however, not endless. Most notably, in *Kirschstein*, the Court stressed that commercial practices should not be confused with the product which is the subject of that transaction.[14] Accordingly, a national rule which "aims to determine the operator who is authorised to provide a service in a commercial transaction, without directly regulating the practices which that operator may subsequently implement to promote or dispose of the sales of that service, cannot be considered to relate to a commercial practice in direct connection with the provision of that service".[15] The Court thus draws the line between, on the one hand, promoting or marketing services and, on the other hand, the authorisation of an operator to provide such services. While the former dimension is covered by the UCPD, the latter falls outside its scope.

Although the outcome of the *Kirschstein* case seems logical, the line between products and commercial practices may in practice be difficult to draw. The Court was faced with similar problems under free movement law when it distinguished between restrictions placed on goods and "selling arrangements".[16] The distinction can be even more challenging when it comes to services, and especially digital services provided on a long-term basis. For example, should the design of a ranking system be treated as a commercial practice, a product feature, or possibly both? As discussed further in this section, rankings have already made their way to the Unfair Commercial Practices Directive but have also been analysed under the Digital Services Directive.[17] Ultimately, either the UCPD or the DSD will likely be applicable to different activities of platform operators and both acts can influence each other. In the following, the focus remains on the former, considering that its recent reforms explicitly engage with the platform economy.

[13] Judgement of the Court of Justice of 16.4.2015 in case C-388/13 *UPC Magyarország*, ECLI:EU:C:2015:225, paras. 41, 42 and 60.

[14] Judgment of the Court of Justice of 4.7.2019 in case C-393/17, *Kirschstein*, ECLI:EU:C:2019:563, para. 42.

[15] Ibid, para. 45.

[16] For a comparison with free movement law, see Jabłonowska (2019a), p. 244.

[17] On the relationship between the regulation of commercial practices and contractual conformity, see Schmidt-Kessel and Möllnitz (2022), pp. 106–109.

The prohibition of unfair commercial practices in the UCPD has a multi-layered structure. Firstly, Article 5(2) contains a general clause defining unfair commercial practices as practices which (a) are contrary to the requirements of professional diligence, and (b) materially distort or are likely to materially distort the economic behaviour with regard to the product of the consumer. Professional diligence is defined in Article 2(h) as the "standard of special skill and care which a trader may reasonably be expected to exercise towards consumers, commensurate with honest market practice and/or the general principle of good faith in the trader's field of activity". Unfairness of the practice is analysed from the perspective of the model consumer, who in general is considered to be reasonably well-informed and reasonably observant and circumspect, taking into account social, cultural and linguistic factors ("average consumer"), but in certain cases can also be a person whose characteristics makes him or her particularly vulnerable to unfair commercial practices ("vulnerable consumer").[18] Aside from the general clause, particular cases of unfairness are typified in Articles 6 to 9, covering misleading actions and omissions or aggressive commercial practices. If a given conduct fulfils their relevant conditions, an analysis of the general clause is no longer necessary.[19] Finally, Annex I lays down a black list of practices prohibited in all circumstances.

Broadly framed provisions of Directive 2005/29/EC offer a promising normative framework for the protection of consumers in the platform economy. The adaptable nature of the instrument was reaffirmed in the updated UCPD Guidance, published in 2021. Like its predecessor, the document contains a dedicated section examining the application of the UCPD to the platform economy, including its relationship with other legal acts governing the online sector. It is highlighted, among others, that a platform operator qualifying as a "trader" is required to act with a degree of professional diligence, commensurate to its specific field of activity and, especially, not to mislead the consumers by either action or omission.[20]

According to the Guidance, the UCPD should be considered complementary to the E-Commerce Directive (now the DSA), which is mindful not only of the interests of service providers, but also of consumer protection goals. As already mentioned, whether or not platform operators active in the travel sector can at all be qualified as host providers, and therefore enjoy protection under Articles 6 and 8 DSA (previously Articles 14 and 15 ECD), is not self-evident.[21] Even where this is

---

[18] Both concepts have met with controversy. For recent judicial developments see, in particular judgment of the Court of Justice of 14.11.2024 in case C-646/22, *Compass Banca*, ECLI:EU:C:2024:957, para. 59. On the notion of vulnerability, see Helberger et al. (2022), p. 175. See also Duivenvoorde (2023), p. 177.

[19] Judgment of the Court of Justice of 19.9.2013 in case C-435/11 *CHS Tour Services*, ECLI:EU:C:2013:574, para. 45.

[20] Commission Notice, Guidance on the interpretation and application of Directive 2005/29/EC (2021), sec. 4.2.1.

[21] See, in particular, judgment of the Court of Justice of 12.7.2011 in case C-324/09 *L'Oréal and Others*, ECLI:EU:C:2011:474, paras. 115–116. See also Narciso (2019), pp. 570–573 and Hausemer et al. (2017a), p. 113. Cf. judgment of the Court of Justice of 20.12.2017 in case C-434/15 *Asociación Profesional Elite Taxi (Uber Spain)*, paras. 37–41. For criticism of the latter,

the case, the relevant safe harbour framework may turn out to be more limited than platform providers would wish. As argued by the Commission, a distinction should be made between the liability for own failures of platform operators, resulting in a breach of national provisions implementing the UCPD, and the liability for illegal information stored at the request of third parties.[22] Moreover, a tendency towards increasingly restrictive reading and gradual legislative adjustment of liability exemptions can be observed.[23]

Overall, regardless of the controversial interface with the safe harbour framework, the potential of the UCPD for addressing protection gaps in the platform economy appears to be significant. A number of reference points in this regard can already be derived from the Commission Guidance. While the interpretation proposed in the document has partly been viewed as overstretched,[24] it may nonetheless set the direction for future developments—in the field of unfair commercial practices law, as well as contract law and beyond.

### 7.3.2 Directive 2005/29/EC and Commercial Practices of Platform Operators

Firstly, pursuant to the Guidance on the implementation and application of Directive 2005/29/EC, compliance with the requirements of professional diligence under the general clause in Article 5(2) may imply that providers of online platforms enable relevant third party suppliers to comply with applicable requirements. As noted by the Commission, such a measures could involve, among others, "design[ing] their interfaces in a way that enables third party traders to present information to platform users in compliance with EU marketing and consumer law".[25] This wording closely resembles Article 31 DSA about compliance by design, yet the requirement of the UCPD can be more universal. Even though the Guidance explicitly refers to consumer law *stricto sensu*, a similar argument can, in my view, be made in respect of obligations stemming from other instruments, such as the Services and E-Commerce Directives. As was signalled before, for example, Article 22(1)(c) of the Services Directive requires service providers, whose activity is subject to an authorisation scheme, to inform service recipients about particulars of the relevant competent authority or the single point of contact. The importance of information about the

yet with a persuasive argument that Uber qualifies only as a provider of information society services in the broad sense, and not as a host provider in the meaning of Article 14 of Directive 2000/31/EC on electronic commerce, see Adamski (2018), p. 746.

22 Commission Notice, Guidance on the interpretation and application of Directive 2005/29/EC (2021), sec. 4.2.1.

23 Sartor (2017), pp. 22–23. See also Schulte-Nölke et al. (2020), pp. 35–37.

24 Adam and Micklitz (2017), pp. 70–74.

25 Commission Notice, Guidance on the interpretation and application of Directive 2005/29/EC (2021), sec. 4.2.1. This interpretation also finds support in the national case law. For the example of Germany, see Engert (2018), p. 345.

supplier and the main features of the service is further underlined in both the Services Directive, the E-Commerce Directive and the UCPD itself.[26] To comply with requirements of professional diligence under the UCPD, platform operators could therefore be required to at least allow the suppliers to display this information, while *de lege ferenda* an argument could be made for a further-reaching duty. Building upon the reasoning concerning obligations of the "trader acting in the name or on behalf of another trader",[27] shared responsibility in travel law, as well as Article 6a of the Consumer Rights Directive,[28] the platform operator could be involved even more directly in pre-contractual disclosure, which in turn could serve both information-sharing and warning functions. Increased responsibility of platform operators in this respect could also be derived from applicable codes of conduct, as is elaborated on further below.

On an even more extensive reading, the reasoning set out above in relation to information duties could be extended to the compliance with other regulatory provisions. The Guidance indeed makes reference to such norms—this time, however, outside the context of the platform economy. Specifically, in relation to car rental companies, the Commission takes note that national or local regulations can be of relevance to the analysis of the trader's compliance with the standard of professional diligence.[29] For illustration, an example of a German requirement for all vehicles to be equipped with snow tyres in winter is provided. According to the Commission, aside from the trader's obligation to provide vehicles with snow tyres, consumers should be informed about any additional, non-optional costs of this equipment at the start of the booking process.[30] In the platform economy, this could translate, for instance, into information about compliance with requirements to equip the accommodation with smoke and carbon monoxide detectors or to offer passenger transport services only with vehicles, which are adequately inspected and insured. It is worth recalling that confirming compliance with similar requirements had been recognized as important for consumers engaged in cross-border travel. To

[26] Cf. Article 22(1) of Directive 2006/123/EC on services in the internal market, Article 5(1) of Directive 2000/31/EC on electronic commerce and Article 7(4) of Directive 2005/29/EC on unfair commercial practices. By way of illustration, in the case of short-term accommodation rental mandatory information about the main features of the service could, potentially, extend to the presence of smoke and carbon monoxide detectors. Note that information about the existence of such detectors or the lack of corresponding data is already disclosed on Airbnb platform. See also Hausemer et al. (2017b), pp. 17–18.

[27] See judgment of the Court of Justice of 24.2.2022 in case C-536/20 *Tiketa*, ECLI:EU:C:2022:112, para. 31.

[28] See Article 4(5) of Directive 2019/2161 on better enforcement and modernisation of Union consumer protection rules, which imposes a duty on the providers of online marketplaces to inform the consumer "whether the third party offering the goods, services or digital content is a trader or not, on the basis of the declaration of that third party". For a further-reaching proposal, extending beyond the declaration-based approach, see Report of the European Law Institute: Model Rules on Online Platforms (2019).

[29] Commission Notice, Guidance on the interpretation and application of Directive 2005/29/EC (2021), sec. 4.3.5.

[30] Ibid.

recall, Article 4(2)(a) of the previously applicable Directive 90/314/EEC on package travel in conjunction with point c) of the Annex required the package travel contract to contain, among others, information about the compliance of the relevant accommodation with the rules of the host Member State concerned.

While the UCPD is not directly applicable to the underlying peer-to-peer relationships, platform operators, as the only professional parties involved, might be expected to bear a certain degree of responsibility in safeguarding consumer interests. In a similar vein, a 2018 study assessing the regulatory aspects affecting the collaborative economy in the tourism accommodation sector concludes that "cooperation of platforms with the authorities to facilitate compliance by accommodation providers […] would be beneficial".[31] Platform operators could potentially assume a share of responsibility in this regard based on the codes of conduct developed for this field. Such codes could, among others, promote the design of relevant web structures so that suppliers are prompted to make a statement about a variety of recurring elements in national requirements or to otherwise confirm their compliance with applicable norms.

Notably, a connection between the analysed framework of fairness control and codes of conduct has explicitly been established in the UCPD. More specifically, Article 6(2)(b) of Directive 2005/29/EC defines the conditions under which noncompliance by the trader with commitments contained in codes of conduct by which the trader has undertaken to be bound constitutes a misleading practice. Aside from the general prerequisite of behaviour distortion, the provision specifies that, for the non-compliance to qualify as misleading, the commitment must not be aspirational, but instead must be firm and capable of being verified, while the commercial practice must contain an indication that the trader is bound by the code. While the treatment of codes of conduct in the final text of the UCPD is not as well-articulated as in the original proposal,[32] the act does offer a starting point for greater accountability. Against this background, the development of codes of conduct for online platforms active in the travel sector, with regard to ensuring compliance with regulatory requirements and providing functionally equivalent mechanisms for reaching their objectives, is to be encouraged.[33] A robust data-sharing framework coordinated at the EU level, similar to the one established by Regulation 2024/1028, would greatly facilitate their operation.[34]

Also aside from the compliance of relevant third-party suppliers with applicable EU or national norms, Directive 2005/29/EC on unfair commercial practices can potentially assist consumers in getting verifiable information about their

[31] Ypma et al. (2018), p. 53.

[32] See also Cafaggi (2007), p. 171. Unfortunately, the Court of Justice has so far missed the opportunity to clarify the functioning of this framework. See judgment of the Court of Justice of 19.9.2018 in case C-109/17 *Bankia*, ECLI:EU:C:2018:735, para. 52–59 and Jabłonowska (2019b), pp. 30–31.

[33] Note that similar steps have already been taken in other areas, most notably in terms of counteracting online disinformation and hate speech as well as improving the presentation of information to consumers, see Podstawa (2019).

[34] Stemler (2017), pp. 130–132; Finck (2018b), p. 271.

counter-parties. In particular, a certain degree of platform-specific responsibility can be derived with regard to the criteria of access to the platform, transparency of search results and contractual conditions. Firstly, according to the Commission, platform operators might be expected to inform consumers how they select suppliers operating through their services and whether and, if so, what checks they perform in relation to their reliability.[35] The standard of care expected of platform operators according to this reading is not particularly rigorous. Nonetheless, the assessment should always be made on a case-by-case basis.

Secondly, if the platform operator plays a role in the final display of information to the consumer, for example by determining the ranking of products or certain conditions of the final offer, it should ensure that such presentation is not misleading. This point has been raised by the EU consumer protection authorities in an action taken as part of the Consumer Protection Cooperation (CPC) framework against Airbnb, Booking.com and Expedia. The authorities noted the difficulties in distinguishing between organic and sponsored search results as well as insufficient price information.[36] The operators responded by correcting their practices, while in the meantime increased transparency requirements for search results were explicitly added to the UCPD.[37]

A similar argument can, in my view, be made in respect of choice-enhancing instruments provided on a contractual basis, as is the case for cancellation policies offered by Airbnb and other operators in the travel sector. The Guidance engages with this problem in the context of air transport services, noting that "traders [who] advertise a specific flight ticket [...] should also indicate the cancellation policy that applies to that ticket (e.g. whether there is no refund or whether it is possible to change tickets)".[38] The document goes on to say that transparency of this kind is especially relevant where the fees charged by the carrier or the travel agent for cancelling the ticket amount to the actual cost of the ticket. References to "advertising" the ticket, and not necessarily acting as direct service provider, as well as to the role of travel agents, illustrate the importance of ensuring that standards of professional diligence are complied with in multi-party contexts.[39] The validity of this finding is not reduced by the fact that underlying services in the platform economy are often provided by non-professional suppliers. On the contrary, the fact that the platform

---

[35] Commission Notice, Guidance on the interpretation and application of Directive 2005/29/EC (2021), sec. 4.2.1.

[36] For an overview of CPC actions concerning short-term accommodation rental platforms, see <https://commission.europa.eu/live-work-travel-eu/consumer-rights-and-complaints/enforcement-consumer-protection/coordinated-actions/accommodation-booking_en>.

[37] Article 3(4)(b) of Directive 2019/2161 on better enforcement and modernisation of Union consumer protection rules, adding paragraph 4a to Article 7 of the UCPD, clarifying that general information on the main parameters determining the ranking of products presented to the consumer as a result of the search query and the relative importance of those parameters, as opposed to other parameters, shall be regarded as material information, the omission of which can be qualified as a misleading omission.

[38] Commission Notice, Guidance on the interpretation and application of Directive 2005/29/EC (2021), sec. 4.3.4.

[39] Similarly, from a contractual perspective, see Hauck and Blaut (2018), p. 1428.

operator is the only trader engaged in the transaction seems likely to increase the standard of special skill and care that may be expected of it.

The design of reputational feedback systems is a further field of platform operators' activities, which remains of relevance to consumer protection. Considering the central role of online reputation as the trust-building factor in most analysed platforms, unreliable reputation systems seem rather likely to affect the consumer's ability to make an informed decision, thereby causing him or her to take a transactional decision that he or she would not have taken otherwise.[40] Platform operators do not directly provide reputational information, but play an important role in how relevant ratings and reviews are actually perceived by consumers. It is thus not surprising that the subject is extensively covered by the Guidance document and that certain provisions particularising the standard of skill and care required of platform operators have also been added to the UCPD as part of recent reform.

The key adjustment made to the UCPD is the addition of paragraph 6 to Article 7 on misleading omissions, directed specifically at traders who provide access to consumer reviews, stipulating that information about whether and how the trader ensures that the published reviews originate from consumers who have actually used or purchased the product constitutes material information. Recital 49 of the Modernisation Directive 2019/2161 clarifies that information on relevant processes or procedures includes not only the question of how the checks are made, but also "how reviews are processed, for example, if all reviews, either positive or negative, are posted or whether those reviews have been sponsored or influenced by a contractual relationship with a trader". Such an extensive reading is to be welcomed from a consumer protection perspective, although it is regrettable that it does not feature more prominently in the Directive's normative part. Doubts can further be raised about the very notion of review, to which the provision refers. Arguably, the analysed term could also cover so-called ratings, for instance in the form of stars.[41]

Overall, Article 7(6) UCPD comes close to a disguised information duty, although it must be remembered that the qualification of information as material is only the first step in considering an associated commercial practice as misleading. To qualify as such, the omission of material information should further cause or be likely to cause the average consumer to take a transactional decision that he or she would not have taken otherwise. In any case, such a connection indeed seems rather plausible, considering the central role of online reputation for consumer decision-making in the platform economy. Not equipped with the information in question, consumers may be prompted to rely on reputation systems that, in fact, do not reflect genuine consumer experience and, for example, refrain from taking additional precautions before concluding a contract.

Differently from Articles 6 to 9 of Directive 2005/29/EC, an assessment of the impact on consumers' transactional decisions is not necessary in the case of blacklisted practices. Also in this respect, some small adjustments were made to the UCPD in 2019. Most notably, point 23b was added to Annex I qualifying as a misleading practice prohibited in all circumstances the act of "stating that reviews of a product

---

[40] Narciso (2019), p. 575.

[41] Ibid, p. 559.

are submitted by consumers who have actually used or purchased the product without taking reasonable and proportionate steps to check that they originate from such consumers". The provision should be viewed in the context of previously mentioned Article 7(6) of the UCPD. Against this background, a subtle yet crucial distinction has to be recognized between stating that particular reviews originate from previous buyers or service recipients and stating that steps are being taken to verify whether this is indeed the case. The wording of point 23b leaves room for interpretation and would benefit from additional clarification. Certain reference points can be found in the UCPD Guidance, which refers to steps such as requesting the reviewers to register, verifying IP addresses or deploying tools to automatically detect fraudulent activity.[42]

An openness to interpretation also characterises the second blacklisted practice related to reviews, added in point 23c of the UCPD. The provision refers to "submitting or commissioning another legal or natural person to submit false consumer reviews or endorsements, or misrepresenting consumer reviews or social endorsements, in order to promote products". As was noted before, reputational feedback provided in the form of ratings appear to fall under the notion of a review, while endorsements could be linked to more general expression of opinion, such as "likes" on social media.[43] It is debatable whether the practice of displaying consolidated ratings on the basis of opaque criteria could be analysed a possible case of "misrepresentation" of consumer reviews (German: *falsche Darstellung*, French: *déformer*). Similar concerns can be raised for other types of reputational feedback systems and include, among others, the problematic practice of suppressing genuine negative reviews.[44] At this stage, however, the analysed protection framework may be reaching its boundaries, which implies that safeguards for consumers in the platform economy cannot be based on the UCPD alone. The question can be asked whether, and if so, to what extent Directive 93/13/EEC on unfair terms in consumer contracts is suited for this task.

## 7.4 Directive 93/13/EEC on Unfair Terms as a Safety Net in Relation to Private Governance by Contract

### *7.4.1 Main Elements of the Framework and Its Role in Digital Markets*

Directive 93/13/EEC on unfair terms in consumer contracts belongs to the earliest measures on consumer protection adopted as part of the process of European integration. It applies to non-individually negotiated terms in business-to-consumer

[42] Commission Notice, Guidance on the interpretation and application of Directive 2005/29/EC (2021), sec. 4.2.4.

[43] On the notion of endorsement, see recital 49 of Directive 2019/2161 on better enforcement and modernisation of Union consumer protection rules.

[44] Commission Notice, Guidance on the interpretation and application of Directive 2005/29/EC (2021), sec. 4.2.4.

contracts, many of which found in the so-called standard conditions of business. Such an approach, combining elements of the standard-form contract model with a status-based consumer protection model,[45] excludes both non-individually negotiated terms in relationships other than B2C and individually negotiated terms in consumer contracts from the scope of harmonised safeguards. Unlike Directive 2005/29/EC on unfair commercial practices, the instrument is based on the principle of minimum harmonisation, which allows Member States to adopt or retain more stringent provisions in the relevant field, so as to ensure a greater degree of consumer protection.[46] The Directive is, therefore, by design, merely a contribution to fairness control, and not a comprehensive response to perceived power imbalances in the internal market.

Despite its modest scope and a baseline level of approximated safeguards, the UCTD has been recognized early on as a potential catalyst for further Europeanisation of private law.[47] Indeed, more than a quarter century since its adoption, a gradual development of autonomous EU concepts in the analysed field, supported by a robust procedural framework, can be observed.[48] What is more, legislative steps have recently been taken to also address contractual imbalances in relationships falling outside the scope of the UCTD, as is the case for the previously mentioned Regulation 2019/1150 on promoting fairness and transparency for business users of online intermediation services.[49] As an instrument designed more specifically with digital transactions in mind, the P2B Regulation provides an important point of reference for a possible further development of fairness control in the internal market—away from coherence-oriented adaptations and towards regulatory-instrumentalism.[50] *De lege lata*, however, in respect of the asymmetry between the platform operators and consumers, Directive 93/13/EEC on unfair terms in consumer contracts, and the previously discussed Directive 2005/29/EC on unfair commercial practices, maintain their central role.

The key element of the protection framework established by the UCTD is the statutory test, under which the fairness of contractual terms in B2C relationships is to be assessed, along with the associated transparency requirements.[51] Pursuant to Article 3(1), a contractual term which has not been individually negotiated shall be

---

[45] Wilhelmsson (2004), pp. 53–54.

[46] For a prominent illustration, see judgment of the Court of Justice of 3.6.2010 in case C-484/08 *Caja de Ahorros y Monte de Piedad de Madrid*, ECLI:EU:C:2010:309, para. 40–44, in which the Court found that Member States may authorise a judicial review as to the unfairness of contractual terms which relate to the definition of the main subject-matter of the contract, even in the case where those terms are drafted in plain, intelligible language.

[47] Hondius (1995), p. 242.

[48] Micklitz and Reich (2014), pp. 771–808.

[49] For another illustration, see Schebesta et al. (2018), p. 690.

[50] Twigg-Flesner (2018), pp. 223–224, 230–233. A similar distinction between generalist, adaptive and dedicated approaches is made by Iamiceli (2019), pp. 398–401.

[51] For a detailed overview, see Commission Notice, Guidance on the interpretation and application of Council Directive 93/13/EEC on unfair terms in consumer contracts [2019] OJ C323/4.

regarded as unfair if, contrary to the requirement of good faith, it causes a significant imbalance in the parties' rights and obligations arising under the contract, to the detriment of the consumer. Recital 16 further clarifies that the good faith requirement "may be satisfied by the seller or supplier where he deals fairly and equitably with the other party whose legitimate interests he has to take into account" while its assessment should take into account "the strength of the bargaining positions of the parties". As the Court elaborated in *Aziz*, in making this assessment national courts should consider "whether the seller or supplier, dealing fairly and equitably with the consumer, could reasonably assume that the consumer would have agreed to such a term in individual contract negotiations".[52] In turn, the assessment of a "significant imbalance" should consider, in particular, the rules of national law which would apply in the absence of an agreement by the parties in that regard.[53] This, however, is not the only reference point. In some cases, a "quantitative economic evaluation" may even be sufficient.[54]

Article 4(1) of Directive 93/13/EEC further lays down that the fairness control should take into account the nature of the goods or services for which the contract was concluded and refer, at the time of conclusion of the contract, to all the circumstances attending the contract conclusion and to all the other terms of the contract or of another contract on which it is dependent. As elaborated by the Court of Justice, the relevant circumstances can include, among others, the presence of unfair commercial practices,[55] while reference to other contracts potentially opens the way to the consideration of multi-party relationships.

Article 4(2) narrows down the scope of contractual clauses subject to the harmonised fairness test, stipulating that the assessment shall relate "neither to the definition of the main subject matter of the contract, nor to the adequacy of the price and remuneration, on the one hand, as against the services or goods supplies in exchange, on the other, in so far as these terms are in plain intelligible language".[56] Transparency is further underlined in Article 5, which provides that terms offered to consumers in writing must always be drafted "in plain, intelligible language"—a requirement that

[52] Judgment of the Court of Justice of 14.3.2013 in case C-415/11 *Aziz*, ECLI:EU:C:2013:164, para. 69.

[53] Ibid, para. 68.

[54] Judgment of the Court of Justice of 23.11.2023 in case C-321/22 *Provident Polska*, ECLI:EU:C:2023:911, para. 47.

[55] Judgment of the Court of Justice of 15.3.2012 in case C-453/10 *Pereničová and Perenič*, ECLI:EU:C:2012:144, para. 43 and Durovic (2015), pp. 730–732. See also recital 16 of Directive 93/13/EEC on unfair terms in consumer contracts, which notes that "in making an assessment of good faith, particular regard shall be had to the strength of the bargaining positions of the parties, whether the consumer had an inducement to agree to the term and whether the goods or services were sold or supplied to the special order of the consumer".

[56] Note, however, that the Member States may extend the scope of fairness assessment in line with the principle of minimum harmonisation. See judgment of the Court of Justice of 3.6.2010 in case C-484/08 *Caja de Ahorros y Monte de Piedad de Madrid*, para. 40–44.

has been broadly interpreted by the Court of Justice.[57] Where there is doubt about the meaning of a term, an interpretative rule of *contra proferentem* applies.[58]

The general clause is subsequently complemented with an indicative and non-exhaustive list of the terms which may be regarded as unfair, contained in Annex I. Member States may extend the scope of fairness control or establish further lists of unfair terms, but remain under an obligation to inform the Commission of this fact.[59] Overall, the framework of fairness control in the UCTD reflects a conundrum of different concepts, associated with both individual and collective protection of consumer interests.[60] The same is also true for the framework of remedies and procedural guarantees.[61]

To better understand the potential and limits of Directive 93/13/EEC as an instrument of consumer protection in the platform economy, it is useful to structure the discussion around the functions it assigns to the principle of good faith. In this respect, private law scholarship distinguishes between the functions of specifying/interpreting, complementing and modifying/limiting obligations.[62] Seen through this lens, the substantive fairness assessment provided for under the UCTD appears to aim primarily at limiting and, with important caveats, modifying as well as interpreting obligations. The main consequence of finding unfairness is laid down in Article 6(1), according to which unfair terms shall not be binding on the consumer and the contract shall continue to bind the parties upon those terms if it is capable of continuing in existence without the unfair terms. As the Court has numerously stressed, national courts are generally not empowered to revise the content of an unfair term, as it could weaken the dissuasive effect for sellers or suppliers.[63]

As seen above, the objective pursued by Directive 93/13/EEC consists in restoring the balance between the parties without abolishing all contracts containing unfair terms.[64] It is important to stress, however, that the consequence of removing unfair terms from the contract while preserving its overall validity only applies if the contract is "capable of continuing in existence" without such terms. In the latter regard, the Court of Justice recognized that national courts may exceptionally

---

[57] See generally Jabłonowska and Tagiuri (2023), p. 347.

[58] Note that, under the minimum standard of harmonization introduced, the *contra proferentem* rule does not apply to collective redress. For a comprehensive overview, see Waelkens (2015), p. 47.

[59] Article 8a added to Directive 93/13/EEC on unfair terms in consumer contracts on the basis of Article 32 of Directive 2011/83/EU on consumer rights.

[60] Micklitz and Reich (2014), pp. 773–774.

[61] In this respect, *ex officio* assessment and collective actions assume a major role. For the landmark case law, see judgment of the Court of Justice of 4.6.2009 in case C-243/08 *Pannon GSM*, ECLI:EU:C:2009:350, para. 35, judgment of the Court of Justice of 26.4.2012 in case C-472/10 *Invitel*, ECLI:EU:C:2012:242, para. 43 and judgment of the Court of Justice of 21.12.2016 in case C-119/15 *Biuro podróży Partner*, ECLI:EU:C:2016:987, para. 47.

[62] Pecyna (2009), p. 115.

[63] See e.g. judgment of the Court of Justice of 21.12.2016 in case C-154/15 *Gutiérrez Naranjo*, ECLI:EU:C:2016:980, paras. 56–66, judgment of the Court of Justice of 26.1.2017 in case C-421/14 *Banco Primus*, ECLI:EU:C:2017:60, para. 71 and the case law cited.

[64] Judgment of the Court of Justice of 15.3.2012 in case C-453/10 *Pereničová and Perenič*, para. 31.

replace an unfair contract term with a supplementary provision of national law in order to avoid contract nullity, if nullity would expose the consumer to particularly unfavourable consequences, so that the consumer would thus be penalised.[65] As the Commission summarised in its Guidance document, the finding whether or not continuity of the contract is possible requires a case-by-case inquiry as to whether the contract can, legally or technically, be performed without the unfair term.[66] A prominent instance of non-continuity, endorsed by the Court of Justice, is when a term defining its main subject matter or a term that is essential for the calculation of the remuneration to be paid by the consumer is removed.[67]

The importance of transparency is not limited to its undoubtedly crucial role in delineating the scope of fairness control under Article 4(2) of Directive 93/13/EEC. Transparency in the UCTD also assumes an interpretative and obligation-complementing function and, perhaps most importantly, takes part in substantive fairness assessment. As the Court recalled in *Verein für Konsumenteninformation*, unfairness of a term "may result from a formulation that does not comply with the requirement of being drafted in plain and intelligible language", which in itself must be interpreted broadly.[68] Together with (and as part of) the substantive fairness requirement, the principle of transparency thus prevents the trader from enjoying an unjustified margin of discretion when drafting, changing and applying the terms.[69] Such a conclusion finds additional support in the "grey list" annexed to the Directive, in which terms related to unilateral changes of contract terms and of product or service characteristics as well as termination clauses feature numerously and are only allowed if further conditions are fulfilled.[70] As a result, despite their concise wording, safeguards provided for under the UCTD appear, for the most part, to encompass the requirements of procedural fairness,[71] known among others from the P2B Regulation. The question, nonetheless, remains whether they go any further in

[65] See judgment of the Court of Justice of 30.4.2014 in case C-26/13 *Kásler and Káslerné Rábai*, ECLI:EU:C:2014:282, paras. 80–85 and judgment of the Court of Justice of 26.3.2019 in case C-70/17 *Abanca Corporación Bancaria*, ECLI:EU:C:2019:250, paras. 56–63.

[66] Commission Notice, Commission Notice, Guidance on the interpretation and application of Council Directive 93/13/EEC on unfair terms in consumer contracts (2019), sec. 4.3.2.

[67] See e.g. judgment of the Court of Justice of 30.4.2014 in case C-26/13 *Kásler and Káslerné Rábai*, para. 49, judgment of the Court of Justice of 14.3.2019 in case C-118/17 *Dunai*, ECLI:EU:C:2019:207, paras. 48 and 52 and judgment of the Court of Justice of 3.10.2019 in case C-260/18 *Dziubak*, ECLI:EU:C:2019:819, para. 44.

[68] The Court even went so far to say that "where the effects of a term are specified by mandatory statutory provisions, it is essential that the seller or supplier informs the consumer of those provisions", see judgment of the Court of Justice of 28.7.2016 in case C-191/15 *Verein für Konsumenteninformation*, ECLI:EU:C:2016:612, paras. 68–69.

[69] On transparency as non-arbitrariness, see Jabłonowska and Tagiuri (2023), p. 381.

[70] See especially paragraph 1 of the Annex to Directive 93/13/EEC on unfair terms in consumer contracts under (f), (g), (j) and (k) as well as paragraph 2 of the Annex under (b). For an in-depth analysis, see Loos and Luzak (2016), pp. 67–79.

[71] Iamiceli (2019), pp. 404–405.

"elucidating the actual regulatory regime set into force by [platform] operator[s]"[72] and, eventually, increasing the level of protection enjoyed by consumers in the platform economy.

### 7.4.2 Directive 93/13/EEC and Contract Terms of Platform Operators

The application of the UCTD to the standard terms of platform providers has met with some controversy. In particular, doubts have been raised whether the terms on the relationship between users (and not between users and platform operators) should at all be subject to fairness control. Arguing on the basis of German law, Schweitzer compared platform operators to sports associations, noting that the latter have traditionally enjoyed a broader margin of discretion in their exercise of rule-setting functions, provided they were driven by legitimate goals.[73] According to the author, to the extent that competition exists between distinct platforms, and as long as there are no indications of particular conflicts of interest within a given business model, a higher degree of discretion in the design of platform rules can be accepted.[74] One can nonetheless wonder if the level of competition between the providers of online travel platforms can be deemed sufficient.

A practical example of the potential and limits of Directive 93/13/EEC is the action taken against Airbnb as part of the Consumer Protection Cooperation (CPC) framework. The action focused on the operator's standard terms concerning the following subjects: applicable law and jurisdiction, survival of the terms, waiver by the provider of all liability and consumer's obligation to indemnify the provider, power to unilaterally change terms and conditions, power to remove user-generated content, power to unilaterally suspend or terminate the contract for any reason, refunds and pay-outs, collection of damage claims.[75] The CPC initiative led Airbnb to amend its terms and conditions for European users, which are currently more balanced and transparent, compared both to the previous versions and to the terms applicable to non-EU users.[76]

To illustrate the impact of the UCTD on platform terms, it is worth drawing attention to the clauses on liability, refunds, pay-outs and damage claims collection, singled out in the CPC action. The former are probably the most widely used clauses in online commerce and have long attracted the attention of legal scholars.[77] In par-

---

[72] Wielsch (2019), p. 207.

[73] Schweitzer (2019), pp. 7–8.

[74] Ibid, p. 8.

[75] CPC Authorities, Common Position of National Authorities within the CPC Network Concerning the Commercial Practices and the Terms of Service of Airbnb Ireland, pp. 4–12.

[76] For a US perspective on unfair terms control, see Caruso (2013), pp. 304–306.

[77] Meller-Hannich et al. (2019), p. 406.

ticular, an argument has been made that a full exclusion or a broad limitation of a trader's liability in standard terms significantly affects the balance between the rights and obligations of both parties and can be qualified as contrary to the requirement of good faith.[78] Consumer protection authorities and courts in the EU have taken a similar view in several cases, which has left an impact on the market practice.[79] At the same time, the removal of an unfair term—i.e. the central consequence of its unfairness—is a mere starting point for improving consumer protection. In this respect, a parallel might be drawn to the liability exemption in the E-Commerce Directive. Paraphrasing Peifer, similarly to liability privileges, the provisions on fairness control as applied to liability limitations are merely a filter, not a method.[80]

Secondly, as for refunds and pay-outs, the main objections of CPC authorities concerned the impreciseness of the relevant Airbnb terms. It was argued that the provider should specify, among others, the timeframe applicable to refunds. The document did not engage, however, with the actual crux of the matter, concerning the processes, pursuant to which the platform operator arrives at the conclusion that a certain refund or pay-out indeed needs to be made. The CPC authorities merely remarked that "the consumer should not be deprived of [his or her] right to exercise any legal remedy, particularly by being bound to a procedure which is not provided for by legal provisions".[81] From this, it arguably follows that "in case of a dispute between the parties to the contract, the collection of evidence, the burden of proof and the collection of damages should follow the provisions of the applicable law and should not be defined at the discretion of Airbnb".[82] This rather superficial treatment of the topic provides little clarity about procedural conditions in the dispute-handling procedures of platform operators and their relation to otherwise available enforcement pathways. The CPC action also does not elaborate on the instances in which it is the consumer who seeks redress from the supplier under the operator's contract terms. Thus, the current legal framework and its possible extension at national and EU levels invites further analysis.

## 7.5 Conclusions

The chapter considered the extent to which horizontal EU norms on unfair terms and commercial practices offer protection to consumers contracting via online platforms. It showed that both sets of norms apply to different aspects of private

---

[78] Similarly Loos and Luzak (2016), pp. 79–81, 87; Wauters et al. (2014), pp. 279–282.

[79] See e.g. an overview of the commitments made in 2020 by Expedia <https://commission.europa.eu/document/download/d6d08533-6955-4216-8e0a-67e0e51e0194_en>. See also Rustad and Onufrio (2012), pp. 1144–1148. In the Polish context, see Jagielska and Rauch (2016), p. 244.

[80] Peifer (2017), p. 624.

[81] CPC Authorities, Common Position of National Authorities within the CPC Network Concerning the Commercial Practices and the Terms of Service of Airbnb Ireland, p. 12.

[82] Ibid.

governance frameworks, namely to code and contract. As such, they can counter several problematic practices, such as skewed review systems and far-reaching liability limitations. Enforcement based on the UCPD and the UCTD can moreover inspire legislative action, as it has done in the case of compliance by design.

However, the studied horizontal norms also suffer from limitations. As for the UCPD, a question can be asked about the very notion of the "commercial practice". Indeed, the line between "commercial practices", on the one hand, and "qualities and performance features" of digital services, on the other, is not crystal clear. Also the reach of the UCPD fairness test has been the subject of debate. Much has been written about the concept of the average consumer, which sets a relatively high bar to consumer protection.[83] The recent judgment in *Compass Banca*, in which the Court confirmed that an individual's decision-making capacity may be impaired by constraints, such as cognitive biases, could lower this bar to some degree.[84] This could carry particular weight in the context of Article 5(2) UCPD, which, however, has barely been used so far. Procedural amendments, such as easing the burden of proof placed upon consumers,[85] could lead to increased litigation, and eventually more clarity. The European Commission took note of this issue in its recent Fitness Check report[86] but the possible legislative action is yet to take shape.

The discussion of standard terms control has similarly revealed both potential and limits. Like in the case of the UCPD, the scope of and benchmarks for analysis have been the subject of debate. Focusing on the substantive fairness test, a potential for further development of the current system could be sought in the criterion expressed in *Aziz*, according to which, in assessing the imbalance between the parties, account should be taken of the rules of national law which would apply in the absence of an agreement.[87] It is true that the mismatch between the legal framework at hand and the dynamically evolving market practice constitutes a recurring problem of the platform economy. Arguably, however, the provisions applicable to comparable business models could continue to provide a valid reference point—with necessary adjustments. Prior efforts to define the "Draft Common Frame of Reference" in EU private law could regain their significance in this regard.[88] Furthermore, the advocated approach could guide the assessment of other prominent platform terms, including those on refunds or pay-outs.[89]

---

[83] See e.g. Mak (2013), p. 333; Mak (2016), p. 384; Purnhagen and Schebesta (2020), p. 293.

[84] Judgment of the Court of Justice of 14.11.2024 in case C-646/22, *Compass Banca*, para. 59. For previous signs of this development, see Purnhagen (2017), p. 437.

[85] For a detailed discussion, see Rott (2024), p. 243.

[86] European Commission, 'Commission Staff Working Document. Fitness Check of EU consumer law on digital fairness' (2024) SWD(2024) 230 final.

[87] Judgment of the Court of Justice of 14.3.2013 in case C-415/11 *Aziz*, para. 68.

[88] For an overview, see Beale (2016), pp. 434–436.

[89] This could result in increased safeguards for the platform users in underlying relationships even if the terms of platform-user contracts would remain without, or with a limited, direct effect on the content of those relationships, in line with the principle of privity of contract. See Engert (2018), pp. 345–350. The question whether or not standard terms of platform operators may affect the

A further issue concerns the consequences of finding unfairness. As mentioned before, the existing EU framework is primarily geared towards removing unfair terms from consumer contracts. This does not affect the right of the parties to amend or replace an unfair contract term with a new one, within their contractual freedom, which may, to some extent, incentivise consensual resolution.[90] Similarly, a platform operator forced to remove certain terms can be inclined to amend them accordingly, if failure to do so comes with disadvantages. Still, a question can be asked whether a system more directly geared towards positive results would not be preferable. With this in mind, it is worth recalling another option considered during legislative and policy debates on unfair terms control, namely direct negotiations between the traders and the bodies with legitimate interests in protecting consumers. Such systems, at times coupled with dedicated out-of-court dispute resolution mechanisms, have been functioning in certain European jurisdictions for many years, arguably with promising results.[91] While the concept has not gained traction at the EU level, it may be worth revisiting, possibly "under the modern language of private regulation".[92] Prior research shows that standard-setting mechanisms for contracts, as well as other polycentric processes of co-regulation, could bring benefits in terms of better information and adaptability,[93] and support the EU market integration.[94] As such, a positive system for unfair terms control (or contract standardisation) for online travel platforms may indeed be promising. Regardless of the ultimate model chosen, for it to serve the interests of consumers, more information needs to be available on how standard terms are translated into internal rules and practices,[95] which is something that the DSA can hopefully help with.

In view of the above, while the role of the UCPD and the UCTD should not be underestimated, both directives do not preclude more targeted, positive obligations of platform operators, such as those found in the Digital Services Act. A further notable feature of the DSA is that it moves away from the status-based approach

---

interpretation of underlying contracts depends on national rules of private law. For Germany, see Engert (2018), p. 344; Meller-Hannich et al. (2019), p. 405.

[90] Judgment of the Court of Justice of 14.3.2013 in case C-415/11 *Aziz*, para. 32.

[91] European Commission, 'Report from the Commission on the Implementation of Council Directive 93/13/EEC of 5 April 1993 on Unfair Terms in Consumer Contracts' (2000) COM(2000) 248 final 24–25.

[92] As Hans Micklitz anticipated already a decade ago, noting that "by now there is an upcoming discussion on collective negotiation, mainly under the modern language of private regulation", see Micklitz (2010), p. 361. See also Cafaggi (2007), p. 163. The ideas of Europe-wide recommended general contract terms and a European code of conduct, which could be applied in cross-border ADR procedures, also fall within this line of reasoning, see Calliess (2008), p. 244; Calliess and Zumbansen (2010), pp. 166–180. On a related debate about polycentric co-regulation in the platform economy, see Finck (2018b), pp. 268–273.

[93] Finck (2018a), p. 60.

[94] The impact of private regulation on EU market integration has been demonstrated by Cafaggi and Janczuk (2010), p. 1.

[95] On the lack of transparency about the relevant decision-making processes, see Klonick (2018), p. 1639 and Wielsch (2019), pp. 203–204. On the importance of data-sharing in the co-regulation of the platform economy, see e.g. Finck (2018b), p. 271.

known from the established consumer directives. As noted earlier, some of its provisions are directly applicable to online travel platforms already now, and even extend to the collaborative economy. Other could be the source of inspiration *de lege ferenda*, next to further existing instruments like the E-Commerce[96] and Package Travel Directives[97] as well as passenger rights regulations. Possible adaptations of the existing legal framework with an eye on increased consumer protection in online travel platforms are discussed in the next chapter.

## References

Adam L, Micklitz H-W (2017) Verbraucher und Online-Plattformen. In: Micklitz H-W, Reisch LA, Joost G, Zander-Hayat H (eds) Verbraucherrecht 2.0 – Verbraucher in der digitalen Welt. Nomos, pp 45–102

Adamski D (2018) Lost on the digital platform: Europe's legal travails with the Digital Single Market. CML Rev 55(3):719–751

Beale H (2016) The story of EU contract law – from 2001 to 2014. In: Twigg-Flesner C (ed) Research handbook on EU consumer and contract law. Edward Elgar, pp 431–462

Cafaggi F (2007) Self-regulation in European contract law. EJLS 1(1):163–218

Cafaggi F (2013) From a status to a transaction-based approach? Institutional design in European contract law. CML Rev 50:311–329

Cafaggi F, Janczuk A (2010) Private regulation and legal integration: the European example. Bus Polit 12(3):1–40

Calliess G-P (2008) Transnational consumer law: co-regulation of B2C e-commerce. In: Dilling O, Herberg M, Winter G (eds) Responsible business: self-governance and law in transnational economic transactions. Hart Publishing, pp 225–258

Calliess G-P, Zumbansen P (2010) Rough consensus and running code: a theory of transnational private law. Hart Publishing

Caruso D (2013) Black lists and private autonomy in EU contract law. In: Leczykiewicz D, Weatherill S (eds) The involvement of EU law in private law relationships. Hart Publishing, pp 291–316

Devolder B (2019) Contractual liability of the platform. In: Devolder B (ed) The platform economy: unravelling the legal status of online intermediaries. Intersentia, pp 31–88

Duivenvoorde B (2023) Redesigning the UCPD for the age of personalised marketing – a proposal to redesign the UCPD's consumer benchmarks and general clauses. EuCML 12(5):177–184

Durovic M (2015) The subtle Europeanization of contract law: the case of Directive 2005/29/EC on unfair commercial practices. ERPL 23(5):715–749

Engert A (2018) Digitale Plattformen. AcP 218(2):304–376

Finck M (2018a) Digital co-regulation: designing a supranational legal framework for the platform economy. Eur Law Rev 43(1):47–68

Finck M (2018b) The sharing economy and the EU. In: Davidson NM, Finck M, Infranca JJ (eds) The Cambridge handbook of the law of the sharing economy. Cambridge University Press, pp 261–273

[96] Regarding personal scope, consider the use of default rules in the case of B2B relationships in Articles 10(1), 10(2), 11(1) and 11(2) of Directive 2000/31/EC on electronic commerce.

[97] Consider the more inclusive personal scope with more tailored exceptions reflected in Article 2(2)(c) of Directive 2015/2302 on package travel and linked travel arrangements, which excludes packages and linked travel arrangements purchased on the basis of a general agreement for the arrangement of business travel between a trader and another natural or legal person who is acting for purposes relating to his trade, business, craft or profession.

Hauck R, Blaut H (2018) Die (quasi-)vertragliche Haftung von Plattformbetreibern. NJW 20:1425–1430
Hausemer P, Rzepecka J, Dragulin M, Vitiello S, Rabuel L, Nunu M, Rodriguez Diaz A, Psaila E, Fiorentini S, Gysen S, Meeusen T, Quaschning S, Dunne A, Grinevich V, Huber F, Baines L (2017a) Exploratory study of consumer issues in online peer-to-peer platform markets – final report. European Union
Hausemer P, Rzepecka J, Dragulin M, Vitiello S, Rabuel L, Nunu M, Rodriguez Diaz A, Psaila E, Fiorentini S, Gysen S, Meeusen T, Quaschning S, Dunne A, Grinevich V, Huber F, Baines L (2017b) Exploratory study of consumer issues in online peer-to-peer platform markets: task 4 – case study: AirBnB. European Commission
Helberger N, Sax M, Strycharz J, Micklitz H-W (2022) Choice architectures in the digital economy: towards a new understanding of digital vulnerability. J Consum Policy 45(2):175–200
Hondius E (1995) The reception of the directive on unfair terms in consumer contracts by Member States. ERPL 3(2):241–255
Iamiceli P (2019) Online platforms and the digital turn in EU contract law: unfair practices, transparency and the (pierced) veil of digital immunity. ERCL 15(4):392–420
Jabłonowska A (2019a) Fine lines between national rules on 'products' and 'commercial practices': judicial déjà-vu in case C-393/17 Kirschstein. EuCML 8(6):244–246
Jabłonowska A (2019b) Wpływ dyrektywy 2005/29/WE o nieuczciwych praktykach handlowych na krajowe normy proceduralne – glosa do wyroku Trybunału Sprawiedliwości z 19.09.2018 r., C-109/17, Bankia SA przeciwko Juanowi Carlosowi Mariemu Merinowi i in. EPS 11:25–32
Jabłonowska A, Tagiuri G (2023) Rescuing transparency in the digital economy: in search of a common notion in EU consumer and data protection law. YEL 42:347–387
Jagielska M, Rauch I (2016) Klauzule abuzywne w umowach standardowo zawieranych przez Internet. In: Flaga-Gieruszyńska K, Gołaczyński J, Szostek D (eds) Media elektroniczne: współczesne problemy prawne. CH Beck, pp 235–251
Johnston A (2016) Seeking the EU "consumer" in services of general economic interest. In: Leczykiewicz D, Weatherill S (eds) The images of the consumer in EU law: legislation, free movement and competition law. Hart Publishing, pp 93–138
Karsten J (2007) Passengers, consumers, and travellers: the rise of passenger rights in EC transport law and its repercussions for community consumer law and policy. J Consum Policy 30(2):117–136
Klonick K (2018) The new governors: the people, rules, and processes governing online speech. Harv Law Rev 131(6):1598–1670
Loos M, Luzak J (2016) Wanted: a bigger stick. On unfair terms in consumer contracts with online service providers. J Consum Policy 39(1):63–90
Mak V (2013) The "average consumer" of EU law in domestic and European litigation. In: Leczykiewicz D, Weatherill S (eds) The involvement of EU law in private law relationships. Hart Publishing, pp 333–356
Mak V (2016) The consumer in European Regulatory Private Law. In: Leczykiewicz D, Weatherill S (eds) The images of the consumer in EU law: legislation, free movement and competition law. Hart Publishing, pp 381–400
Meller-Hannich C, Krausbeck E, Wittke R (2019) Der Verbraucher in der Sharing Economy. VuR 11:403–412
Micklitz H-W (2010) Reforming European unfair terms legislation in consumer contracts. ERCL 6(4):347–383
Micklitz H-W, Reich N (2014) The Court and Sleeping Beauty: the revival of the Unfair Contract Terms Directive (UCTD). CML Rev 51(3):771–808
Narciso M (2019) The regulation of online reviews in European consumer law. ERPL 27(3):557–581
Nihoul P (2008) The status of consumers in European liberalisation directives. In: Parry D, Nordhausen A, Howells G, Twigg-Flesner C (eds) The yearbook of consumer law 2009. Routledge, pp 69–108
Nijenhuis A (2013) Electronic communications and the EU consumer. In: Benyon F (ed) Services and the EU citizen. Hart Publishing, pp 47–74

Pecyna M (2009) Naruszenie zobowiązania w świetle harmonizacji prawa zobowiązań. Studium prawnoporównawcze. Wolters Kluwer

Peifer K-N (2017) Platform economy and liability questions – desperately in search of concepts lost in the virtual world or "Störerhaftung" resurrected? IIC Int Rev Intellect Prop Compet Law 48:623–625

Petersen CS, Ulfbeck VG, Hansen O (2018) Platforms as private governance systems – the example of Airbnb. Nord J Commer Law 1:37–60

Podstawa K (2019) Hybrid governance or… nothing? The EU code of conduct on combatting illegal hate speech online. In: Carpanelli E, Lazzerini N (eds) Use and misuse of new technologies: contemporary challenges in international and European law. Springer, pp 167–184

Purnhagen K (2017) More reality in the CJEU's interpretation of the average consumer benchmark – also more behavioural science in unfair commercial practices? EJRR 8(2):437–440

Purnhagen K, Schebesta H (2020) Island or ocean: empirical evidence on the average consumer concept in the UCPD. ERPL 28(2):293–310

Rott P (2024) Burden of proof. In: Helberger N, Kas B, Micklitz H-W, Namysłowska M, Naudts L, Rott P, Sax M, Veale M (eds) Digital fairness for consumers. BEUC

Rustad M, Onufrio M (2012) Reconceptualizing consumer terms of use for a globalized knowledge economy. Univ Pa J Bus Law 14:1085–1190

Sartor G (2017) Providers liability: from the ECommerce Directive to the future. In-depth analysis for the IMCO Committee. European Parliament

Schebesta H, Verdonk T, Purnhagen KP, Keirsbilck B (2018) Unfair trading practices in the food supply chain: regulating right? EJRR 9(2):690–700

Schmidt-Kessel M, Möllnitz C (2022) Qualität von Bewertungsportalen. In: Schmidt-Kessel M, Möllnitz C (eds) Grundfragen des Digitalvertragsrechts. Mohr Siebeck, pp 95–109

Schulte-Nölke H, Rüffer I, Nobrega C, Wiewiórowska-Domagalska A (2020) The legal framework for E-Commerce in the internal market. Study requested by the IMCO committee. European Parliament

Schweitzer H (2019) Digitale Plattformen als private Gesetzgeber: Ein Perspektivwechsel für die europäische "Plattform-Regulierung". ZEuP 27(1):1–12

Sørensen MJ (2016) Private law perspectives on platform services. Uber – a business model in search of a new contractual legal frame? EuCML 5(1):15–19

Stemler A (2017) Feedback loop failure: implications for the self-regulation of the sharing economy. MJLST 18:673–712

Tereszkiewicz P (2018) Digital platforms: regulation and liability in the EU law. ERPL 26(6):903–920

Tereszkiewicz P (2019) Digital platforms: regulation and liability in EU law. In: DiMatteo LA, Cannarsa M, Poncibò C (eds) The Cambridge handbook of smart contracts, blockchain technology and digital platforms. Cambridge University Press, pp 143–159

Twigg-Flesner C (2018) The EU's proposals for regulating B2B relationships on online platforms – transparency, fairness and beyond. EuCML 7(6):222–233

Waelkens J (2015) Article 5 Unfair Terms Directive 93/13/EEC: transparency and interpretation in consumer contracts. In: Samoy I, Loos MBM (eds) Information and notification duties. Intersentia, pp 47–72

Wauters E, Lievens E, Valcke P (2014) Towards a better protection of social media users: a legal perspective on the terms of use of social networking sites. IJLIT 22(3):254–294

Wielsch D (2019) Private law regulation of digital intermediaries. ERPL 27(2):197–220

Wilhelmsson T (2004) The abuse of the "confident consumer" as a justification for EC consumer law. J Consum Policy 27(3):317–337

Ypma P, Chaves M, McNally P, Kazmierska K, Domínguez Gaitán M, Rzepecka J, Dragulin M, Rabuel L, Juskevicius R, Kuuliala V, Peroz T, Plasilova I, Rodriguez Diaz A (2018) Study on the assessment of the regulatory aspects affecting the collaborative economy in the tourism accommodation sector in the 28 Member States. Final report: legal assessment of the regulatory environment surrounding the collaborative economy in the tourism accommodation sector across the 28 Member States. European Commission

# Chapter 8
# Consumer Protection in the Transforming Travel Sector: A Way Forward for European Union Law

## 8.1 Preliminary Remarks

The previous analysis confirmed the significance of consumer protection in both the internal market and the common transport policy. At the same time, the rationale for adopting protective measures may sometimes be elusive, just like the very notion of the consumer. Consumers are generally protected due to their weaker position, which is usually linked to the level of information, economic resources and legal experience.[1] The notion of the consumer in secondary law, particularly in the internal market policy, is often limited to natural persons acting for purposes unrelated to their business or professional activity in relationships with traders, understood in an opposite way.[2] Such an approach, however, does not paint the full picture of neither the position of weakness, nor the consumer notion in both legal theory and European Union law.[3]

As argued by Willett, consumer weaknesses have a dual nature and refer to, firstly, consumers' struggles in exercising self-reliance to protect themselves from detrimental outcomes and, secondly, their weaker position as loss bearers.[4] In the broad sense, represented in the primary law, consumer notion can simply refer to passive market participants,[5] persons not offering goods or services in the market, but seeking access to them, regardless of purposes for which they—or their counterparties—act. Such a more comprehensive perspective is more useful in the context

---

[1] Judgment of the Court of Justice of 4.10.2018 in case C-105/17 *Kamenova*, ECLI:EU:C:2018:808, para. 34.

[2] Karsten (2007), p. 127. See e.g. Articles 2(1) and 2(2) of Directive 2011/83/EU on consumer rights.

[3] Reich (2008), pp. 18–25, 62.

[4] Willett (2018), p. 187.

[5] Reich and Micklitz (2014), p. 53.



A. Jabłonowska, *Consumer Protection and Online Travel Platforms*, Law, Governance and Technology Series 73, https://doi.org/10.1007/978-3-031-90170-6_8

of new market developments, particularly if consumer protection is to assume a more self-standing role in the process of harmonisation.

To fully grasp the rationale and roles of consumer protection in EU integration, and respond to the potential shortcomings of current legal rules, it is thus necessary to detach the consumer notion from the B2C orientation and to take the dual nature of consumer weaknesses into account. Clearly, consumers' weaker position, and therefore the need for a "high level" of protection, may be especially pronounced in standard B2C transactions, while formally defined "traders" may be best placed to take on increased duties. However, when entire regulatory attention is directed at two-sided B2C transactions, a risk of disconnection of the legal norms from the increasingly complex, multi-party market reality becomes significant. Before considering what can be done to remedy this disconnect and improve consumer protection in online travel platforms, it is useful to restate the arguments for doing so in the first place, and particularly at the EU level.

## 8.2 Case for Improving Consumer Protection in the Transforming Travel Sector

### *8.2.1 Internal Market Policy*

Acknowledging the dual nature of consumer weaknesses and the broad scope of the consumer notion is the fundamental starting point, ensuring that any subsequent analysis does not fall into the trap of path dependence. However, such a finding is not in itself sufficient to establish a case for increased consumer protection in a specific context. The latter is closely intertwined with the scope and nature of the Union's competences, governed by the principles of conferral, proportionality and subsidiarity. Although the scope of competences conferred upon the Union by the Member States has been evolving over time, Treaty provisions related to the establishment and functioning of the internal market continue to provide the principal legal basis in the field of consumer protection. Accordingly, confirming the case for enhanced consumer protection under Article 114 TFEU carries more practical weight than pointing to the legal bases that have been barely used.

As seen from the previous analysis, the expansion of consumer protection framework in the EU generally accompanies the process of bringing down the barriers to cross-border trade. Aside from providing benefits in terms of choice and potentially lower prices, the implementation of EU policies is also liable to exacerbate consumer weaknesses, to which EU legislature should respond, in line with Article 12 TFEU. Consumers may struggle to exercise self-reliance in view of an increasing number and variety of suppliers and find themselves in a weaker position as loss bearers, especially in cross-border contexts.[6] At the same time, the connection

[6] Willett (2018), p. 187.

between consumer protection and the internal market is not fully captured by the image of two consecutive processes. Measures aimed at consumer protection also remain an inherent part of the internal market project. To recall, pursuant to Article 169(2)(a) TFEU, the Union contributes to the attainment of a high level of consumer protection *through* measures adopted pursuant to Article 114 TFEU in the context of the completion of the internal market. This results in a complex dynamic and, at times, conceptually inconsistent outcomes. On the one hand, when legislating on the basis of Article 114 TFEU a "high level" of consumer protection needs to be pursued.[7] As the Court of Justice recognized, consumer protection may even be a "decisive factor" in the choices made, as long as the measures taken *also* make a market-making contribution.[8] On the other hand, the market-making contribution can be especially strong when both consumers and suppliers are encouraged to engage in the internal market, which may favour pragmatic solutions, manageable to both parties.

The notion of "consumer confidence" aims to reconcile the tension between market-related goals and a high level of consumer protection. If the building of consumer confidence is accepted as a valid rationale, then the personal scope and instruments of protection should depend primarily on the nature of consumer weaknesses, which underlie the lack of confidence. Consumer confidence-building so understood may require the adoption of measures associated with both need and self-reliance ethics, providing for diverse personal scopes.[9] The available regulatory toolbox should not be limited to information and choice-enhancing instruments, but may also include direct regulation of products and services[10] as well as measures aimed at facilitating consumers' access to a counterparty.[11] The relevant obligations may convincingly be located with the parties who are best placed to achieve the internal market goals, including by ensuring a high level of consumer protection, which at times may lead to shared responsibility. While the vision laid out above is not a golden mean, appropriate for all areas of the internal market and all aspects of consumer protection, it fits well with the reality of digital markets and the travel sector. Indeed, the path has already been followed in those areas, as illustrated by Directive 2000/31/EC on electronic commerce, the Digital Services Act and Directive 2015/2302 on package travel and linked travel arrangements.

In view of the above, the case for an increased protection of consumers from travel-related risks in the platform economy is not *prima facie* excluded by the fact that relevant relationships may qualify as P2P. The question to be asked is rather whether consumers in such relationships find themselves in a position of weakness and whether relevant weaknesses result in lack of confidence detrimental to the

---

[7] Article 114(3) TFEU.

[8] Judgment of the Court of Justice of 8.6.2010 in case C-58/08 *Vodafone and Others*, ECLI:EU:C:2010:321, para. 36. See also Weatherill (2016), p. 210.

[9] Wilhelmsson (2004).

[10] Twigg-Flesner (2016), p. 200.

[11] Wilhelmsson (2004).

internal market. In my view, the answer to this question is affirmative, in respect of both types of weaknesses identified by Willett.[12]

Firstly, due to the distant nature of established contracts and a very wide variety of service providers, consumers may struggle to exercise self-reliance to protect themselves from detrimental outcomes. In particular, the asymmetry of information remains significant, which explains why all analysed platform operators have taken steps to promote information provision, most notably by means of reputation systems.[13] Consumers required to make down-payments may additionally find it difficult to claim their money back if anything goes wrong, particularly if they would need to argue with the parties residing in other Member States. This argument, of course, does not apply to relationships where no payments take place. Still, as described in Chap. 2, the analysed transformation of the travel sector is primarily driven by platforms attracting suppliers with economic motives. Remuneration in those models is generally charged in advance and the possibility of reimbursement depends on mechanisms deployed by platform providers, vis-à-vis whom consumers are also structurally weaker.[14]

Secondly, and equally importantly, due to the nature of the underlying services, which involve personal experience, often in an unknown environment, consumers can also find themselves in a weaker position as loss bearers. While a similar argument may be raised in relation to the peer suppliers, particularly those sharing their private accommodation with strangers, the latter are still much better placed to protect themselves from the associated detriment, e.g. by removing valuable items from the property.[15] In the case of services provided against remuneration, the principle of *cuius commodum eius periculum* can further be invoked to justify a focus on the consumers' side.

The fact that the weaknesses identified above are not addressed in the analysed sector-specific measures suggests that more could be done at the EU level to promote consumer confidence in the transforming travel sector. Besides the role of horizontal norms, which were addressed before, two arguments can be brought against such a submission, pointing, respectively, to the role of national law and private governance. Indeed, both frameworks can mitigate the identified protection gaps to some extent and need to be assessed case-by-case. On the whole, however, both also come with limitations. Firstly, due to the volume of cross-border transactions in online travel platforms, a harmonised solution may be preferable to divergent national norms from both axiological and market-related perspectives. A set of

---

[12] Willett (2018), p. 185.

[13] On the role of online reputation as a source of information and its relationship to trust, see Ranchordás (2018), pp. 131–133.

[14] Smorto (2018), pp. 433–436.

[15] For an opposite view, according to which peer consumers and peer suppliers in the platform economy are equal to each other, see Kucharska (2019), p. 32.

common basic safeguards reduces the need of getting to know national laws every time one travels abroad. Moreover, negative experiences with platform-based services on one occasion, in a country with a lower level of protection, could discourage consumers from making use of them even in jurisdictions with stronger safeguards. This is true for both tourism accommodation and passenger transport services, including in the model of rides-on-demand, which are further discussed in the context of the common transport policy. Finally, divergent development of national norms aimed more directly at the platform economy may trigger more traditional rationales for harmonisation, associated with the emergence of obstacles to trade.

The same key question, as to whether the identified weaknesses are not, or cannot, be mitigated against more suitably through other means, can also be posed in relation to private governance frameworks. Mechanisms of this kind, deployed by platform operators, reflect an instrumentalist, pragmatic approach, similar to the one endorsed by the EU, yet their goals may not entirely cohere with those derived from EU legislation. According to the narrative endorsed by key industry players, online platforms create environments with primarily positive impacts and a strong capacity to self-regulate, while the operators' role is to assist the users in seizing opportunities.[16] Arguably, they provide an equal common standard of protection, which users can rely upon, regardless of the jurisdiction. However, private governance frameworks by no means guarantee a level of protection aligned with user's expectations, consistent application or operators' neutrality. On the contrary, the existence of network effects may create a tendency towards concentration, making platform operators less receptive to individual complaints.[17] Aspects of private governance frameworks, such as reputational feedback systems, may fail to protect consumers as a result of inherent limitations, biases and manipulation.[18] When it comes to acting on key matters, especially when detriment is experienced during an offline interaction, most analysed platforms retain a margin of discretion and rarely share more data than required. Confidence, which consumers derive from private governance frameworks, may therefore be based on a rather thin ground.[19] Crucially, the relationship between users and platform operators is also one in which users can be described as weaker parties.[20] Overall, the role of platform providers does not necessarily weaken the case for an increased consumer protection, but rather discloses the need for new regulatory strategies, taking this role into account.

---

[16] Dredge and Gyimóthy (2015), p. 298.

[17] Smorto (2018), p. 436.

[18] Ranchordás (2018), pp. 134–138.

[19] Petersen et al. (2018), p. 59. On a similar distinction between trust and trustworthiness, see Helberger et al. (2022), p. 189.

[20] Smorto (2018), p. 440.

### 8.2.2 Common Transport Policy

When it comes to *passenger* protection, the special position of the transport sector in EU integration must be kept in mind. As far as the rationales for consumer protection measures are concerned, most notably related to the protection of weaker parties, an overall congruity between the internal market and the common transport policies can be identified. A convergence of this kind is not coincidental. Consumer protection belongs to the objectives of the Treaties, which, with respect to transport, are pursued within the framework of a common transport policy, as per Article 90 TFEU. At the same time, the key competence norm in Article 91 TFEU seems to be framed even more broadly than Article 114 TFEU, and can be read as supporting a self-standing role of consumer protection in the common transport policy—in both axiological and market-making perspectives. Not only does it explicitly authorise harmonised action aimed at increased safety, but it also refers more broadly to "any other appropriate provisions" in the area of road transport.

It may be due to this broad framing that the recourse to applicable competence norms in the transport sector has been largely unquestioned. The focus of the case law has rather remained on the *exercise* of competences. Also in this respect, however, the Court accepted a very broad margin of appreciation enjoyed by the EU legislature. For example, in *IATA and ELFAA* the Court observed that in areas which, like regulation of passenger rights, "involve political, economic and social choices" and require "complex assessments", invalidity on grounds of proportionality would only be conceivable if the measure was "manifestly inappropriate" having regard to the objective which the competent institution was seeking to pursue.[21] Crucially, pursuing a high level of passenger protection, taking account of the requirements of consumer protection in general, has been treated as a valid objective.[22]

Overall, existing rules on passenger protection reflect the role of consumer protection in EU integration rather comprehensively. The emphasis is placed on the weaker position of passive market participants. To avoid terminological confusion, the "passenger" notion is most commonly used in the analysed regulations, yet it is clear that the framework is driven by broadly understood consumer protection requirements, in line with Article 12 TFEU. Both facets of consumer weaknesses are taken into account, namely consumer struggles in exercising self-reliance to protect themselves from detrimental outcomes and their weaker position as loss bearers.[23] Despite the distinct position of the transport sector, a connection between the internal market and the common transport policies remains strong and many safeguards put in place in the latter field appear to be well-suited for the former.

---

[21] Judgment of the Court of Justice of 10.1.2006 in case C-344/04 *IATA and ELFAA*, ECLI:EU:C:2006:10, para. 80.

[22] Ibid, paras. 69, 82.

[23] Willett (2018), p. 185.

While the conceptual underpinnings of consumer protection in the common transport policy are well-developed and well-founded, the protection gaps identified in respect of passenger transport in the platform economy are even more significant than in the context of short-term accommodation rental. This is due to the piecemeal nature of harmonisation in the analysed field, providing a high level of consumer protection in the areas covered, but leaving other passengers without significant safety nets. Passenger transport services are therefore largely excluded from the scope of more general acts, such as the Services Directive and the Consumer Rights Directive. At the same time, consumer weaknesses elucidated previously in the internal market context are also at play in the platform-based models focused more specifically on transport, such as ride-sharing and rides-on-demand. Consumer struggles in exercising self-reliance can be linked, similarly, to the distant nature of established contracts and a very wide variety of service providers. Due to the nature of relevant services, involving personal experience in a potentially unknown environment, consumers can also find themselves in a weaker position as loss bearers.

In view of the above, existing EU norms in the common transport policy appear unlikely to establish a high level of consumer protection and promote consumer confidence following the platform-driven transformation of the travel sector. Admittedly, the same two arguments mentioned earlier can be brought against such a submission. By way of an analogy, a similar set of counter-arguments can be invoked against them. As regards the role of national and local regulators, it goes without saying that they are generally well-placed to improve the level of passenger protection in analysed domains. Still, reliance on national or local standards only may fail to provide the protection needed for the EU market to prosper, especially when the truly mobile consumers are taken as a reference point. Platform companies make it possible for consumers not only to conclude contracts beyond borders (e.g. in ride-sharing) but also to access transport services in different EU locations, using a single user account and online interface. Consumers experiencing detriment in one Member State may therefore be deterred from using similar services while being physically present in other countries, even if the corresponding level of protection is considerably higher in those jurisdictions. Room thus remains for an EU action. Furthermore, while protection provided by platform-based mechanisms is clearly very valuable, one can doubt whether platform operators can alone be entrusted with the key task of protecting the weaker parties, particularly as relationships between users and operators are themselves asymmetrical.

### *8.2.3 Interim Conclusions*

The importance of consumer protection in both the internal market and the common transport policies is beyond doubt. While the structure of relevant competence norms is not identical, both Article 114 and Article 91 TFEU provide a strong basis for EU measures to protect consumers in the travel sector. The distinction between both policies does not support a markedly different approach to different travel services. The rationales for protecting consumers as passive market participants, in line with Article 12 TFEU, are essentially the same in all policy areas.

Admittedly, the self-standing role of consumer protection in the internal market policy is not as obvious as in the common transport policy. However, established grounds for recourse to Article 114 TFEU, including the confidence-building argument, open the way to consumer-oriented legal action in the travel sector. As was already mentioned, due to the strong cross-border potential of online travel platforms, reliance on the confidence reasoning appears to be well-founded in this area. Following Karsten and Petri, one can conclude that there are, indeed, "good arguments for giving priority to travel and tourism in a first attempt for better regulation, regulatory simplification, removal of remaining trade barriers, and filling gaps in consumer law."[24] Almost two decades after these lines were written, the goal is still far from being achieved. What is more, the EU legislature is now faced with a new set of challenges, arising from the platform-driven transformation of the travel sector.

By now, a high level of protection has been afforded to the recipients of travel services in most traditional business models, such as package travel or transport by bus or coach. Having reached this objective, the EU legislature appears to have assumed that the main issues in the travel sector are now duly addressed. This might explain its decision to exclude travel services from the scope of other legislation, such as the Consumer Rights Directive or the E-Commerce Directive, which is particularly prominent in the transport sector. Also in the field of tourism accommodation rental, a great deal of attention has been devoted to the package travel model while the role of stand-alone contracts for single travel services has been marginalized. To the extent such models remained of minor socio-economic importance compared to the established ones, the problem could be overlooked. Nonetheless, the platform-driven transformation of the travel sector has radically changed the picture. A disconnection between the legal norms and the socio-technological state of the art became increasingly apparent. As a result, the instruments currently in place are unlikely to provide a high level of consumer protection in a major—and growing—part of the travel sector, and promote consumer confidence in relevant fields.

As the analysis has shown, consumers of both short-term accommodation rental services and passenger transport services, contracted for via online platforms, find themselves in a weaker position vis-à-vis their counterparties in respect of the ability to both exercise self-reliance and bear potential losses. As such, they appear to be equally in need of protection as the travellers making use of the business models characteristic of the pre-platform age. In fact, the problems that both groups may face are not at all dissimilar. National lawmakers can certainly play a part in addressing them. Nonetheless, due to the scale and the cross-border nature of relevant activities, a common—or, at any rate, coordinated—approach to core aspects of consumer protection may be preferable. Platform operators can counterbalance the identified

[24] Karsten and Petri (2005), p. 43.

consumer weaknesses to some degree and support consumer confidence.[25] However, it is important not to lose sight of the fact that platform users are also weaker parties vis-à-vis the operators.[26] Consequently, the role of platform providers does not necessarily weaken the case for an increased consumer protection, but underlines the need for new regulatory strategies, taking this role into account.[27]

## 8.3 Case for Including Platform Operators in Consumer Protection

The previous section addressed the case for harmonised protection of consumers contracting through online travel platforms on grounds of specific consumer weaknesses and the associated internal market impacts. A finding that such increased protection is justified paves the way to a more detailed analysis of the possible protection framework. Core aspects of protection—such as information, choice enhancement, safety and performance—can be identified on the basis of Article 169(1) TFEU as well as prior law-making practice. What counts as a high level of protection will depend on the context, yet it is generally accepted that the EU legislature does not need to adopt the highest possible level of protection,[28] and that instruments based on the need ethic afford a higher level of protection than those guided by self-reliance.[29] With this in mind, an overarching question concerns the parties to be involved in the protection framework and, especially, the associated role of platform operators. Notably, arguments in favour of directing regulatory and, potentially, co-regulatory measures at platform operators could additionally reinforce the role of EU institutions in the entire process.

The involvement of platform operators can be supported by the effectiveness arguments. The plurality of actors involved in the protection framework also remains in line with the prior law-making practice in the travel sector. What is more, the analysis of existing rules on package travel and passenger rights points to varying degrees of such involvement, thus laying out a spectrum based upon which an approach suitable to the platform economy can be devised. In particular, a distinction can be made between responsibility for actions or inactions of another party (e.g. responsibility of the organiser for statements of the retailer in Directive 2015/2302 on package travel and linked travel arrangements or responsibility of the carrier for actions of the performing carrier in Regulation 181/2011 on the rights of passengers travelling by bus and coach) and responsibility of multiple actors for

---

[25] Cf. Petersen et al. (2018), pp. 46–50.

[26] Smorto (2018), pp. 444–445. See also Petersen et al. (2018), p. 59.

[27] Finck (2018b), pp. 267–268.

[28] Judgment of the Court of Justice of 13.5.1997 in case C-233/94 *Germany v Parliament and Council*, ECLI:EU:C:1997:231, para. 48.

[29] Willett (2018), p. 185.

safeguarding consumer interests within their respective areas of competence (e.g. responsibility for information provision shared between carriers and terminal managing bodies in Regulation 181/2011 and specific disclosure duties imposed on the providers of online marketplaces in amended Directive 2011/83/EU on consumer rights).

On the other hand, the approach previously taken to the digital market may be cited as an argument for limiting the involvement of platform operators. In particular, the safe harbour framework, originally set out in the E-Commerce Directive, has traditionally been invoked as an argument in favour of a special treatment of online intermediaries. Indeed, Articles 6 and 8 of the Digital Services Act confirm that hosting providers should not only be shielded from liability for third-party content, but also not exposed to any associated general monitoring obligations. From this one could extrapolate that online intermediaries may potentially be removed from the general dynamic, in which measures aimed to increase market freedoms and measures aimed at ensuring a high level of consumer protection are being developed side by side.

While in the early days of the digital economy arguments of this kind could be deemed convincing, they certainly lose force more recently. Firstly, the category of online intermediaries and their potential sub-groups are much less clear today than it was in the early days of the digital economy. What is more, as the *Uber* jurisprudence shows, many platform operators may not be sure of their status not only as host providers, but even as providers of information society services.[30] Secondly, a tendency to narrow down safe harbours and increase the involvement of platform operators in risk mitigation is clearly visible in current policy and legislation—at both national[31] and EU levels. The previously mentioned Digital Services Act is a prominent case in point and other, platform-specific measures[32] are even more striking.

Overall, a case can not only be made for increased consumer protection in the transforming travel sector but also for the involvement of platform operators in reaching this objective.[33] Considering that any potential measures taken by the EU

---

[30] See judgment of the Court of Justice of 20.12.2017 in case C-434/15 *Asociación Profesional Elite Taxi (Uber Spain)*, ECLI:EU:C:2017:981, paras. 37–41. Cf. judgment of the Court of Justice of 19.12.2019 in case C-390/18 *Airbnb Ireland*, ECLI:EU:C:2019:1112, paras. 39–69.

[31] See German Network Enforcement Act (Netzwerkdurchsetzungsgesetz, BGBl. I S. 3352) and Loi n° 2016-1321 pour une République numérique of 7.10.2016 (JORF n°0235 of 8.10.2016).

[32] For video-sharing platforms, consider Directive (EU) 2018/1808 of the European Parliament and of the Council of 14 November 2018 amending Directive 2010/13/EU on the coordination of certain provisions laid down by law, regulation or administrative action in Member States concerning the provision of audiovisual media services (Audiovisual Media Services Directive) in view of changing market realities [2018] OJ L303/69. For platforms with copyrighted content, see Directive (EU) 2019/790 of the European Parliament and of the Council of 17.4.2019 on copyright and related rights in the Digital Single Market and amending Directives 96/9/EC and 2001/29/EC [2019] OJ L130/92.

[33] Finck (2018b), pp. 268–269.

will involve a range of "political, economic and social choices",[34] the subsequent discussion will not seek to lay out a single correct solution but instead draw a spectrum of options. Such an approach makes it possible to connect the present analysis on the travel sector with a broader debate on modern challenges to consumer protection. Indeed, at least certain proposals can equally be considered in other areas of the platform economy, e.g. broader categories of online marketplaces.

In the first place, the potential of existing EU rules and their moderate adaptions will be explored, particularly with respect to the functioning of platform-based protection mechanisms. The shape of possible new initiatives will further be examined. Throughout this process, the provisions on comparable forms of travelling existing prior to platform-driven transformation will be used as a reference point, taking into account the specificity of the analysed relationships, in particular the non-professional nature of service provision and the role of data-driven architectures.

## 8.4 Existing Norms and Adaptive Approaches

### *8.4.1 Information*

Among the obligations aimed at improving consumer information and choice mandatory disclosure duties feature particularly prominently. Even though the limits of protection through information in light of behavioural economics are being recognized,[35] there appears to be a certain level of consensus that well-crafted information duties[36] can provide an important baseline of protection, improving the conditions in which consumers exercise their autonomy and self-reliance, increasing their overall willingness to contract and supporting the demand-side competitive pressure.[37] The same can also be the case for choice-enhancing instruments, such as the right of withdrawal or termination at a fee, in which case, however, careful drafting is required particularly to avoid placing an excessive burden on the suppliers.[38] Generally speaking, choice-enhancing instruments tend to offer a higher degree of consumer protection than information duties, more akin to need ethics than to self-reliance.

Due to their soft nature and a broader growth-enhancing potential, information duties belong not only to the most widely used instruments of consumer protection in EU law but also to the instruments most frequently transcending the status-based

[34] Judgment of the Court of Justice of 10.1.2006 in case C-344/04 *IATA and ELFAA*, para. 80.

[35] Howells (2005), pp. 356–362.

[36] Elshout et al. (2016), pp. 96–103.

[37] Busch (2016b), pp. 222–224, 230–232. For an in-depth discussion of the meaning of 'autonomy' in the context of regulating transactions from the freedom of contract and fairness-oriented perspectives, see Willett (2005), pp. 1–6.

[38] Watson (2016), pp. 241–245, 246–249.

approach. Consequently, the scope of the identified protection gaps in respect of protection through information is significantly smaller compared to other core aspects of consumer protection. For this reason, it is worth reiterating how existing information norms apply to the analysed area and, particularly, whether and to what extent platform operators are involved in information provision. Due to comparably non-controversial nature and already extended scope of information duties, opting for an adaptive approach in this regard may turn out to be promising.

As far as information on underlying services is concerned, Article 22 of Directive 2006/123/EC on services in the internal market assumes a prominent role. The provision requires service providers to disclose information about themselves and their activity, including the particulars of the relevant competent authority or the single point of contact where the activity is subject to an authorisation scheme, as well as about the subject matter of the transaction, including the price and main features of the service and available insurance or guarantees. Importantly, the information requirements at issue are in addition to other disclosure duties provided for in EU law and do not prevent Member States from imposing additional requirements applicable to providers established in their territory.[39] The indicated obligations should be complied with by all service recipients falling within the remit of the Services Directive and their scope is broadly in line with the items of information recognized as important to the recipients of services in the travel sector. As a matter of fact, the provisions of package travel law appear to be well-placed to clarify the scope of certain information items *per analogiam*, such as the main features (characteristics) of the service, of course with necessary adjustments.[40]

Translating the above to online travel platforms, Article 22 of Directive 2006/123/EC covers suppliers of tourism accommodation rental services via platforms like Airbnb and Booking.com, regardless of their formal status. Suppliers of passenger transport services, however, fall outside the scope of relevant provisions, as per Article 2(2)(d) of the Services Directive. This limitation can be criticised in light of the observed market developments. Indeed, there are good reasons to believe that prospective passengers searching for rides via BlaBlaCar would benefit from a similar set of information as prospective guests searching for flats via Airbnb. Even in the case of rides-on-demand, where consumer decision-making is more dynamic, room for improved disclosure remains.[41] The extent of harmonisation in the Services Directive is therefore more limited than it seems at first sight. At the same time, the analysed legal instrument does not appear to provide for shared responsibility similar to the one known from Directive 2015/2302 on package travel and linked travel arrangements, even for tourism accommodation rental services that fall within its scope. If at all, such a shared responsibility can be derived from Directive 2011/83/

[39] Article 22(5) of Directive 2006/123/EC on services in the internal market.

[40] Cf. Article 5(1)(a) of Directive 2015/2302 on package travel and linked travel arrangements. Interpretation by analogy would, for example, exclude the provision of information about "itinerary", where the relevant contract only involves the purchase of a single travel service on a standalone basis.

[41] Hausemer et al. (2017), p. 32.

EU on consumer rights, via the notion of the trader acting in the name or on behalf of another trader.[42] However, a corresponding reading is of no practical use should the underlying contracts be excluded from the scope of the Consumer Rights Directive, as is the case for peer-to-peer relationships and, for the most part, contracts for passenger transport services.

Beyond the Services Directive, a notable idea, which until recently was considered by EU institutions, concerns the so-called "European services e-card".[43] In 2017, the Commission submitted a proposal envisaging a card, also referred to as a "services passport", to be used voluntarily by service providers wishing to show compliance with applicable national rules. However, the initiative—which anyway was more focused on providers who actively move across borders—did not meet with political support and was eventually withdrawn.[44] Still, the idea seems promising from a consumer protection perspective and is therefore worth keeping in mind. Possibly, sector-specific measures could turn out to be more successful, with the travel sector as a prominent candidate.

The abovementioned perspective finds support in the recently adopted Regulation 2024/1028 on data collection and sharing relating to short-term accommodation rental services.[45] The act provides that Member States may impose a requirement on online short-term rental platforms to transmit data to competent authorities but if they do so, they should establish or maintain a specific registration procedure for units located in their territory.[46] Such a procedure should make it easy for the hosts to indicate to national authorities that they are active on the platform.[47] To the extent a reporting duty has been introduced, online short-term rental platforms are required to collect and transmit activity data to the relevant Member State. As the preamble observes, authorities may need such access "to assess the actual impact of short-term accommodation rental services and develop and enforce appropriate and proportionate policy responses".[48] Moreover, the Regulation includes a provision on compliance by design, similar to the one known from Article 31 DSA but going

[42] Judgment of the Court of Justice of 24.2.2022 in case C-536/20 *Tiketa*, ECLI:EU:C:2022:112, para. 31. See also de Vries and Jabłonowska (2019), p. 107. Cf. Adam and Micklitz (2017), p. 64; Wendehorst (2016), p. 33; Devolder (2019), pp. 54–56, 59–60.

[43] European Commission, 'Proposal for a Regulation of the European Parliament and of the Council Introducing a European Services E-Card and Related Administrative Facilities' (2017) COM(2016) 824 final, European Commission, 'Proposal for a Directive of the European Parliament and of the Council on the Legal and Operational Framework of the European Services E-Card Introduced by Regulation ….[ESC Regulation]' (2017) COM(2016) 823 final.

[44] Delimatsis (2018), pp. 197, 209–211.

[45] Regulation (EU) 2024/1028 of the European Parliament and of the Council of 11.4.2024 on data collection and sharing relating to short-term accommodation rental services and amending Regulation (EU) 2018/1724 [2024] OJ L.

[46] Article 4(2) of Regulation 2024/1028.

[47] See also judgment of the Court of Justice of 22.9.2020 in Joined Cases C-724/18 and C-727/18 *Cali Apartments*, ECLI:EU:C:2020:743 and Jabłonowska (2021), p. 273.

[48] Recital 1 of Regulation 2024/1028.

beyond B2C transactions.[49] For example, platform providers are required to design and organise their online interfaces in a way that, among others, ensures that hosts who declared that a unit offered for short-term accommodation rental services is located in an area covered by the registration procedure have provided a registration number before they are allowed to offer their services and that the registration number is clearly displayed.[50] *Prima facie*, such a requirement would seem extremely valuable to consumers wishing to verify whether relevant providers are legitimate. However, the Regulation does not apply to the whole EU territory but only to selected areas. This is because the act is not designed with consumer interests in mind but rather addresses the platforms' external effects in areas suffering from overtourism, such as the shortage of long-term rental housing and the increase in housing prices.[51]

Overall, despite its initial appeal, Regulation 2024/1028 does little to enhance consumer information in online travel platforms. Also the DSA suffers from limitations, at least as far as peer-to-peer transactions are concerned. As noted, its provisions on the traceability of traders and compliance by design are unfortunately limited to B2C transactions. The situation is not necessarily improved with the new information duty for contracts concluded on online marketplaces in the CRD. The duty, laid down in Article 6a of Directive 2011/83/EU on consumer rights, appears to primarily have a warning function and seeks to sustain the status-based approach.

As recounted in Chap. 4, under Article 6a of the CRD, providers of online marketplaces are required to inform consumers, among others, whether a third party offering the goods, services or digital content is a trader or not, on the basis of the latter's declaration as well as that the consumer rights stemming from EU consumer protection law do not apply to the peer-to-peer relationships. Aside from the rightful criticism of the declaration-based approach,[52] the provision appears to be of little use for the analysed areas of the travel sector, where protection gaps are linked to the material scope of the otherwise applicable rules, and not only the personal one. The norm is complemented with a well-intended, yet practically rather problematic, duty to inform, where applicable, how the obligations related to the contract are shared between the third party offering the goods, services or digital content and the provider of the online marketplace. Given the lack of harmonised provisions on such sharing of obligations, one can expect this information to be based either on platform-user contracts or, at best, the applicable provisions of national law. The opportunity has not been taken to at least include platform providers in compliance with already applicable duties of the peer suppliers (e.g. under the Services Directive and, as I argue below, the E-Commerce Directive), not to mention the possible elaboration of these obligations. Considering that even a consumer who is reasonably

[49] The involvement of platform operators as regulatory intermediaries has been advocated in the scholarship. See Sundararajan (2016), pp. 155–158; Finck (2018a), pp. 60–64; Busch (2020), pp. 120–125.

[50] Article 7 of Regulation 2024/1028.

[51] Ibid, recital 1.

[52] Prastitou Merdi (2020), pp. 360–361.

well-informed, observant and circumspect[53] may have difficulties in defining the scope of "Union consumer protection law", an impression may eventually be created that no harmonised protection can be expected in peer-to-peer relationships.

Against this background, a question can be asked whether increased protection at least through information could not be derived from other instruments of EU law, most notably Directive 2000/31/EC on electronic commerce. As was elaborated before, the E-Commerce Directive applies to the provision of information society services, defined as services normally provided for remuneration, at a distance, by electronic means and at the individual request of a recipient of services. The intermediation services consisting of connecting consumers and suppliers by means of an online platform, in principle, meet the criteria for classification as "information society services" within the meaning of Article 2(a) of the E-Commerce Directive.[54] Only in more recent case law, most notably in *Uber Spain*, did the Court consider the relevant intermediation services to be so strongly interlinked with underlying services that instead they were regarded as an integral part of an overall service whose main component was a service coming under another legal classification (in that case: service in the field of transport).[55]

Despite its exceptional nature, the line of reasoning developed by the Court in *Uber Spain* has met with mixed reactions. On the one hand, the distinction between platform operators qualifying as providers of information society services or not has been treated as a mark of support by the authors arguing in favour of increased contractual liability of particular types of online intermediaries.[56] On the other hand, analyses focused more directly on the respective provisions of the ECD point to the flaws in the Court's reasoning. It is argued that the exclusion of Uber activities from the scope of the E-Commerce Directive undermines the coherence of the framework, in a way which is neither justified nor necessary.[57]

Indeed, instead of developing an interpretation of the notion of information society services for a special category "composite services", a distinction could have been drawn between the online and offline aspects of relevant activities. Following recital 18 of Directive 2000/31/EC, and the judgment in *Ker-Optika*, the Court could have found the service that enables the transfer, by means of a smartphone application, of information concerning underlying services to fall within the scope of the E-Commerce Directive. Such a finding would trigger the applicability of not only the relevant liberalisation framework, but also the norms on the protection of service recipients. This includes Article 5 of the E-Commerce Directive, which

[53] The characteristics describe the "average consumer" image, which is the common point of reference in EU law. For an in-depth analysis, see Mak (2016), pp. 384–386.

[54] Orti Vallejo (2019), p. 1006.

[55] See judgment of the Court of Justice of 20.12.2017 in case C-434/15 *Asociación Profesional Elite Taxi (Uber Spain)*, paras. 37–41. Cf. judgment of the Court of Justice of 19.12.2019 in case C-390/18 *Airbnb Ireland*, paras. 39–69. For a doctrinal reconstruction of the reasoning, see Hacker (2018), pp. 87–88.

[56] Busch et al. (2020), p. 62.

[57] Schaub (2018), p. 62 and Adamski (2018), pp. 744–748.

defines general information to be provided to service recipients, as well as Article 10, which refers to information to be provided prior to the order being placed by the recipient of the information society service. The scope of the former does not significantly differ from that required by Article 22 of the Services Directive and aims to allow the user to see whom he or she is dealing with already at a very early stage.[58] The latter, in turn, relates to the contract, which does not have to be performed electronically, but the conclusion of which is either initiated or completed by the customer placing an order.[59] The underlying offline services would, in turn, be excluded from the scope of the E-Commerce Directive and the associated requirements, applicable to services not provided by electronic means, would remain outside the coordinated field. Arguably, a distinction of this kind could have been drawn even if, from the contractual perspective, the platform operator was deemed to be the consumer's sole counterparty.

A yet another avenue is presented by Directive 2019/770 on digital services. As noted, the DSD requires digital services to, among others, possess the qualities and performance features normal for digital services of the same type and which the consumer may reasonably expect. The potential of using the Directive as a means of platform regulation has been discussed in scholarship.[60] Possibly, the DSD could fill some gaps in the scope of other instruments, like the DSA. With respect to information provision, an argument could be made that the traceability of suppliers is not just a duty under Articles 30 DSA but also a normal feature of digital services that consumers can reasonably expect, regardless of the status of their counterparties, at least in the travel sector. Directive 2005/29/E on unfair commercial practices could also assume a role in this regard; as previously discussed, the relationship between both acts requires more elaboration in the future.

To conclude, as far as protection through information is concerned, the identified protection gaps are potentially not as difficult to resolve as it seems at first sight. Due to its broad personal scope and the focus on online trade, the E-Commerce Directive appears to be well-placed to serve this goal. Also the scope of information to be communicated by the providers of information society services remains in line with items recognized as important to the recipients of other types of services, including those provided in the travel sector. However, despite its good intentions, the line of reasoning adopted by the Court in *Uber Spain* makes it more difficult for the E-Commerce Directive to fulfil this function. *De lege lata*, strict interpretation of the judicial criteria of "market maker" and "decisive influence" can therefore be endorsed. *De lege fereda*, the reversal of the judgment's effects in terms of consumer information and further elaboration of norms on information provision in online commerce, with a focus on shared responsibility, can be considered.[61] In

[58] Nordhausen (2005), p. 103.

[59] Wendehorst (2016), p. 31. See also Lubasz and Namysłowska (2020), pp. 420–425.

[60] See, with respect to social media and video-sharing platforms, Voß (2022), p. 31 and Hennemann (2022), p. 77.

[61] Delimatsis (2018), pp. 246, 249.

particular, the extension of the DSA traceability requirement to peer-to-peer transactions, at least in online travel platforms, would seem advisable: with respect to both short-term accommodation rental and passenger transport. For the time being, Directive 2019/770 on digital services may help achieve this outcome. The DSD has one additional advantage: it is not tied to the notion of an information society service and therefore could also apply to platforms such as Uber.

### 8.4.2 Choice Enhancement

In contrast to instruments of protection through information, in which case the solution is readily available, the situation is significantly less consumer-friendly for choice-enhancing instruments. As a matter of fact, none of the relationships associated with the platform-driven transformation of the travel sector appear to be covered by the right of withdrawal, the right of termination at a fee or the right to contract transfer. Logically, there can also be no question of shared responsibility in this regard. The same is true for the right to reimbursement or rerouting following travel complications, which—as an instrument closely related to safety and performance—will be addressed in the following section.

Considering the broad range of potential instruments of choice enhancement, the question can be asked which of them could provide the most suitable model for the travel sector in the platform age, should additional safeguards in this regard be considered desirable. On the one hand, the right of withdrawal in Directive 2011/83/EU on consumer rights reflects a model of choice for distance B2C transactions. On the other hand, the right does not apply to the main types of contracts concluded in the travel sector, including contracts for the provision of accommodation and passenger transport, even if the status-based criteria are fulfilled. This suggests that a more balanced solution might be more suitable for this domain.[62] Indeed, a solution which considers the interests of both parties appears to be better aligned to the specificity of the travel services as well as the variety of parties involved on the supply and demand sides.[63]

From this perspective, the right of termination at a fee and the right to contract transfer, envisaged in Directive 2015/2302 on package travel and linked travel arrangements, provide a promising avenue for choice enhancement in the widely understood travel sector. A conclusion of this type finds support in recital 21 of the Package Travel Directive, which notes that Member States may maintain or introduce national legislation corresponding to the provisions of the Directive—in whole or in part—in relation to contracts that fall outside its scope, such as certain standalone contracts regarding single travel services. An extension to "the rental of holiday homes" is explicitly mentioned and, indeed, already finds support in some

[62] Bech Serrat (2016), pp. 370–372.

[63] Bech Serrat (2012), pp. 130–131.

national jurisdictions.[64] The reasons why the same should not apply to passenger transport services provided in the platform economy are not immediately apparent. On the contrary, the current market practice shows that instruments of choice enhancement are also well conceivable in this domain and can be easily implemented by electronic means. As a matter of fact, the existence of platform infrastructures opens new, promising possibilities for balanced choice enhancement. For example, termination at a fee could be envisaged as a common basic safeguard, with an additional possibility of reducing the fee if a contract on the same or comparable terms is concluded by another party. As an alternative to top-down regulation, platform operators could also be encouraged to address this issue in their contract terms.[65]

### *8.4.3 Safety and Performance*

As far as safety and quality of services are concerned, the analysis of existing norms and adaptive approaches shows a mixed picture. In both respects the level of consumer protection can be improved via reputation systems, provided their design ensures reliable outcomes. Harmonised norms already in place can contribute to this objective. This is especially the case for Directive 2005/29/EC on unfair commercial practices, whose applicability to reputation systems is beyond doubt. Still, the UCPD is not a miracle solution that cures all problems associated with reputation systems.[66] Considering the importance of reputational feedback in the platform economy, more targeted regulatory or co-regulatory initiatives could be worth exploring.[67]

Moreover, although reputation systems can certainly be very helpful, one should not lose sight of their important limitations. Firstly, sources of bias in the perception of reviews may remain, despite operators' best efforts.[68] Furthermore, reputation systems may be ineffective in protecting users against problems that are not visible[69] and in mitigating risks, which are outside either party's control.[70] In those domains, minimum standards and appropriate insurance frameworks offer a superior approach to consumer protection.[71] However, although such safeguards often apply to the

---

[64] See e.g. judgment of the German Federal Court of Justice (*Budesgerichtshof*) of 20.5.2014 in case X ZR 134/13, NJW 2013, 308, para. 25 and the case law cited. On the possibility of extending the right to contract transfer to such relationships of this kind, see Harke (2020), p. 211.

[65] For a similar emphasis on contract-based solutions, with a potential of harmonisation e.g. via an optional instrument, see Bech Serrat (2012), pp. 130–134.

[66] Narciso (2019), pp. 580–581.

[67] Busch (2016a), pp. 223–244; Ranchordás (2018).

[68] Codagnone et al. (2018), p. 67.

[69] Edelman and Geradin (2016), p. 317.

[70] Martens (2016), p. 6.

[71] Similarly Smorto (2018), pp. 443–445.

established business models, like package travel or transport by bus and coach, they tend to miss novel mobility patterns associated with online platforms.

A modest set of safeguards for consumers contracting for tourism accommodation rental can be found in Directive 2006/123/EC on services in the internal market, which includes provisions on authorisation schemes, professional liability insurance and/or guarantees and policies on quality of services. The relevant norms, however, leave a broad margin of discretion to the Member States, while the corresponding standardisation efforts on the safety and quality of tourism accommodation services have yielded limited results.[72] Consequently, they do little to inspire consumer confidence that a certain level of protection—for example, from fraudulent providers or unsafe accommodations—can be expected regardless of their travel destination.

In view of the above, it is surprising that neither Regulation 2024/1028 on data collection and sharing relating to short-term accommodation rental services takes consumer perspective into account, nor the consumer-centred initiatives, such as the Green Paper on the safety on tourism accommodation services of 2014,[73] have been followed-up with more specific measures.[74] Such a course of action could be linked to the apparent reluctance of many stakeholder groups, including public authorities and the hospitality industry, to change the *status quo*.[75] However, in public consultations accompanying the Green Paper, consumer associations were a prominent group of respondents who did not consider existing rules to be sufficient.[76] Moreover, even stakeholders who were generally satisfied with the legal landscape to date, agreed on the importance of various safety issues, such as carbon monoxide related risks, and showed openness to a certain degree of coordination, particularly through softer approaches, such as guidelines, standards, labels and data-sharing practices.[77] A recurrent remark was also made in relation to potentially higher safety concerns in what was referred to as "shadow hospitality", covering tourism accommodation rental via online platforms.[78]

The continued expansion of the platform economy may result in a renewed interest at the EU level, especially in health and safety aspects of services concerned. The measures taken in response to the COVID-19 pandemic confirm that the EU can have a role to play. In 2020, the Commission issued a Guidance document for

---

[72] van Leeuwen (2017), pp. 143–144.

[73] European Commission, 'Green Paper on the Safety of Tourism Accommodation Services' (2014) COM(2014) 464 final.

[74] See e.g. question E-015013/2015 raised by the Member of the European Parliament, Claudia Tapardel, for written answer to the Commission as regards the Green paper follow-up actions, as well as answer given by Ms Jourová on behalf of the Commission.

[75] European Commission DG Justice, 'Summary Report on the Public Consultation on the Green Paper on the Safety of Tourism Accommodation Services' (2015) Ref.Ares(2019)5989518-26/09/2019 (on file with the author), p. 4.

[76] Ibid, pp. 4, 11.

[77] Ibid, pp. 15–16, 19.

[78] Ibid, pp. 15, 18, 20–21.

health protocols in hospitality establishments,[79] which appears to be a first concrete move in this direction since the 1986 Council Recommendation on fire safety in existing hotels.[80] A similar set of guidelines was also issued for transport services, encompassing a wide variety of transport modes, from airlines to transport by car and urban mobility.[81] Further steps along these lines, extending to the platform-based models of service provision and potentially beginning with the softer approaches discussed above, could additionally contribute to improving consumer protection in the analysed sector. The corresponding role of platform operators remains to be explored.

In the transport sector, requirements applicable to broad groups of traffic participants are not entirely unprecedented.[82] However, even in this domain, harmonisation of the basic safeguards has been facing obstacles. In some areas, Member States have remained reluctant to a common action, leading the EU institutions to propose softer measures, as illustrated by the Commission Recommendation on maximum permitted blood alcohol content for drivers of motorised vehicles.[83] Not infrequently, common measures have focused on particular transport modes or even their subsegments. For example, additional requirements for drivers engaged in the carriage of passengers have been harmonised only for larger vehicles and, as such, do not extend to the platform-based mobility patterns.

Furthermore, the approximation of tort law at EU or international level has been controversial, as the unsuccessful proposal for a directive on the liability of suppliers of services and the convention on the liability for damage caused by motor vehicles show.[84] In established business models, this was compensated either with the harmonisation of contractual liability (as in the case of package travel[85]) or with a dedicated set of pragmatic norms addressing consumer weaker position in case of travel complications (as in the case of bus and coach transport[86]). In the analysed platform-driven models, however, neither of the paths has so far been explored.

The most important harmonised protection framework in the transport sector concerns insurance coverage, addressed by Directive 2009/103/EC. Considering that the Directive has consistently been interpreted by the Court in a

---

[79] European Commission, 'Communication from the Commission. COVID-19: EU Guidance for the Progressive Resumption of Tourism Services and for Health Protocols in Hospitality Establishments' (2020) C(2020) 3251 final, pp. 5–21.

[80] Council Recommendation 86/666/EEC on fire safety in existing hotels.

[81] European Commission, 'Communication from the Commission. COVID-19: Guidelines on the Progressive Restoration of Transport Services and Connectivity' (2020) C(2020) 3139 final 6–15.

[82] Consider, for example, the broadly applicable norms on driving licenses addressed in Chap. 6.

[83] Commission Recommendation of 17.1.2001 on the maximum permitted blood alcohol content (BAC) for drivers of motorised vehicles [2001] OJ L43/31.

[84] See generally Knetsch (2017), pp. 355–356; Bussani and Infantino (2019), pp. 1033–1035.

[85] Magnus and Micklitz (2006), p. 551.

[86] Cf. Articles 7–8 of Regulation 181/2011 on the rights of passengers in bus and coach transport and the associated legislative proposal.

passenger-friendly way,[87] such coverage should even extend to passengers travelling with drivers who do not have an authorisation required under national law or whose insurance policy does not fully reflect the nature of their use of the car. Even if this interpretation is accepted, however, insurance coverage does not in itself ensure a "high level" of passenger protection. For the latter to be established, both safety and performance would need to be considered seriously, taking into account the triangular nature of relevant relationships.

The involvement of platform operators, especially with regard to safety, finds support in national developments, in Europe and beyond. A prominent example is the regulation of rides-on-demand platforms, or "transportation network companies" (TNC), in the United States.[88] The availability of insurance coverage, maintained by either the platform operator, the driver or the combination of both, constitutes a recurring theme.[89] Most TNC regulations in the United States also establish minimal requirements, which drivers must fulfil before platform operators can allow them to use the application.[90] Other proposals, reflected in the actions of some public authorities, concern a possible expansion of legislative and non-legislative initiatives to ensure that features that increase passenger safety are implemented.[91] Features of this kind could assist in incident avoidance, for example by way of verifying drivers' identities and monitoring routes or identifying patterns of behaviour indicating suspected activity as well as analysing and responding to user reports. Platform operators' assistance could potentially be of value also during and following events causing damage, e.g. in the course of subsequent investigations carried out by competent authorities.

While sector-specific discussions and the exchange of best practices is already quite advanced in the United States, EU developments appear to largely miss the travel sector. Still, the Digital Services Act can be regarded as a step in the right direction. As noted, in addition to the adjustments to the liability safe harbour,[92] the DSA contains detailed provisions among others on content moderation, accompanied by reporting duties. Crucially, these provisions apply to all key online travel platforms, regardless of the status of the platform user. A set of further-reaching obligations applies to very large online platforms, which currently include one online travel platform: Booking.com. *De lege ferenda*, such duties—for example, the risk mitigation requirement—could be extended to other platforms active in this sector. After all, it is not only the number of users but also the nature of underlying interactions that may lead to increased risks.

---

[87] Davey (2017), pp. 264–265, 271.

[88] Wyman (2018), pp. 134–135.

[89] Ibid, pp. 135–136.

[90] Ibid, p. 136.

[91] For a similar solution indirectly adopted in London, whereby the weaknesses of the operator's system, which made it possible for unauthorised drivers to upload their photos to other Uber driver accounts, resulted in the revocation of the operator's licence, see Burridge (2019) Uber loses licence to operate in London, available at: <www.bbc.com/news/business-50544283>.

[92] See Chap. 4.

A further DSA provision which holds significant protective potential is Article 31(3) *in fine* on compliance by design. To recall, it requires providers of online platforms allowing consumers to conclude distance contracts with traders to "make reasonable efforts to randomly check in any official, freely accessible and machine-readable online database or online interface whether the products or services offered have been identified as illegal". As noted, however, the requirement has two important limitations. The first one concerns the exclusion of peer-to-peer transactions and could potentially be solved through an expansive reading of the Digital Services Directive, among other things. The second limitation is more serious and concerns the limited availability of databases identifying "illegal services", although this issue could also be of relevance to online travel platforms.[93] For the provision to have an added value, this aspect needs closer attention. A positively framed duty could also be envisaged, e.g. explicitly requiring the providers of passenger transport platforms to verify driver's licenses and perform background checks. A requirement to take reasonable steps to protect platform users in response to reports of misuse, whenever such reporting facilities are put in place, could moreover be derived from contract law.[94]

While the scope of harmonised legal norms concerning the performance of services provided by platform operators is generally not extensive, the situation is slightly different with respect to payment services. Until recently, also in this respect the legal framework applicable to platform operators has not been clear. Specifically, some of the Member States interpreted the previously applicable Directive 2007/64/EC on payment services[95] in a way that allowed for the exclusion of platform operators acting as intermediaries on behalf of buyers and sellers from the scope of harmonised provisions.[96] As a result, consumers (payment service users) were unable to address platform operators with their claims concerning, for example, unauthorised or incorrectly executed payment transactions.[97] This has partly changed with the entry into force of the second directive on payment services (PSD2), which clarified that exclusion from the scope of the act of commercial agents applies when agents act on behalf of only the payer or only the payee.[98]

Under updated rules, agents who act on behalf of both parties are excluded from the Directive's scope only if they do not, at any time enter into possession or control of client funds.[99] The Directive further expands the consumer protection framework

---

[93] For example, a driver removed from one platform could continue to provide services through another one.

[94] See Engert (2018), p. 371.

[95] Directive 2007/64/EC of the European Parliament and of the Council of 13.11.2007 on payment services in the internal market amending Directives 97/7/EC, 2002/65/EC, 2005/60/EC and 2006/48/EC and repealing Directive 97/5/EC [2007] OJ L319/1.

[96] Cf. recital 11 of Directive 2015/2366 on payment services.

[97] See Article 60 and 61 of Directive 2007/64/EC on payment services.

[98] Article 3(b) of Directive 2015/2366 on payment services.

[99] Ibid, Article 3(e) and recital 11. Note that the business model of Booking.com could continue to fall outside the scope of the relevant norms.

due to heightened payment security requirements and better protection in case of unauthorised payments.[100] Still, the practically most relevant questions of charge-back in the event of non-performance or inadequate performance in underlying contracts remain unanswered at the EU level, aside from the narrow context of credit card payments.[101] As the market practice shows, platform operators may provide charge-back systems on a contractual basis.[102] These, however, remain outside the scope of the harmonised safeguards, aside from the possible control of unfair contract terms.

Arguably, therefore, a potential for a consumer-oriented extension of the existing framework remains, possibly even going beyond the charge-back claim. Putting aside the more far-reaching proposals on joint and several liability between platform operators and suppliers,[103] a narrower, sectoral approach could include a specific duty of the platform operator to assist the traveller affected by delays or cancellations in obtaining redress, at the minimum in the form of reimbursement (charge-back), and potentially also re-routing (re-booking, alternative performance). To complete the protection framework, a corresponding measure of harmonisation could also extend to the underlying relationships. The approach of performance rules in previously applicable Directive 97/7/EC could provide a reference point in this regard.

### *8.4.4 Interim Conclusions*

The analysis shows that, in many respects, existing instruments of EU law provide a basis for improving consumer protection in online travel platforms. In the field of protection through information, the foundations have already been laid. As an instrument with a broad personal scope of application and a direct focus on online trade, the E-Commerce Directive appears to be particularly well-suited for this task. In the field of short-term accommodation rental, Directive 2006/123/EC on services in the internal market provides another, often overlooked framework, from which

---

[100] For example, the liability of payment service users in case of an unauthorised payment has been reduced from a maximum of EUR 150 to EUR 50, except in cases of gross negligence, see Articles 73 and 74 of Directive 2015/2366 on payment services.

[101] Article 27 Directive (EU) 2023/2225 of the European Parliament and of the Council of 18 October 2023 on credit agreements for consumers and repealing Directive 2008/48/EC [2023] OJ L2225/1, which maintained the approach of Directive 2008/48/EC. See ECC-Net, 'Chargeback in the EU/EEA' 8–9 <https://commission.europa.eu/document/download/3b971d58-4627-4e33-b5a0-968222e44893>. See also Cortés (2017), pp. 36–37; Quirk and Rothchild (2018), pp. 324–325.

[102] Katsch and Rabinovich-Einy (2017), p. 61.

[103] Research Group on the Law of Digital Services (2016), pp. 165, 168, Busch et al. (2020), p. 65, European Law Institute (2019) Report of the European Law Institute: Model Rules on Online Platforms, pp. 19–20 <www.europeanlawinstitute.eu/fileadmin/user_upload/p_eli/Publications/ELI_Model_Rules_on_Online_Platforms.pdf>. For a more detailed discussion, see Sect. 8.5.

increased consumer protection can be derived. Nevertheless, a number of points remain to be addressed.

First and foremost, the applicability of the E-Commerce Directive to platform operators requires reconsideration in light of the prior judgments, most notably in *Ker-Optika*. While the reading put forward in *Uber Spain* was well-intended, its conceptual coherence is open to question. Rather than focusing on the angle of "composite services" and their inherent parts, the Court could have distinguished between the digital and non-digital dimension of services provided. After all, if selling goods online can be qualified as an information society service, why should this not be the case for an online booking of services? As was argued before, such a conclusion does not necessarily preclude the qualification of platform operators as the consumer's main contracting counterparty.[104] Should the latter conclusion be reached by the competent national court—be it on the basis of *Wathelet*-like criterion of the "objective addressee perspective" (German: *objektiver Empfängerhorizont*), decisive influence reasoning modelled on *Uber Spain*, or any other legal doctrine[105]—from the perspective of the E-Commerce Directive the platform operator would be treated just like a seller operating his or her own web-shop. Considering the scope of the coordinated field, the advocated reasoning would not significantly reduce Member States' regulatory discretion and would ensure that the consumer protection layer of the harmonised e-commerce framework remains applicable. Platform operators could further be subject to the rules on services justified by reasons of consumer protection, subject to their adequate notification.

While the applicability of the E-Commerce Directive to online platforms can be regarded as a central issue, clarification of its scope alone does not exhaust the range of possibilities for increasing the level of consumer information via information on the basis of existing norms and adaptive approaches. Certainly, the long-standing criticism of consumer disclosures in light of behavioural economics should not be disregarded and alternatives to sub-optimal walls of text are to be promoted. Due to their central position, including as developers and controllers of the underlying digital architectures, platform operators should also play their part in this regard. Existing examples of shared responsibility, derived from sector-specific measures, as well as more recent developments in the Consumer Rights Directive and the Digital Services Act provide a starting point. Also the Digital Services Directive and the Unfair Commercial Practices Directive can play a role in this regard.

A significant role of the UCPD can also be identified with respect to the instruments of choice-enhancement. According to the view advocated here, the Directive can be interpreted as requiring the platform operator to indicate the cancellation policy applicable to the transaction. Responsibility of this kind should without doubt exist where the operator directly defines the cancellation options. Aside from this transparency-oriented framework, *de lege ferenda* two further-reaching measures can be identified. Firstly, a choice-enhancing instrument, preferably in the

[104] Schaub (2018), p. 113.

[105] For a more in-depth analysis, see Tereszkiewicz (2018), pp. 908–919.

form of cancellation at a fee, could be introduced as a mandatory consumer right, following the approach of the Package Travel Directive. Alternatively, a bottom-up approach, building upon the idea of collective negotiations or a different polycentric process of co-regulation, could come into play.[106]

Regarding safety and quality of services, recent attempts to clarify the application of the UCPD to reputation systems are certainly noteworthy. However, existing norms on reputation systems are far from comprehensive. Moreover, due to their inherent limitations, even very well-functioning reputation systems do not render minimum standards and insurance frameworks obsolete. To support this direction, existing provisions of Directive 2009/103/EC on motor insurance should continue to be interpreted broadly. For increased effect, a common approach to insurance in the travel sector could be elaborated, taking into account the role of platform operators. Key concepts emerging from both the Motor Insurance Directive and Article 23 of the Services Directive can provide a valuable baseline. As far as minimum standards are concerned, the focus on safety seems most suitable at this point, considering its pivotal role and the prior harmonisation difficulties. In this respect, the DSA provisions on content moderation, traceability of traders, compliance by design and risk mitigation are especially noteworthy. However, they come with limitations, which the consumer *acquis* can resolve only partly.

Finally, when it comes to performance of underlying contracts, existing norms and adaptive approaches do not point to a clear direction. Like in the case of choice-enhancement, two major avenues can be identified: a bottom-up approach, for example modelled on the system of collective negotiations, and a top-down approach, in which mandatory rules on liability assume a central role. Within the latter group, a further set of options can be identified, differing as to the intensity of the burden imposed on platform operators. Firstly, Directive 2015/2302 on package travel and linked travel arrangements provides a reference point which could be most far-reaching for platform operators. Under this approach, operators could be subjected to liability standards comparable to the ones imposed on travel organisers.[107] Secondly, a more moderate approach could take Directives 2015/2366 on payment services and 2023/2225 on consumer credit as its point of departure. To recall, the former is already applicable to many platform operators and provides consumer protection in the event of unauthorised payments.[108] The latter elaborates on charge-back claims in the event of non-performance or inadequate performance in underlying contracts, but only applies to credit card payments.[109] Building upon these instruments, a stronger framework for consumer protection could be devised.

---

[106] On the benefits of co-regulation as a form of governance of the platform economy, see Finck (2018b), pp. 268–271.

[107] For a discussion of the liability framework in package travel law as one of the available models for the platform economy, see Tereszkiewicz (2018), pp. 916–919. Along similar lines Tonner (2018), p. 402.

[108] See Articles 73 and 74 of Directive 2015/2366 on payment services on the protection in case unauthorized payments.

[109] See Article 27 of Directive 2023/2225.

In the travel sector, this could include, for example, a specific duty to assist the traveller affected by delays or cancellations in obtaining redress, in the form of reimbursement (charge-back) or, potentially, re-routing (re-booking). To complete the protection framework, a corresponding measure of harmonisation could also extend to the underlying relationships. The approach of performance rules in previously applicable Directive 97/7/EC could provide a reference point in this regard.

## 8.5 Beyond Existing Norms and Adaptive Approaches

The previous analysis sought to identify possibilities for further action aimed at increasing consumer protection in the travel sector, taking existing norms and their moderate adaptations as the principal point of reference. *Prima facie*, measures following such an approach may be viewed as an expression of a coherentist rationality, placing a particularly high value on the internal consistency and integrity of legal rules, as opposed to a regulatory-instrumentalist mindset.[110] However, one should keep in mind that the legal *status quo* analysed in the present book originates primarily at the EU level and, as such, by design, leans towards the latter.[111] It is therefore not surprising that also the existing norms lend themselves to further adaptations geared towards enhancing consumer protection and, in part, can even be infused with technocratic elements.[112] While this already offers plenty of food for thought, to present a comprehensive overview of the possible regulatory measures, it is worth taking a look at an alternative vision, favouring novel, and to some degree "exceptionalist", interventions.[113] From this perspective, an academic proposal of a platform-specific liability regime, recently put forward by the European Law Institute (ELI), deserves particular attention.

The final text of the ELI report, referred to as "Model Rules on Online Platforms",[114] was published in early 2020, in the midst of legislative discussions on the Digital Services Act.[115] This concurrence is not entirely coincidental. In light of the growing socio-economic importance of online platforms, the suitability of the

[110] Brownsword (2019), pp. 194–195.

[111] Michaels (2011), p. 142.

[112] In particular involving platform operators as regulatory intermediaries, see Busch (2020), pp. 120–125.

[113] The notion of exceptionalism describes a position, according to which an online or offline context of an interaction does make a difference from the regulatory point of view. See, in particular, Post (2009), p. 167. For an analysis in the EU legal context, see Brownsword (2019), pp. 168–169, 198–204.

[114] Report of the European Law Institute: Model Rules on Online Platforms (2019). For an earlier draft, see Research Group on the Law of Digital Services (2016).

[115] For an example of the influence of the ELI Model Rules on public consultations concerning the Digital Services Act, see BEUC, 'Making the Digital Services Act Work for Consumers. BEUC's Recommendations' (2020) <www.beuc.eu/publications/beuc-x-2020-031_making_the_digital_services_act_work_for_consumers_-_beucs_recommendations.pdf>.

E-Commerce Directive and its possible reform have attracted growing attention.[116] Instead of following a piecemeal approach, the Model Rules show how online platforms could comprehensively be addressed in private law. Their focus remains on triangular relationships established via online marketplaces regardless of the formal status of the parties involved, thereby corresponding with the subject matter of the present book.[117]

The Model Rules address a broad spectrum of issues: from pre-contractual disclosure, over the design of reputational feedback systems, to platform operator's liability. Of particular interest from the present perspective is the rule in Article 20, concerning the liability of the platform operator with predominant influence for the proper performance of underlying contracts. Pursuant to the proposed provision, if the customer can reasonably rely on the platform operator having a predominant influence over the supplier, the customer can exercise the rights and remedies for the non-performance available against the supplier under the supplier-customer contract also against the platform operator. The subsequent paragraph includes a non-exclusive list of criteria to be considered when assessing such reasonable reliance. The catalogue is conceptualized as a moveable (flexible) system (German: *bewegliches System*), whereby the weight of particular criteria is assessed by the courts on a case-by-case basis.[118] The list refers, among others, to the circumstances of contract conclusion and the influence of the platform operator on the terms of underlying contracts and, as such, overlaps to some degree with the *Uber* case law.[119]

The proposed provision extends the protection of customers in case of non-performance, without making the platform operator party to the underlying contract.[120] In contrast to the previous wording, the notion of "joint liability" is not explicitly mentioned, but instead reference is made to exercising rights and remedies. This formulation makes it clear that additional protection of the customer is not limited to the platform operator's liability for damages, but can also include a claim for specific performance. As observed in the literature, contrary to what one may expect, such a solution may often be aligned with the economic interest of platform operators, who may actually prefer fulfilment in kind over direct liability for damages.[121] This may, nonetheless, depend on the specific area in which the platform operates.[122] Moreover, since the claim for specific performance is not har-

116 Sartor (2017), pp. 19–23; Schulte-Nölke et al. (2020), pp. 21–24, 36–37.

117 More specifically, online marketplaces formed the starting point for and remain most comprehensively addressed by the Model Rules. The scope of several rules has subsequently been extended to other business models as part of the so-called 'modular approach', see Busch et al. (2020), pp. 63–64.

118 Ibid, p. 63. The authors refer to the previous work of Wilburg (1950).

119 See especially the judgment of the Court of Justice of 20.12.2017 in case C-434/15 *Asociación Profesional Elite Taxi (Uber Spain)*, para. 39.

120 Pecyna (2019), p. 159.

121 On the interpretative difficulties under previous wording, see Maultzsch (2018), pp. 223–224.

122 For doubts about practicability of platform operator's liability for specific performance, see Purnhagen and Wahlen (2017), p. 213.

monised at the EU level, joint liability extending to such claims may achieve different results depending on applicable national contract law, which does not seem preferable from the internal market perspective.[123] Thus, an alternative proposal put forward in the literature provides only for liability for damages and reimbursement.[124] A scholarly discussion also extends to the optimal design of the redress framework between the platform operator and the supplier.[125]

Despite some similarity, Article 20 of the ELI Model Rules should be distinguished from the framework for assessing whether the platform operator provides the underlying service, endorsed by the Commission in the 2016 communication on the collaborative economy,[126] as well as the criteria for qualifying a provider as an "organiser" under Directive 2015/2302 on package travel and linked travel arrangements.[127] The Model Rules, therefore, opt for a third-way solution, purportedly adjusted to the specifics of online platforms.

Critics argue, however, that the triangular scenario, addressed by the ELI working group, is not as unique as it may seem at first sight. In his extensive analysis of an earlier version of the Model Rules, Felix Maultzsch draws parallels, on the one hand, to franchising contracts and, on the other hand, to agency models.[128] According to the author, despite important similarities between the business models potentially covered by the scope of Article 20 of the Models Rules and either of these categories, the proposal does not take due account of the principles they reflect. To illustrate, even though predominant influence is not unusual in traditional franchising agreements, it is not viewed as justified to hold the franchisor jointly liable with the franchisee.[129]

Despite this conceptual critique, Maultzsch is not necessarily against enhancing platform liability for the sake of consumer protection. In particular, the author observes that operators could bear increased responsibility for the performance of underlying contracts where they bear all significant chances and risks of the transaction but the formal construction of a peer-to-peer contract deprives the consumer of the special protection available to him or her in B2C exchange.[130] The proposal follows the example of the German rules on agency, as interpreted by the Federal Supreme Court (*Bundesgerichtshof*). Building upon the same line of case law, Purnhagen and Wahlen argue in favour of, firstly, re-classifying peer-to-peer

---

[123] Maultzsch (2018), p. 224.

[124] Meller-Hannich et al. (2019), p. 407. See also Meller-Hannich (2019), pp. 127–132.

[125] For a solution taking into account the weaker position of the supplier vis-à-vis the platform operator, see Pecyna (2019), p. 165. Cf. Article 25 of the ELI Model Rules.

[126] European Commission, 'Communication from the Commission to the European Parliament, the Council, the European Economic and Social Committee and the Committee of the Regions. A European Agenda for the Collaborative Economy' (2016) COM(2016) 356 final, p. 6.

[127] Article 3(8) in conjunction with Article 3(2)(b) of Directive 2015/2302 on package travel and linked travel arrangements.

[128] Maultzsch (2018), pp. 227, 232.

[129] Ibid, p. 228.

[130] Ibid, p. 232.

transactions to B2C exchange in cases of this kind, and, secondly, involving platform operators, in cooperation with the supplier, in the performance of the contract.[131]

The described agency-inspired solutions are geared towards one specific field of market transformation, i.e. the collaborative economy. Focusing on the travel sector, however, one should not lose sight of the fact that the EU law has still to keep up with the previous stage of the transformation: from package travel as a major model of cross-border travelling to travel services provided on a stand-alone basis. To complete the protection framework, EU lawmakers should therefore also draw attention to this more traditional field of B2C contracting.[132]

## 8.6 Conclusions

The analysis of previous initiatives undertaken at the EU level confirms a major role of consumer protection in both the internal market and the common transport policies. Significant efforts have been made over past decades to approximate and increase the level of consumer protection in the travel sector, as evidenced by the instruments on package travel and the established modes of passenger transport. The process of harmonisation has been complex and progressed gradually. As the pace of changes in the market practice has rapidly accelerated, the law- and policy makers must take on novel challenges.

The development of online platforms has resulted in the creation and expansion of markets that previously remained of marginal economic importance, such as peer-to-peer tourism accommodation, ride-sharing and rides-on-demand. Arguably, recipients of such services find themselves in a weaker position vis-à-vis their suppliers in respect of the ability to both exercise self-reliance and bear potential losses. Platform operators are able to balance this asymmetry to some degree and support consumer confidence. However, platform users are also weaker parties in relation to the operators. Consequently, the role of platform providers does not necessarily weaken the case for an increased consumer protection, but underlines the need for new regulatory strategies, taking this role into account.

Bearing in mind that any potential upgrades of the EU consumer *acquis* will involve a range of "political, economic and social choices",[133] the chapter did not aspire to identify a single correct solution, but instead to elucidate the range of possible options. In the first place, the potential of existing EU rules and their moderate adaptations has been explored. The analysis showed that, in many respects, existing instruments of EU law provide a viable basis for increasing the level of consumer protection following the platform-driven transformation of the travel sector. As far

[131] Purnhagen and Wahlen (2017), pp. 213–215.

[132] Tonner (2018), p. 402.

[133] Judgment of the Court of Justice of 10.1.2006 in case C-344/04 *IATA and ELFAA*, para. 80.

as protection through information is concerned, the E-Commerce Directive provides a strong reference point. The extent to which the Directive can serve this role, however, depends on the interpretation of its scope of application, whereby the reading in *Ker-Optika* provides a higher level of consumer protection than the more recent case law in *Uber Spain* and *Uber France*. Consumer information can further be improved through the combined application of the Digital Services Act, the Digital Services Directive, and the Unfair Commercial Practices Directive.

A transparency-oriented framework can also serve the goal of consumer choice enhancement, for example by equipping consumers with information about the applicable terms of cancelling the contract. Should a further-reaching instrument be considered desirable, existing norms for the established business models provide a spectrum of options: from the right to withdraw to the right of contract transfer and cancellation at a fee. Alternatively, a bottom-up approach, building upon the idea of collective negotiations or a different polycentric process of co-regulation, could be considered.

As far as safety and quality of services are concerned, the analysis of existing norms and adaptive approaches shows a mixed picture. In both respects, the level of consumer protection can be improved via reputation systems, provided their design ensures reliable outcomes. It is worth keeping in mind, however, that protection via reputation may not bring adequate results in relation to risks that are hard to perceive or control. The DSA provisions on content moderation, traceability of traders, compliance by design, and risk mitigation could fill certain protection gaps. However, they come with limitations, which the consumer *acquis* can resolve only partly. *De lege ferenda*, an extension of Articles 30 and 31 DSA to online travel platforms facilitating peer-to-peer exchange, and an elaborated policy on the safety of services, are worth considering. Moreover, obligations currently envisaged for very large online platforms could be applied more generally to online travel platforms.

Finally, when it comes to performance of underlying contracts, existing norms and adaptive approaches do not point in a clear direction. Should mandatory rules on liability of platform operators be considered the right way forward, a set of corresponding options can be identified, differing as to the intensity of the burden imposed on operators. Firstly, Directive 2015/2302 on package travel and linked travel arrangements provides the reference point which could be most far-reaching for platform operators. Under this approach, operators could be subjected to liability standards comparable to the ones imposed on travel organisers. Secondly, a more moderate approach could take Directives 2015/2366 on payment services and 2023/2225 on consumer credit as its point of departure. Building upon these instruments, a stronger framework for consumer protection could be devised. In the travel sector, this could include, for example, a specific duty to assist the traveller affected by delays or cancellations in obtaining redress, in the form of reimbursement (charge-back) or, potentially, re-routing (re-booking). If an entirely novel approach was preferred, the provisions of ELI Model Rules on the liability of platform operators with predominant influence set a direction worth exploring.

Regardless of the substantive approach ultimately followed, its effectiveness will certainly be linked to the enforcement norms in place. Because the former remains up in the air, detailed proposals on the associated enforcement framework seem premature. Prior experience of the EU law points to the direction of a hybrid framework, combining elements of public and private enforcement, including through alternative dispute resolution. Ultimately, the availability of different enforcement avenues provides the best chance of ensuring a high level of consumer protection following the platform-driven transformation of the travel sector.

## References

Adam L, Micklitz H-W (2017) Verbraucher und Online-Plattformen. In: Micklitz H-W, Reisch LA, Joost G, Zander-Hayat H (eds) Verbraucherrecht 2.0 – Verbraucher in der digitalen Welt. Nomos, pp 45–102

Adamski D (2018) Lost on the digital platform: Europe's legal travails with the Digital Single Market. CML Rev 55(3):719–751

Bech Serrat JM (2012) Selling tourism services at a distance: an analysis of the EU consumer *acquis*. Springer

Bech Serrat JM (2016) Consumer travel law. In: Twigg-Flesner C (ed) Research handbook on EU consumer and contract law. Edward Elgar, pp 360–387

Brownsword R (2019) Law, technology and society: reimagining the regulatory environment. Routledge

Busch C (2016a) Crowdsourcing consumer confidence. How to regulate online rating and review systems in the collaborative economy. In: De Franceschi A (ed) European contract law and the digital single market: the implications of the digital revolution. Intersentia, pp 223–244

Busch C (2016b) The future of pre-contractual information duties: from behavioural insights to big data. In: Twigg-Flesner C (ed) Research handbook on EU consumer and contract law. Edward Elgar, pp 221–240

Busch C (2020) Self-regulation and regulatory intermediation in the platform economy. In: Cantero Gamito M, Micklitz H-W (eds) The role of the EU in transnational legal ordering. Edward Elgar, pp 115–134

Busch C, Dannemann G, Schulte-Nölke H, Wiewiórowska-Domagalska A, Zoll F (2020) The ELI model rules on online platforms. EuCML 9(2):61–70

Bussani M, Infantino M (2019) Harmonization of tort law in Europe. In: Marciano A, Ramello GB (eds) Encyclopedia of law and economics. Springer, pp 1029–1043

Codagnone C, Karatzogianni A, Matthews J (2018) Platform economics: rhetoric and reality in the "sharing economy". Emerald Publishing Limited

Cortés P (2017) The law of consumer redress in an evolving digital market: upgrading from alternative to online dispute resolution. Cambridge University Press

Davey J (2017) A compulsory diet of chickens and eggs: the EU motor insurance directives as a shadow tort regime. In: Giliker P (ed) Research handbook on EU tort law. Edward Elgar, pp 239–272

de Vries A, Jabłonowska A (2019) Article 11: duty to inform about platform operator and supplier. In: Busch C, Dannemann G, Schulte-Nölke H, Wiewiórowska-Domagalska A, Zoll F (eds) Discussion draft of a directive on online intermediary platforms. Commentary. Jagiellonian University Press, pp 105–119

Delimatsis P (2018) From *Sacchi* to *Uber*: 60 years of services liberalization, ten years of the Services Directive in the EU. YEL 37:188–250

Devolder B (2019) Contractual liability of the platform. In: Devolder B (ed) The platform economy: unravelling the legal status of online intermediaries. Intersentia, pp 31–88
Dredge D, Gyimóthy S (2015) The collaborative economy and tourism: critical perspectives, questionable claims and silenced voices. Tour Recreat Res 40(3):286–302
Edelman BG, Geradin D (2016) Efficiencies and regulatory shortcuts: how should we regulate companies like Airbnb and Uber? STLR 19:293–328
Elshout M, Elsen M, Leenheer J, Loos, Luzak J (2016) Study on consumers' attitudes towards terms conditions (T&Cs). Final report. European Commission
Engert A (2018) Digitale Plattformen. AcP 218(2):304–376
Finck M (2018a) Digital co-regulation: designing a supranational legal framework for the platform economy. Eur Law Rev 43(1):47–68
Finck M (2018b) The sharing economy and the EU. In: Davidson NM, Finck M, Infranca JJ (eds) The Cambridge handbook of the law of the sharing economy. Cambridge University Press, pp 261–273
Hacker P (2018) UberPop, UberBlack, and the regulation of digital platforms after the Asociación Profesional Elite Taxi judgment of the CJEU. ERCL 14(1):80–96
Harke JD (2020) Vertragsübertragung als allgemeines Verbraucherrecht? VuR 35(6):209–215
Hausemer P, Rzepecka J, Dragulin M, Vitiello S, Rabuel L, Nunu M, Rodriguez Diaz A, Psaila E, Fiorentini S, Gysen S, Meeusen T, Quaschning S, Dunne A, Grinevich V, Huber F, Baines L (2017) Exploratory study of consumer issues in online peer-to-peer platform markets: task 4 – Uber – case study report. European Commission
Helberger N, Sax M, Strycharz J, Micklitz H-W (2022) Choice architectures in the digital economy: towards a new understanding of digital vulnerability. J Consum Policy 45(2):175–200
Hennemann M (2022) Qualität von Video-Sharing-Plattformen. In: Schmidt-Kessel M, Möllnitz C (eds) Grundfragen des Digitalvertragsrechts. Mohr Siebeck, pp 77–94
Howells G (2005) The potential and limits of consumer empowerment by information. J Law Soc 32(3):349–370
Jabłonowska A (2021) Joined cases C-724/18 and C-727/18: Cali Apartments – the potential and limits of national authorisation schemes for providers of accommodation services in the platform economy. R.E.D.C. (2):273–282
Karsten J (2007) Passengers, consumers, and travellers: the rise of passenger rights in EC transport law and its repercussions for Community consumer law and policy. J Consum Policy 30(2):117–136
Karsten J, Petri G (2005) Towards a handbook on European contract law and beyond: the Commission's 2004 communication "European contract law and the revision of the *acquis*: the way forward". J Consum Policy 28(1):31–51
Katsch E, Rabinovich-Einy O (2017) Digital justice: technology and the internet of disputes. Oxford University Press
Knetsch J (2017) European tort law in Western Europe. In: Giliker P (ed) Research handbook on EU tort law. Edward Elgar, pp 342–358
Kucharska A (2019) Bezpieczeństwo konsumentów w świecie gospodarki współpracy z perspektywy prawa Unii Europejskiej – analiza wybranych problemów. iKAR 8(8):25–35
Lubasz L, Namysłowska M (2020) Article 5. General information to be provided. In: Schulze R, Staudenmayer D (eds) EU digital law: article-by-article commentary. C.H. Beck/Hart/Nomos, pp 415–426
Magnus U, Micklitz H-W (2006) Liability for the safety of services. Nomos
Mak V (2016) The consumer in European Regulatory Private Law. In: Leczykiewicz D, Weatherill S (eds) The images of the consumer in EU law: legislation, free movement and competition law. Hart Publishing, pp 381–400
Martens B (2016) Economic policy perspective on online platforms. Institute for Prospective Technological Studies – Digital Economy Working Paper 2016/05. European Commission
Maultzsch F (2018) Contractual liability of online platform operators: European proposals and established principles. ERCL 14(3):209–240

Meller-Hannich C (2019) Wandel der Verbraucherrollen: das Recht der Verbraucher und Prosumer in der Sharing Economy. Duncker & Humblot

Meller-Hannich C, Krausbeck E, Wittke R (2019) Der Verbraucher in der Sharing Economy. VuR 11:403–412

Michaels R (2011) Of islands and the ocean: the two rationalities of European private law. In: Brownsword R, Niglia L, Micklitz H-W (eds) Foundations of European private law. Hart Publishing, pp 139–158

Narciso M (2019) The regulation of online reviews in European consumer law. ERPL 27(3):557–581

Nordhausen A (2005) Information requirements in the E-Commerce Directive and the proposed directive on unfair commercial practices. In: Janssen A, Howells G (eds) Information rights and obligations: a challenge for party autonomy and transactional fairness. Routledge, pp 93–114

Orti Vallejo A (2019) Contractual relationships in collaborative economy platforms. ERPL 27(5):995–1022

Pecyna M (2019) Article 18: liability of the platform operator for the non-performance of suppliers. In: Busch C, Dannemann G, Schulte-Nölke H, Wiewiórowska-Domagalska A, Zoll F (eds) Discussion draft of a directive on online intermediary platforms. Commentary. Jagiellonian University Press, pp 157–165

Petersen CS, Ulfbeck VG, Hansen O (2018) Platforms as private governance systems – the example of Airbnb. Nord J Commer Law 1:37–60

Post DG (2009) In search of Jefferson's Moose: notes on the state of cyberspace. Oxford University Press

Prastitou Merdi T (2020) The 2018 New Deal on better enforcement and modernisation of EU consumer law: an actually good digital deal? In: Synodinou TE, Jougleux P, Markou C, Prastitou T (eds) EU internet law in the digital era: regulation and enforcement. Springer, pp 347–365

Purnhagen K, Wahlen S (2017) Der Verbraucherbegriff, § 13 BGB und die Sharing Economy. In: Micklitz H-W, Reisch LA, Joost G, Zander-Hayat H (eds) Verbraucherrecht 2.0 – Verbraucher in der digitalen Welt. Nomos, pp 185–220

Quirk P, Rothchild JA (2018) Consumer protection and the Internet. In: Howells G, Ramsay I, Wilhelmsson T (eds) Handbook of research on international consumer law, 2nd edn. Edward Elgar, pp 308–339

Ranchordás S (2018) Online reputation and the regulation of information asymmetries in the platform economy. CAL 5(1):127–147

Reich N (2008) Crisis or future of European consumer law? In: Parry D, Nordhausen A, Howells G, Twigg-Flesner C (eds) The yearbook of consumer law 2009. Routledge, pp 3–68

Reich N, Micklitz H-W (2014) Economic law, consumer interests, and EU integration. In: Reich N, Micklitz H-W, Rott P, Tonner K (eds) European consumer law. Intersentia, pp 1–66

Research Group on the Law of Digital Services (2016) Discussion draft of a directive on online intermediary platforms. EuCML 5(4):164–169

Sartor G (2017) Providers liability: from the ECommerce Directive to the future. In-depth analysis for the IMCO Committee. European Parliament

Schaub MY (2018) Why Uber is an information society service: case note to CJEU 20 December 2017 C-434/15 (Asociación Profesional Élite Taxi). EuCML 7(3):109–115

Schulte-Nölke H, Rüffer I, Nobrega C, Wiewiórowska-Domagalska A (2020) The legal framework for E-Commerce in the internal market. Study requested by the IMCO committee. European Parliament

Smorto G (2018) The protection of the weaker parties in the platform economy. In: Davidson NM, Finck M, Infranca JJ (eds) The Cambridge handbook of the law of the sharing economy. Cambridge University Press, pp 431–446

Sundararajan A (2016) The sharing economy: the end of employment and the rise of crowd-based capitalism. MIT Press

Tereszkiewicz P (2018) Digital platforms: regulation and liability in the EU law. ERPL 26(6):903–920

Tonner K (2018) Die Pauschalreise und ihr Recht – was kommt danach? VuR 33(11):401–402

Twigg-Flesner C (2016) The importance of law and harmonisation for the EU's confident consumer. In: Leczykiewicz D, Weatherill S (eds) The images of the consumer in EU law: legislation, free movement and competition law. Hart Publishing, pp 183–202
van Leeuwen B (2017) European standardisation of services and its impact on private law: paradoxes of convergence. Hart Publishing
Voß W (2022) Regulierung von Social Media-Anbietern durch Qualitätsstandards. In: Schmidt-Kessel M, Möllnitz C (eds) Grundfragen des Digitalvertragsrechts. Mohr Siebeck, pp 31–56
Watson J (2016) Withdrawal rights. In: Twigg-Flesner C (ed) Research handbook on EU consumer and contract law. Edward Elgar, pp 241–265
Weatherill S (2016) Empowerment is not the only fruit. In: Leczykiewicz D, Weatherill S (eds) The images of the consumer in EU law: legislation, free movement and competition law. Hart Publishing, pp 203–222
Wendehorst C (2016) Platform intermediary services and duties under the E-Commerce Directive and the Consumer Rights Directive. EuCML 5(1):30–33
Wilburg W (1950) Entwicklung eines beweglichen Systems im bürgerlichen Recht. Kienreich
Wilhelmsson T (2004) The abuse of the "confident consumer" as a justification for EC consumer law. J Consum Policy 27(3):317–337
Willett C (2005) Autonomy and fairness: the case of public statements. In: Janssen A, Howells G, Schulze R (eds) Information rights and obligations: a challenge for party autonomy and transactional fairness. Routledge, pp 1–16
Willett C (2018) Re-theorising consumer law. CLJ 77(1):179–210
Wyman KM (2018) The novelty of TNC regulation. In: Davidson NM, Finck M, Infranca JJ (eds) The Cambridge handbook of the law of the sharing economy. Cambridge University Press, pp 129–140

The manufacturer's authorised representative in the EU is Springer
Nature Customer Service Centre GmbH, Europaplatz 3, 69115 Heidelberg,
Germany. If you have any concerns regarding our products, please
contact ProductSafety@springernature.com

Printed and bound by CPI Group (UK) Ltd, Croydon, CR0 4YY
30/09/2026
02225589-0002